"This work is mandatory reading for anyone interested in contemporary Catholic theological anthropology and thus the humanism of the Incarnation. As the author declares, 'the full and final revelation given in Christ shows the indissoluble, paradoxical unity between the human being as such and God.' Grace transfigures nature and with this move reason is illumined by faith. The critical couplets of nature and grace, faith and reason, work together in the process by which the human person, made in the image of God, grows into the likeness of Christ. This work is also highly original in so far as it connects Mariology and the metaphysics of Erich Przywara, SJ, with the discipline of theological anthropology. Quite simply, it is a synthetic masterpiece."

—TRACEY ROWLAND,
St. John Paul II Chair of Theology, University of Notre Dame, Australia

"For too long there has persisted a sharp divide between Mariology and other domains of theology, namely the study of Christ and of the human person. This work represents an illustrative step in the right direction, treating the Catholic theology of the Virgin Mary as a foremost dimension of theological anthropology. How is our human condition enlightened by theological consideration of Mary, and what does her mystery tell us about the future of the human race and the church? Here these questions are engaged with inspiration taken from Erich Przywara, who saw in the Virgin an epitome of the creature under grace. At the same time, this work helpfully engages with emergent philosophical challenges and recent theological resources to forge a new Mariological vision of Catholic theology. It embodies a profound Christian vision of our created personhood, one undertaken in the light of its most noble representative."

—THOMAS JOSEPH WHITE, OP,
Rector, Pontifical University of St. Thomas, Angelicum, Rome

"Good theology is both 'faith seeking understanding' and the soul rejoicing. In this dazzling book, Joseph Terry argues for a Marian theological anthropology along lines that speak both to reason and to joy. How could contemplation of the Theotokos not bring wondrous joy and insight into mere human creatureliness in God's plan of redemption and deification? In these pages one attends to the voices of an extraordinarily catholic range of theologians and philosophers, as Terry brings to bear the whole tradition."

—MATTHEW LEVERING,
James N. Jr. and Mary D. Perry Chair of Theology, Mundelein Seminary

"The dogma of the Assumption is also that of our humanity. This is what Joseph Terry's book shows us. The approach is certainly theological, but also and above all philosophical. For it is by being woman and human, as a mother at the same time as the Mother of God, that the Virgin Mary comes to meet us today."

—EMMANUEL FALQUE,
Faculté de Philosophie, Institut Catholique de Paris

"Joseph Terry follows the train of some of the greatest Marian thinkers in the church, gathering breath-taking insights from them and bringing it all into a novel synthesis. He shows that Mary is not just an important figure for personal piety, but ought to be seen as having a central place in theology and even metaphysics: the Mother of God reveals—in a surprising but intellectually compelling way—the most fundamental meaning of being and the human person. Terry's book takes a decisive step forward in Mariology and will be of great interest to anyone working in metaphysics and anthropology from within the light of faith."

—D. C. SCHINDLER,
Professor of Metaphysics and Anthropology, Pontifical John Paul II Institute, Washington, DC

"In this impressive work, which combines philosophical acumen with a profound theological sensibility, Joseph Terry aims to explain the metaphysical significance of Mary for anthropology. He more than succeeds. I can think of no work that offers a more robustly metaphysical explanation of Mary's significance as the one who, as a human person, perfectly images her divine Son. Rather than Mariology competing with Christology, this book shows with admirable clarity how they complement one another—how Marian doctrine not only 'safeguards the hominization of God and the deification of *anthropos*,' but also 'fleshes out,' so to speak, the logic of the hypostatic union. In short, for those who want to start thinking more deeply about Mary, there is no better place to begin."

**—JOHN BETZ,**
Associate Professor, Department of Theology, University of Notre Dame

"Joseph Terry's remarkable new book shows how there can be no adequate anthropology that does not put Mary, the Mother of the Lord, at the center of its theorizing. With great originality he provides Mariology with a much fuller metaphysical development."

**—JOHN MILBANK,**
Professor Emeritus of Religion, Politics and Ethics,
University of Nottingham

"*Human, All Too Human: Mariology as Theo-Philosophical Anthropology* is a rare text of Mariological reflections. It is rare because it seeks to ground Mariology within the depths of a robust analogical metaphysics. There is much talk (and debate) today, within theological circles, of Christ the concrete analogy of being. Terry is keen to show that the Mother of God is also and likewise a concrete analogy of being, as Karl Barth was afraid she was. But, for Terry, one must never fear this reality without which we lose sight of what it means to be a creature, to be human all-too-human. Indeed, this Marian truth, viewed from within the light of the Triune God's revelatory activity, is the very secret of our humanity. This text is a conversation starter. Highly recommended."

**—PHILIP JOHN PAUL GONZALES,**
Professor of Philosophy, St. Mary's Seminary and University, Baltimore

"In his *Human, All Too Human: Mariology as Theo-Philosophical Anthropology*, Joseph Terry has rendered a unique service to contemporary theology. Placing himself in the line of the twentieth-century Catholic Ressourcement, he has produced the first systematic account of the Marian dogmas as the touchstone of the trinitarian logic of creation and revelation. At the center of his account stands the Theotokos, the human icon of triune perichoresis, who embodies, as pure creature, the interplay of God and the creature, nature and grace, faith and reason. Anyone working in dogmatics—particularly theological anthropology, Mariology, fundamental theology, and philosophical theology--will profit from reading this path-breaking work of creative theological retrieval."

**—ADRIAN J. WALKER,**
Professor of Philosophy and Dogmatics, Saint Patrick's Seminary and University

"Given the uneven post-Vatican II theological landscape, Joseph Terry's necessary book on Mariology is at once an intervention in that he exposes the marginalization and relative vacuity of discussion of Mary in contemporary theology; a concerted ecumenical retrieval of the Marian tradition from the Patristic to the modern period in which Mary was central to figuring both the church and persons; an apologetic on behalf of the Marian doctrines of immaculate conception, perpetual virginity, and assumption that not only pleads for their intelligibility, but argues for their theological and philosophical centrality when it comes to understanding the human person; and, finally, a constructive and synthetic proposal in its own right that if it takes its cues from the likes of Erich Przywara and Louis Bouyer it strikes out in innovative ways. Perhaps one of the deepest insights in this wonderful book is that figurally Mary is as much—if not more—an eschatological as a protological figure. Even without this emphasis, perhaps this book might represent an opening towards a Renaissance in Mariology. With this emphasis, perhaps in our time in which the person seems to be under erasure, reflection on Mary as well as Christ can guide us to a future beyond doubt and beyond violence."

**—CYRIL O'REGAN,**
Catherine F. Huisking Professor of Theology, University of Notre Dame

"Joseph Terry here offers a wide-ranging work in theological anthropology, weaving Mariological themes with contemporary philosophy into a seamless vision of human origin, identity and vocation. It is a rigorous and insightful contribution to contemporary Catholic thought."

—**AARON RICHES,**
Associate Professor of Theology, Benedictine College

# Human, All Too Human

# VERITAS

## Series Introduction

"... the truth will set you free" (John 8:32)

In much contemporary discourse, Pilate's question has been taken to mark the absolute boundary of human thought. Beyond this boundary, it is often suggested, is an intellectual hinterland into which we must not venture. This terrain is an agnosticism of thought: because truth cannot be possessed, it must not be spoken. Thus, it is argued that the defenders of "truth" in our day are often traffickers in ideology, merchants of counterfeits, or anti-liberal. They are, because it is somewhat taken for granted that Nietzsche's word is final: truth is the domain of tyranny.

Is this indeed the case, or might another vision of truth offer itself? The ancient Greeks named the love of wisdom as *philia*, or friendship. The one who would become wise, they argued, would be a "friend of truth." For both philosophy and theology might be conceived as schools in the friendship of truth, as a kind of relation. For like friendship, truth is as much discovered as it is made. If truth is then so elusive, if its domain is *terra incognita*, perhaps this is because it arrives to us—unannounced—as gift, as a person, and not some thing.

The aim of the Veritas book series is to publish incisive and original current scholarly work that inhabits "the between" and "the beyond" of theology and philosophy. These volumes will all share a common aspiration to transcend the institutional divorce in which these two disciplines often find themselves, and to engage questions of pressing concern to both philosophers and theologians in such a way as to reinvigorate both disciplines with a kind of interdisciplinary desire, often so absent in contemporary academe. In a word, these volumes represent collective efforts in the befriending of truth, doing so beyond the simulacra of pretend tolerance, the violent, yet insipid reasoning of liberalism that asks with Pilate, "What is truth?"—expecting a consensus of non-commitment; one that encourages the commodification of the mind, now sedated by the civil service of career, ministered by the frightened patrons of position.

The series will therefore consist of two wings: (1) original monographs; and (2) essay collections on a range of topics in theology and philosophy. The latter will principally be the products of the annual conferences of the Centre of Theology and Philosophy (www.theologyphilosophycentre.co.uk).

Conor Cunningham and Joseph Terry, *Veritas Series Editors*

### *Available from Cascade Books*

| | |
|---|---|
| Anthony D. Baker | *Diagonal Advance: Perfection in Christian Theology* |
| D. C. Schindler | *The Perfection of Freedom: Schiller, Schelling, and Hegel between the Ancients and the Moderns* |
| Rustin Brian | *Covering Up Luther: How Barth's Christology Challenged the* Deus Absconditus *that Haunts Modernity* |
| Timothy Stanley | *Protestant Metaphysics After Karl Barth and Martin Heidegger* |
| Christopher Ben Simpson | *The Truth Is the Way: Kierkegaard's* Theologia Viatorum |
| Richard H. Bell | *Wagner's Parsifal: An Appreciation in the Light of His Theological Journey* |
| Antonio Lopez | *Gift and the Unity of Being* |
| Toyohiko Kagawa | *Cosmic Purpose*, translated and introduced by Thomas John Hastings |
| Nigel Zimmerman | *Facing the Other: John Paul II, Levinas, and the Body* |
| Conor Sweeney | *Sacramental Presence after Heidegger: Onto-theology, Sacraments, and the Mother's Smile* |
| John Behr et al. (eds.) | *The Role of Death in Life: A Multidisciplinary Examination of the Relation between Life and Death* |
| Eric Austin Lee et al. (eds.) | *The Resounding Soul: Reflection on the Metaphysics and Vivacity of the Human Person* |
| Orion Edgar | *Things Seen and Unseen: The Logic of Incarnation in Merleau-Ponty's Metaphysics of Flesh* |
| Duncan B. Reyburn | *Seeing Things as They Are: G. K. Chesterton and the Drama of Meaning* |
| Lyndon Shakespeare | *Being the Body of Christ in the Age of Management* |
| Michael V. Di Fuccia | *Owen Barfield: Philosophy, Poetry, and Theology* |
| John McNerney | *Wealth of Persons: Economics with a Human Face* |
| Norm Klassen | *The Fellowship of the Beatific Vision: Chaucer on Overcoming Tyranny and Becoming Ourselves* |
| Donald Wallenfang | *Human and Divine Being: A Study of the Theological Anthropology of Edith Stein* |
| Sotiris Mitralexis | *Ever-Moving Repose: A Contemporary Reading of Maximus the Confessor's Theory of Time* |
| Sotiris Mitralexis et al. (eds.) | *Maximus the Confessor as a European Philosopher* |
| Kevin Corrigan | *Love, Friendship, Beauty, and the Good: Plato, Aristotle, and the Later Tradition* |
| Andrew Brower Latz | *The Social Philosophy of Gillian Rose* |
| D. C. Schindler | *Love and the Postmodern Predicament: Rediscovering the Real in Beauty, Goodness, and Truth* |

1. Note: Nathan Kerr, *Christ, History, and Apocalyptic*, although volume 3 of the original SCM Veritas series, is available from Cascade as part of the Theopolitical Visions series.

| | |
|---|---|
| Stephen Kampowski | *Embracing Our Finitude: Exercises in a Christian Anthropology between Dependence and Gratitude* |
| William Desmond | *The Gift of Beauty and the Passion of Being: On the Threshold between the Aesthetic and the Religious* |
| Charles Péguy | *Notes on Bergson and Descartes* |
| David Alcalde | *Cosmology without God: The Problematic Theology Inherent in Modern Cosmology* |
| Benson P. Fraser | *Hide and Seek: The Sacred Art of Indirect Communication* |
| Philip John Paul Gonzales | *Exorcising Philosophical Modernity: Cyril O'Regan and Christian Discourse after Modernity* |
| Caitlin Smith Gilson | *Subordinated Ethics: Natural Law and Moral Miscellany in Aquinas and Dostoyevsky* |
| Michael Dominic Taylor | *The Foundations of Nature: Metaphysics of Gift for an Integral Ecological Ethic* |
| David W. Opderbeck | *The End of the Law? Law, Theology, and Neuroscience* |
| Caitlin Smith Gilson | *As It Is in Heaven: Some Christian Questions on the Nature of Paradise* |
| Andrew T. J. Kaethler | *The Eschatological Person: Alexander Schmemann and Joseph Ratzinger in Dialogue* |
| Emmanuel Falque | *By Way of Obstacles: A Pathway through a Work* |
| Paul Tyson (ed.) | *Astonishment in Science: Engagements with William Desmond* |
| Darren Dyk | *Will & Love: Shakespeare and the Motion of the Soul* |
| Matthew Vest | *Ethics Lost in Modernity: Reflections on Wittgenstein and Bioethics* |
| Hanna Lucas | *Sensing the Sacred: Recovering a Mystagogical Vision of Knowledge and Salvation* |
| Philip Gonzales et al. (eds.) | *Finitude's Wounded Praise: Responses to Jean-Louis Crétien* |
| Martin Koci et al. (eds.) | *God and Phenomenology: Thinking with Jean-Yves Lacoste* |
| Steven E. Knepper (ed.) | *A Heart of Flesh: William Desmond and the Bible* |
| James Madden | *Thinking About Thinking: Mind and Meaning in the Era of Techno-Nihilism* |
| Tyler Dalton McNabb | *An Analytic Theology of Evangelism: A Classical Theist's Approach* |
| Duncan Reyburn | *The Roots of the World: The Remarkable Prescience of G. K. Chesterton* |
| Pablo Irizar et al. (eds.) | *To Die of Not Writing: Doing Philosophy of Religion with Emmanuel Falque* |
| Rachel M. Coleman | *Matter as an Image of the Good: Ferdinand Ulrich's Metaphysics of Creation* |
| Christine Stephenson | *Remembering Augustine: The Symphonic Forms and Fundamental Affordances of Memory in His Theology of Memoria* |
| Aimé Forest | *Consent to Being* |

# Human, All Too Human

*Mariology as Theo-Philosophical Anthropology*

JOSEPH TERRY

*foreword by Caitlin Smith Gilson*

CASCADE *Books* • Eugene, Oregon

HUMAN, ALL TOO HUMAN
Mariology as Theo-Philosophical Anthropology



Cascade Books
An Imprint of Wipf and Stock Publishers
199 W. 8th Ave., Suite 3
Eugene, OR 97401

www.wipfandstock.com

PAPERBACK ISBN: 979-8-3852-5551-1
HARDCOVER ISBN: 979-8-3852-5552-8
EBOOK ISBN: 979-8-3852-5553-5

*Cataloging-in-Publication data:*

Names: Terry, Joseph, author.

Title: Human, all too human : Mariology as theo-philosophical anthropology / Joseph Terry.

Description: Eugene, OR: Cascade Books, 2026. | Veritas. | Includes bibliographical references.

Identifiers: ISBN: 979-8-3852-5551-1 (paperback). | ISBN: 979-8-3852-5552-8 (hardcover). | ISBN: 979-8-3852-5553-5 (ebook).

Subjects: LCSH: Theological anthropology. | Theological anthropology—Catholic Church. | Theological anthropology—Christianity. | Mary, Blessed Virgin, Saint.

Classification: BT701.2 T22 2026 (print). | BT701.2 (epub).



Emphasis added to Scripture quotations.

# Contents

# Acknowledgments

THIS BOOK, WHICH IS ESSENTIALLY my doctoral dissertation, would not have been possible without the generous support of many. I am indebted to the Mariological Society of America for their affirming confidence in my research and their substantial financial support through the Arthur W. Clinton Jr. Scholarship, awarded to me twice during my years of study. I hope that their trust in my work was not misplaced and that this book will redound to the honor of our Lady, demonstrating her singular role in the church and the world.

My doctoral supervisor, Dr. Conor Cunningham, has offered prophetic insight, warm hospitality, spiritual direction, and joyful banter throughout the entirety of my research. His friendship, critical eye, deep insight, and loving encouragement made it possible for me to research and write from a joyful and discerning space. He was decisive in my swim across the Tiber as I returned home to Rome.

In addition, many thanks to those academics and friends who have offered incalculable feedback at various stages of my project. I am grateful to Dr. Philip Gonzales for his advice on my initial research proposal, taking the time to both affirm and critique where needed. Dr. Adrian Walker shared critical feedback at the beginning of my work, helping me to think through the trajectory and approach I would eventually take. Without his initial guidance, this book would undoubtedly be different. Thanks to Rev. Dr. Thomas Joseph White, OP, for offering encouraging feedback at certain stages of my work and helping me think through some questions I wrestled with before my return to the Catholic Church. His prayerful advice continues with me. Special thanks to Rev. Dr. John Behr, who graciously accepted me into his seminars on Irenaeus and Maximus the Confessor at St. Vladimir's Seminary, where I could sit under a master, such as he is, and learn. His insightful comments on my initial research layout were critical as well. I am incredibly grateful to Dr. Caitlin Smith Gilson for her friendship and generous reading of my work. Our conversations have been inspiring and illuminating. Her prayers continue to embrace my family, and it is a deep honor to have her contribute the foreword to this work. I am also grateful to Dr. John Milbank, Dr. John Betz, and Dr. Matthew Levering for their friendly and encouraging comments regarding the initial portion of my writing. Special thanks to Dr. Erich Groat for his editing assistance and for the generative conversations we typically have.

Thanks to my colleagues at the City University of New York, Kingsborough, who have encouraged me to pursue my doctorate, especially Dr. Tara Weiss and Dr. Rick Repetti. My profound gratitude to my home parish, Our Lady Queen of Martyrs, Forest Hills, for being a spiritual home to my wife and me, and now to our beautiful son, Isaac Joseph. Special thanks to Bishop Paul R. Sanchez, Rev. Francis J. Passenant, Rev. Antonin Kocurek, the late Msgr. Joseph L. Cunningham, and Deacon Greg Kandra for their faithful service to the Lord in the holy sacrifice of the Mass, of which I continue to receive much-needed nourishment. Furthermore, this work is a testament to my friends' many encouraging words and faithful support during my years of research and writing. Thank you.

I am incredibly grateful to my family, whose loving and joyful support was a source of encouragement. Words cannot express my gratitude to my mother, who has been a bottomless font of strength, joy, and profound love throughout my life. I would not be the man I am today if it were not for her heart. Her guidance and perseverance have brought me to where I am today.

While the dissertation was written and defended before his arrival, I am nevertheless grateful to my son, who now fills my heart with so much happiness and joy. I pray that this work will find a place in his hands and heart in the future.

It goes without saying that I could not have undertaken the journey of research and writing without my wife, my "Caramelita." Her sacrificial presence has sustained my heart and mind, and words fail to express how truly grateful I am to her. At every step, she was there, always ready to pull me up to reality, where I could once again rest in her arms. She embodies so much of what this book seeks to articulate.

Finally, I would like to express my most heartfelt thanks to my father, whose light continues to burn bright despite his departure to be with the Lord at the beginning of my research. As a wounded healer, he taught me to embrace all God has for me. I pray that what is found in these pages will faintly express what he so easily did through his music. This book is dedicated to him.

# Foreword

## *Mary, Cause of our Joy, Undoer of Knots*

*I saw my mother's face again, and felt, for the first time, how the stones of the road she had walked on must have bruised her feet. I saw the moonlit road where my father's brother died. And it brought something else back to me, and carried me past it, I saw my little girl again and felt Isabel's tears again, and I felt my own tears begin to rise. And I was yet aware that this was only a moment, that the world waited outside, as hungry as a tiger, and that trouble stretched above us, longer than the sky.*

—James Baldwin, *Going to Meet the Man*

*Human, All Too Human: Mariology as Theo-Philosophical Anthropology* is a stunning work, a treasury of riches. Its pages are the concrete realization of what each of us glimpsed when drawn, as if by magnet, to Christian revelation, to the life of the Holy Church, and into the arms of the Mother of God as womb of the world. Dr. Joseph Terry's magnificent book is one of those realizations where we know that those inklings of glory glimpsed all those years ago, in our studies and in our personal faith, are truly well and present. They are not mirage; instead they are an effective grace, and we find that our all too human reason and faith are now fortified in relentless gentleness and nourished in majestic strength. This is quite simply a watershed moment in Marian scholarship: truth springing from spiritual fecundity overflowing into pristine wisdom radiating the Word itself. Our Lady truly is Queen of Heaven, Star of the Sea, Mother of Mercy, *anthropologically* the Cause of Our Joy and *ontologically* the Undoer of Knots.

This work begins with an in-depth exploration of Our Lady as the existential icon of a creaturely metaphysics. Dr. Terry shows us the many effects and gifts of her astonishing and singular metaphysical position as the expressed concretization of Erich Przywara's "God in-and-beyond creation" and the *analogia entis*. This situates her as the archetypal human being who manifests the dynamic relationship between nature and grace, reason and faith, philosophy and theology. Throughout the work, our guide creates phenomenological spaces to reflect on Mary's whole and inexhaustible donative relationality. She is *entirely* the daughter of the Father, *entirely* the mother of the Son, and *entirely* the spouse of the Holy Spirit. This Marian *entirety* is the locus of all human expression and vocation, the mere creature as perfect human correlate to God in every way.

> Mary is uniquely and vividly positioned as creature to behold *in her* the interplay of these relations, such that they find their culminating and integrated expression only ever as *this* historically positioned, materially petite, existentially bound *mere* creature, in her words, decisions, actions—in short, the totality of her life both on earth and in glory. Neither do we behold these relations accidentally in her, as if to say *despite* her creaturely personhood, but truly, really, and substantially in and through her finite, bounded, and beautiful person. It is *as* human person, *as* mere creature, she *is* the unifying matrix of reality, the theoanthropocosmic synthesis, coextensively complementing her Son who is this synthesis as God, the Synthesis of syntheses. Thus, she reveals the depth and height, the meaning and purpose, the origin and end of *anthropology*.[2]

*Human, All Too Human* constructs a vigorous theo-philosophical anthropology grounded in Mariology, specifically focusing on the four Marian dogmas of the Catholic Church: divine maternity, perpetual virginity, immaculate conception, and assumption. Mary, in union with her Son Jesus Christ, unveils prismatically what it means to be human,[3] offering profound and ever-relevant insights into perennial anthropological questions concerning our origin, identity, vocation, and end. Dr. Terry provides a comprehensive and constructive methodology, integrating

2. This book, 48–49; emphasis in original.

3. See Dante Alighieri, *Paradiso* (1984), 2.142–44: "Because of the glad nature from which it flows, this many-faceted power shines through that body as through the living eye the glad soul glows."

theological and philosophical truths to reveal breathtaking conclusions that come from Mary's unique place in the divine economy. Our Lady is, again, crucial for understanding the human person as a theoanthropocosmic synthesis.

The book's clarion coordination of Marian dogmas with perennial anthropological questions brings us so thoroughly beyond any of the anemic yet persistent rejections of Mariology as excessive, idolatrous, and displacing Christ as intercessor. Mary's singular and exalted role in the economy of salvation is a "prism that refracts the white light of the hypostatic union between divinity and humanity, grace, and nature."[4] It is truly this image of a prism that sheds light on the Theotokos as pure self-*gift* who *gifts* Christ in his flesh, as the hypostatic *gift* beginning and ending all time. She is the open and effulgent icon of God who inhabits so perfectly an interpenetrating relationality in and to the undivided Trinity.

> It must be stressed that Mary's role in revealing this analogical interval in no way stands in competition with, let alone in contradistinction to, her Son. Rather, it is *in* and *through* her Son that she unfolds in an illuminative fashion the way a prism reveals what is already present—the full spectrum of visible light—as does Eve with Adam. We can say that Mary images her Son in a way that parallels the Son's image of the Father.[5]

One of the numerous contributions of *Human, All Too Human* to Christian philosophy is how it exposes the neglect of Our Lady as the real source of the disastrous displacement of Christ, promoting "a myopic *Christomonistic* style."[6] Christ, together with Mary, is the paradigmatic fulfillment of all dialogic tensions—time and eternity, finite and infinite, reason and faith, philosophy and theology. Her maternal union to her Son is the most intimate and most universal "undivided relational dynamic" through which all relations flow and return.[7] What our guide presents is no less than a redemptive anthropological pilgrimage from Nazareth to heaven:

1. Our human identity is truly revealed through the workings of divine maternity.

4. This book, 24.
5. This book, 43; emphasis in original.
6. This book, 19; emphasis in original.
7. This book, 16.

2. Our human vocation is given its direction "as radical openness to the Other" in her perpetual virginity.
3. What it means to be a human person, entirely creaturely and yet wholly shot through with the infinite, is extrapolated through her immaculate conception.
4. The destiny of the only creatures God willed for himself is revealed exquisitely in the mystery of the assumption.

> Mary's divine maternity unfolds the maternal identity of anthropos; her perpetual virginity identifies anthropological vocation; her immaculate conception reveals the decisive origin of the human being; and her assumption details the end, the destiny of the anthropos as such.[8]

Etienne once remarked: "In metaphysics the choice does not lie for us between the old and new but rather between the false and true."[9] This is precisely the quandary of the philosopher when presented not with religious ideas in general, but Christ, the God who became man, who *as existence* has forever changed the way we encounter Being. The metaphysical choice is, again, between the false and the true. It would be a falsehood to deny what is clearly revealed to us.

> "Jesus' conception and birth signify a new involvement in history that exceeds the uniqueness of belonging to every single human being. . . . What begins here has the quality of a new creation, owing to God's own totally specific interventions.[10]

Refusing to encounter this decisive incarnational change to existence does not retain philosophical footing but impoverishes its soil. Such a closed and warped philosophy forces reason to postulate ideas opposed to meaning and reality. Dr. Terry is in a rare intellectual circle: he lets reason *see* what is to be *seen* and faith hold dear what it has received:

> Our initial observation draws us to the fact that she is *a* creature. And while revelation taken up and received in faith sees her as *the* one, *the* Mother, and thus, notes her *perennial* significance and scope, reason can also begin with what is merely observed and deduced: the particular in relation to the universal, such

8. This book, 187–88.
9. Gilson, *Art of Misunderstanding Thomism*, 7.
10. Ratzinger, *Daughter Zion*, 47–48.

> that the universal and the particular are bound together. She is *a* human creature—*a* woman—within *a* given cultural and historical milieu. But by way of causality, philosophy also observes that she is the effect of multiple causes, especially that of a transcendent ground that holds all things together in being at every moment—the ontological cause both of her and of all.[11]

Philosophy after the Christ event has its being on a higher plane while retaining its direction to understand what *is*.[12] The Theotokos gifted philosophy with inexhaustibly *more* to understand, and genuine philosophy, such as this remarkable book, responds to the call. Revelation and its interpretation belong to theology, but its implications are open to philosophy. Philosophy has always had a way of sighting Being; this is the philosophical act as wonder. And what is more wondrous than pondering the philosophical implications of the incarnation? These sage writings deepen our reception of philosophical wonder. We grasp with awe that the Theotokos, as mere creature and Mother of God, has offered to metaphysics a higher, far richer anthropological perspective for viewing Being:

> Our Lady's conception indeed secures her as the perfect *icon* of the God-man, ever only as a mere creature, and so she is the center and channel of the highest aesthetic reality as a creature of God, who is the apex of creation.[13]

Dr. Terry never loses sight of the relational demands that signify the intrinsic dignity of the anthropos. We reside as flesh and spirit, from Mother to Son and Son to Mother. His writing intensively enacts,

11. This book, 75.

12. See Balthasar, *Theology of History*, 74: "Christ can be called the 'concrete analogy of Being,' *analogia entis*, since he constitutes himself, in the unity of his divine and human natures, the proportion of every interval between God and man. And this unity is his person in both natures. The philosophical formulation of the analogy of Being is related to the measure of Christ precisely as is world history to his history—as promise to fulfillment, the preliminary to the definitive. He is so very much what is most concrete and most central that in the last analysis we can only think by starting with him; every question as to what might be if he did not exist, or he had not become man, or if the world had to be considered without him, is now superfluous and unnecessary. . . . When God reveals his inner intention—that he willed creation from all eternity; that now, bound up with the world in the indissoluble bond of the hypostatic union, he will never again be without the world; that he designed and predestined man as the brother of his eternal Son become man—then it becomes clear how, without losing its validity, the plane of philosophy is transcended."

13. This book, 130; emphasis in original.

reenacts, and heightens those relational structures through each of the five chapters. The truth, goodness, and beauty unveiled lead us towards ultimacy while avoiding those well-traveled echo chambers and ideological dead ends. The human person is placed into the mystery of our humanity as reverberation of the *interior-exteriorized* union that Mary enacts united in self-giving to her Son:

> Thus, observing reality "in Christ"—which is also to say "in Mary," though in a different metaphysical register—furnishes us with the tools to observe the relationship between nature and grace (since Christ is the hypostatic union between divinity and humanity, which Mary enacts as the *interior-exteriorized* union that is internal to her Son, as we saw in our first chapter), perceiving that "the natural is not transformed into the supernatural, just as sacraments are not magic pills, religious ones at that, no, rather it is the transformation of the old into the new; more, it is the revelation of the new in the old, the old was always meant for the new."[14]

The metaphysical implications of Our Lady address most profoundly the uncreated ground and immediate relation with God at root in all creational meaning. This ground must be held and continually approached even if only in our acknowledged failure to enact it. Only Mary, mere creature, is truly granted to enact this convertible union. The womb of the Theotokos holds the trembling enactment of cresting waves mingling the uncreated with the created; she illuminates "a Trinitarian ontology via *analogia entis* by way of her unique placement in the divine economy."[15]

> Through her we can speak of God as a zygote, embryo, fetus, child, son of Adam, and so on, for she is the door to the

14. This book, 115; quoting C. Cunningham, "Natura Pura," 253; emphasis in original.

15. This book, 187. See further Balthasar and Ratzinger, *Mary*, 82–83: "The scene of the Annunciation merits consideration for another reason, too: it is not only wholly Christological; it is wholly trinitarian as well. It is strikingly obvious that its structure amounts to a first revelation of God's triunity. The angel's initial salutation, which calls Mary the one full of grace par excellence, brings her the greeting of the 'Lord,' Yahweh, the Father, whom she knows as a Jewish believer. And she ponders what this greeting might mean, the angel responds with a second speech that reveals that she will give birth to the 'Son of the Most High,' who will at the same time be the Messiah from the house of Jacob. And when she asks what is expected of her in all this, the angel offers a third explanation in which he reveals to her that the Holy Spirit will overshadow her, so that her child can legitimately be called the Holy One and the Son of God."

> *communicatio idiomatum* ever only possible by this ineffable union between the uncreated and created.[16]

*Human, All Too Human* decisively provides the harmonization of the creational world to its inexhaustible and maternal uncreated ground as key to a living anthropos. Without it we get variations of personhood severed from flesh and transcendence—mind or machine, it is no matter, thought has perniciously sidelined what it is to be human. In our fallen state we are more comfortable with the fragmented, partial, and ephemeral, considering what is vaguely grasped in our blindness to be substantial.[17] An anthropological orientation estranged from the Theotokos moves too quickly; it touches all and caresses nothing. This estrangement misses both our prevenient openness to the divine in the immaculate conception and the assumption's revelation and completing of the human being who, on earth, is the *"apophatically concealed, eschatologically deferred being*."[18] This is not a concessionary Mariology that tries to eke out a place of relevance for Our Lady by sequestering her contributions and placing them on insufficient grounds. Dr. Terry consistently shows how she is the situatedness of a Trinitarian ontology, the pleromatic suspended middle through which every human being must enter and emerge to be a person. Mary is the non-reductive expression of the human being because she is the pure overflowing icon of love and surrender to Christ. In the assumption we discover:

> The hermeneutical lens through which we see the *total* human being, but ever only partially—through a dark glass, as it were—since this end, this culmination is, as stated above, ineffably mysterious; thus, the human being is the *apophatically concealed, eschatologically deferred being*. This is the meta-anthropology given at the end, an anthropology that transcends any reductionistic account.[19]

16. This book, 31.

17. See Dante Alighieri, *Paradiso* (1984), 22.51: "The little threshing floor that so incites our savagery."

18. This book, 164; emphasis in original.

19. This book, 174; emphasis in original.

## FIVE POWERFUL ONTOLOGICAL IMPLICATIONS OF DR. JOSEPH TERRY'S MARIAN ANTHROPOLOGY

Our Lady's fiat is the home of our underlying ontological freedom, which lives at the interplay of the unchanging and the changing, the permanent and the conditional, the horizontal and the vertical. When we do not work to approach or enact her freedom, we find ourselves immanentized into entity or ego. The common state of the human person both within and outside the church is one akin to the machinist, remnant finitude treated as parts and moving pieces of an enclosed timepiece with nowhere to go beyond their immediate coordination of horizontal time. We have divested our finitude of its nuptial intimacy with the infinite, severed flesh from its specific transcendent dignity. But the Theotokos ontologically instructs us as "a nurse tenderly caring for her own children" (1 Thess 2:7 NRSVCE) and in travail with a "sword of suffering piercing the soul of His Blessed Mother."[20] Through Our Lady, we hear the groaning of our creational ends, forever the creaturely mirroring of the uncreated. Understanding the Marian *theoanthropocosmic synthesis* enables us to recognize and overturn the artificial structures protracted over and against nature and grace (and with an intentional infidelity to the eternal) that cater only to the death of the human person. Dr. Joseph Terry magnificently provides a living and corresponsive key to understanding and appreciating Our Lady's supreme and life-giving instructions. Here are but a few of these graced guidelines to be seen in full in this masterpiece:

1. *Mary's Maternal Identity as Central to Human Identity*

   Mary's fiat is the archetypal expression of human finitude capable of receiving the infinite. Her maternal identity is enacted through her fiat, gestation, birth, and parenting of the Word revealing the human as an intrinsically maternal being who embodies the call-and-response to the divine. The emphasis on Mary's maternal identity as the paradigmatic human identity vigorously challenges anthropologies that neglect the relational and receptive dimensions of being human.

2. *Perpetual Virginity as Anthropological Vocation and Eschatological Exocentricity*

20. Chardon, Cross of Jesus, 166.

Mary's perpetual virginity points to an eschatologically oriented vocation marked by radical openness to the Other and a proleptic embodiment of the "angelic state," signifying the spousal character of human vocation in relation to God. This profound vocational responsiveness includes not only her bodily integrity but is more wholly viewed as virginal luminosity of seamlessly united body, mind, and sense, ever free from the seed of sin so that Our Lady can be the magnificent situation for creaturely transcendence. This holy virginity signifies Our Lady's glorious spousal character bound in God as wholly *for God*.

3. *The Immaculate Conception Revealing Human Origin as Graced Personhood and Pneumatic Time*

Mary's immaculate conception signifies the preemptive grace that shapes human origin, emphasizing the human being as a graced person whose origin is both temporal and eternal, realized in a temporal/eternal dynamic originally termed by Dr. Terry as "pneumatic time." This richly layered temporal/eternal dynamic wedded to Our Lady and realized through her to the anthropos raises time into Being, so that history and all its contingencies are "nevertheless definitively shaped by an eschatological, eternal grammar."[21] As the analogical interval, both mere creature and Theotokos, Our Lady enables history to recover its fractured eschatological destination.

> She is the end upon which a longing gaze searches for the way *to* the Unconditioned. She is the gate *through* which glory is revealed. In her there is no room for an idolatrous quicksand but instead a bridge to the invisible *through* the visible.[22]

The original concept of pneumatic time is a central contribution. It offers a way of integrating time and eternity in a way that avoids extrinsicism. Pneumatic time recognizes the problems of placing "grace" immaturely atop "nature" as one layer of cake rests atop another but, in reality, is separated from it.[23] Without a fully integrated understanding of time and eternity in our anthropological

21. This book, 102n15.

22. This book, 131; emphasis in original.

23. "The subtle and supple understanding of nature and grace advocated by St. Thomas turned into an ossified extrinsicism, a layer-cake theology of two separable and impermeable realms" (Wood, "Flannery O'Connor, Benedict XVI," 38).

reflection, the eschatological dimensions of human existence degenerate into wish fulfillment or fantasy. Our Lady's self-gift of her Son is the estuary where time and eternity are convertible while remaining distinct and without reduction. A Marian ontology recovers the many coextensive mysteries of our eschatological dimensions.

4. *The Assumption as the Anthropological Telos: The Human as Eschatologically Deferred*

   Our eschatologically deferred nature is a stunning insight and the culmination of this interrogative masterpiece, one that has done all the careful conceptual development with striking attentiveness to the essential teachings of the faith. Dr. Terry's analysis of the human as eschatologically deferred being, realized through Our Lady, is the linchpin through which this masterpiece can be read yet again. Understanding this crucial insight allows the book to become altogether new with more truths to encounter. The assumption dramatically reveals our human destiny as an eschatologically deferred being, underscoring the completion and glorification of the human person in union with God, and affirming the theoanthropocosmic synthesis. The assumption of Our Lady enacts and recapitulates human ending, showing us in all its ineffability the way forward forever bound to her pure self-gifting divine maternity.

5. *The Significance of a Theo-Philosophical Approach Combining Theology and Philosophy*

   *Human, All Too Human* emphasizes the necessity of integrating both theology and philosophy to fully apprehend Mary's role in anthropology, arguing that a purely Christomonistic approach neglects the Trinitarian and analogical complementarities revealed through Mary. By grounding the study in both theology and philosophy, it avoids reductionism and enriches anthropological inquiry through a dual lens that respects faith and reason. I stress this cornerstone of the book because it provides a living rubric for the theologian and philosopher when approaching Christian teaching, one that recognizes and avoids the uninformative strictures suffocating our courtship with divine meaning.

> Theology is the science of grace though never to the exclusion of nature, but instead always in and through nature as its

> presupposition. (Healthy) philosophy is the science of nature but never as "pure nature," but instead always in and through grace from which it springs forth and in which it is sustained.[24]

Dr. Terry's theo-philosophical approach underscores the importance of this integrative dialogue in theology and philosophy, affirming that neither discipline alone can fully grasp the mystery of the human person as revealed in Mary. Through his scholarship, we genuinely experience what we may have grasped only speculatively: it is *relation* from the beginning to the end, every experience is *relation*, it is a union of poles, intensities, of otherness as self and self as given to the other, it *is* the persons of the Trinity, from Mother to Son, and Son to Mother, from bride to bridegroom, and bridegroom to bride. Only from the seat of relationality do we begin to approach the divine love that undergirds it all. Our Lady's fiat teaches this: "It is only a yes to life, to love, to light, to Reality itself, that can be the genesis for new and real life, deep and abiding love, a luminosity that truly enlightens, that grounds the self via anamnesis in what is true, good, and beautiful."[25]

*Human, All Too Human* is a remarkable work, a wisdom text with the fruits of grace illuminating its sentences as if each word speaks directly to the readers' hearts and minds. Perhaps this is how Our Lady, the anthropological Cause of Our Joy and ontological Undoer of Knots, speaks to us . . .

Our lives need Mary's prismatic maternal light if we are to see what is before us and to live truly for the kingdom of heaven, for we are not our own light.

> And she said such strange things! To her own mother she had said—without warning "Woman! do you ever look inside? Do you ever look inside and see what you are not? God!" she had cried sinking down again and staring at her plate, "Malebranche was right: we are not our own light. We are not our own light!"
> —Flannery O'Connor, "A Good Man Is Hard to Find"

24. This book, 32.

25. This book, 48–49.

# Abbreviations

| | |
|---|---|
| BETL | Bibliotheca Ephemeridum Theologicarum Lovaniensium |
| *Comp. Theol.* | *Compendium of Theology*. By Thomas Aquinas. Translated by Richard J. Regan. Oxford: Oxford University Press, 2009 |
| *De Ver.* | *Quaestiones Disputatae de Veritate* |
| *Dorm.* | *In Dormitionem Sanctae Dei Genitricis Mariae Orationes* |
| FC | Fathers of the Church: A New Translation |
| *LG* | "*Lumen Gentium*: Dogmatic Constitution on the Church." Promulgated by Paul VI. Vatican, Nov. 21, 1964. https://www.vatican.va/archive/hist_councils/ii_vatican_council/documents/vat-ii_const_19641121_lumen-gentium_en.html |
| *NBf* | *New Blackfriars* |
| PG | Patrologia Graeca[= *Patrologiae Cursus Completus*: Series Graeca]. Edited by Jacques-Paul Migne. 162 vols. Paris, 1857–86 |
| *ST* | *Summa Theologiae: A Concise Translation*. By Thomas Aquinas. Edited by Timothy McDermott. Notre Dame, IN: Ave Maria, 1989 |

# Introduction

## BACKGROUND

Christianity is a humanism insofar as the apex of revelation is centered upon a human being: Jesus the Christ. In other words, God reveals God's self definitively and finally in and through the Son by the Spirit (Heb 1:1–3)—an act accomplished through the incarnation, wherein God becomes human without ceasing to be God. Thus, the human being is at once the focal point of divine disclosure, such that both God *and* the human being are coextensively revealed in the unity of Christ's person—without confusion or separation.

Implicit within Christianity, then, is a distinct anthropology—indeed, *the* anthropology—one that is theandric in scope. It is in Christ that the true and authentic expression of anthropos is revealed: its being and purpose, and its origin and end.[1] The human being, therefore, can be fully understood only in the light of God, just as God is most fully apprehended in and through *the* human being, Jesus the Nazarene. Consequently, *anthropology* and *theology* are intrinsically and indivisibly united.

Moreover, because the whole sweep of creation is also revealed in and through this one who is both God and man, the unity of divinity and humanity becomes the very cipher of creation itself (Col 1:15–22). At the heart of Christianity's revelatory arc, then, is a *theo-anthropo-cosmic* synthesis—the anthropology given to us, a *meta*-anthropology.

This awareness has caused Christians since apostolic times to examine both the meaning and implication of such a revelation that has at its

1. Consider John Paul II's encyclical *Redemptor Hominis* for a description of the way in which Christ reveals both God and anthropos in a coextensive manner.

heart the human being.[2] Since any reflection upon God or creation in the final analysis cannot be done without recourse to anthropos, Christian theologians and philosophers—just to consider these two vocations—always at least implicitly engage in a priori anthropological truths, regardless of how remote those truths are to their current study. In addition, whenever studies or reflections are offered by Christians on any aspect of creation or God, such reflections, especially within the Catholic tradition, bring to bear the full resources of both *faith* and *reason*, since both *grace* and *nature* are revealed to be inextricably bound without confusion within the one person, Jesus of Nazareth. To put it differently, the incarnation essentially removes any possibility of using either faith or reason *alone*, contra Luther, since what is revealed in Christ is the coextensive unity—no doubt paradoxical, given their difference—between divine and human natures. Thus, despite what is already presupposed within the Catholic metaphysical tradition regarding ontological participation in God (Acts 17:28), the full and final revelation given in Christ shows the indissoluble, paradoxical unity between the human being as such and God—God, therefore, not destroying but building upon and transfiguring *nature* transcendently by grace—and so the salvation of *reason* revealed *to faith*. Reason, therefore, is not destroyed but elevated and completed through faith; and faith is reflected upon and explored by reason, spurred on by faith: *fides quaerens intellectum*. Given all this, we can discern why a Catholic examination of any aspect of creation and/or God (1) at the very least *implicitly* operates within a priori anthropological truths revealed, and (2) does so by having recourse to what has explicitly been revealed to *faith* and, having been illumined by this light, *reason*.[3]

2. Consider, for example, Fr. John Behr's brief work titled *Becoming Human* regarding how patristic sources explored the significance of the indissoluble marriage between the anthropos and God. See also Steenberg, *Of God and Man*, to observe how theology and anthropology were tightly bound within early fathers like Irenaeus, Tertullian, Cyril of Jerusalem, and Athanasius of Alexandria. For a view on Maximus's theology as anthropology, see Thunberg, *Man and the Cosmos*. For a fuller treatment on the how certain theologians, including the Reformer Calvin, possess a nonreductive anthropology, see the following: Wingren, *Man and the Incarnation*; Duffy, "Anthropology"; Lehrberger, "Anthropology"; Torrance, *Calvin's Doctrine of Man*.

3. John Paul II's encyclical *Fides et Ratio* explores the critical relation between faith and reason, arguing their fundamental compatibility within the Catholic tradition since they essentially belong together. Reason divorced from faith leads to nihilism, and faith divorced from reason is superstitious. See also the collection of essays edited by Foster and Koterski, *Two Wings of Catholic Thought*, which reflects on this encyclical.

Historically, both before and within the postconciliar period, theological and philosophical reflection on anthropos has been explicitly taken up. Various philosophical anthropologies from Enlightenment thinkers such as Descartes, Locke, Hume, and Kant had a decisive influence in shaping the way the anthropos was understood, primarily through an egocentric, anthropocentric lens in which God was factored in only tertiarily, or sometimes not at all. As Kelly M. Kapic notes, these modern philosophers influenced the shape of anthropological considerations for professing believers and their theological ruminations.[4] Schleiermacher's (1768–1834) "feeling of absolute dependence," for example, offered a critical response to Kant's anthropology by thinking about the human being in embodiment through terms like "feeling" or "intuition" (*Gefühle*).[5] Another German Protestant theologian, Ernst Troeltsch (1865–1923), in light of the new scientific and psychological writings of Darwin and Freud, provided a "religious anthropology" that focused on the "soul," since "the religious concept of the soul has absolutely *nothing* to do with the scientific anthropology and experimental psychology; it is rather an object of faith."[6] Responding to what he perceived as trends within (Protestant) Christian anthropologies that tended to have an optimistic and progressive view of the human being predicated on a certain reading of evolutionary theory, James Orr (1834–1913) argued, before the great world wars, that such tendencies water down the Christian teaching on sin and the fallenness of anthropos. As he would state, "The myth of the fall of man is replaced by the scientific theory of the ascent of man."[7] Other Protestant theologians, like Charles Hodge (1797–1878) and B. B. Warfield (1851–1921) attempted to think through anthropology in view of scientific discoveries around evolution and human origins, either by rejecting or correlating theology with what science was articulating; while, from the Catholic side, Fr. Pierre Teilhard de Chardin (1881–1955) developed an anthropology profoundly shaped by evolutionary science.[8]

With the continuation of the twentieth century and the beginning of the twenty-first comes a twofold trend in theological anthropology: contextualized anthropologies[9] and renewed Christocentric and dogmat-

4. Kapic, "Anthropology," 123.

5. Kapic, "Anthropology," 126. See also Thandeka, *Embodied Self.*

6. Troeltsch, *Christian Faith*, 225; as cited in Kapic, "Anthropology," 131.

7. Orr, *God's Image in Man*, 11; as cited in Kapic, "Anthropology," 133.

8. See Chardin: *Future of Man*; *Human Phenomenon*.

9. Some salient examples are Teevan, "Challenges to the Role"; Clifford, "When

ically informed anthropologies—from the crowning twentieth-century Protestant theologian Karl Barth and successors like Dietrich Bonhoeffer, Wolfhart Pannenberg, and T. F. Torrance;[10] and from Catholic theologians such as Henri de Lubac, Hans Ur von Balthasar, Pope John Paul II (Karol Wojtyła), and Pope Benedict XVI (Joseph Ratzinger), to name just a few.[11] With the advent of the Second Vatican Council, and in particular sections 12–22 in the document *Gaudium et Spes*, Catholic theological and philosophical anthropology established the importance of grounding anthropological reflections within the orbit of Christology, which was later reaffirmed by the writings of Pope John Paul II and Pope Benedict XVI.[12] A number of documents coming from the International Theological Commission, a group commissioned by Paul VI in order to bridge theologians with the magisterium after the Second Vatican Council, have extended the church's thinking on theological and philosophical anthropology. The following three documents have been particularly fruitful in this: "Theology, Christology, Anthropology" (1982), "The Dignity and Rights of the Human Person" (1983), and "Communion and Stewardship: Human Persons Created in the Image of God" (2004). As Tracey Rowland notes, during the celebration of the commission's fiftieth anniversary, Philippe Vallin remarked that the documents of the commission (from 1969 to 2019) "have contributed to the development of a theological anthropology based on a metaphysical vision of the human person made in the image of God that finds its dynamics in a sacramentality of

Being Human"; Gutiérrez, *Theology of Liberation*.

10. Barth, *Doctrine of Creation*, 16–19; Pannenberg, *Anthropology in Theological Perspective*; Bonhoeffer, *Act and Being*; Woznicki, *Torrance's Christological Anthropology*.

11. Lubac, *Mystery of the Supernatural*; Balthasar, *Dramatis Personae*; John Paul II, *Man and Woman*; Benedict XVI, *Anthropology and Culture*.

12. Tracey Rowland identifies the significance and scope of the magisterial writings of John Paul II and Benedict XVI for anthropology: "The combined magisterial works of the papacies of John Paul II and Benedict XVI read as an exercise in unpacking and re-presenting what the young Ratzinger identified as a theological anthropology explicitly trinitarian and Christocentric. Central to this anthropology is an understanding of the missions of the Persons of the Trinity in the life of the world and the spiritual development of the human person. Common themes are the work of the theological virtues—faith, hope, and love—on the faculties of human soul, and the soul's receptivity to truth, goodness, and beauty. The trinitarian encyclicals of John Paul II (*Redemptor hominis; Dives in misericordia*; and *Dominum et vivificantem*) and the theological virtues trilogy of the papacy of Benedict XVI (*Deus caritas est*; *Spe salvi*; and *Lumen fidei*) outline the major principles of this trinitarian Christocentric anthropology. To obtain a comprehensive account of this anthropology it is necessary to combine the content of all six encyclicals" ("Theological Anthropology," 9).

active imitation of Jesus Christ and in a moral theology of eschatological responsibility."[13] Within the Catholic Church, there now seems to be a twofold trend regarding the styles in which theologians reflect on anthropology, much of which could be categorized as belonging to either the *concilium* or the *communio* camps. As Rowland states,

> It is something of an academic cliché to say that Catholic theological anthropology in the twenty-first century is divided into Rahnerian and Balthasarian camps, with the "open-to-history" existential Thomists finding themselves welcome within the Balthasarian camp, but nonetheless this *is* how the territory looks at the beginning of the twenty-first century. The root cause of the division would appear to be Rahner's openness to Kant and the general legacy of German Idealism and the contrary belief, shared by Newman, Scheeben, Gilson, Balthasar, and Ratzinger, that reason is never theologically neutral.[14]

Finally, another central postconciliar fruit was the production of the *Catechism of the Catholic Church*, promulgated by Pope John Paul II, of which the third part, titled "Life in Christ," offers the church's teaching on theological and philosophical anthropology.[15] All this reveals the church's mind on the question concerning anthropology, and there have been no signs indicating a waning of such theological and philosophical reflections and clarifications.

Notwithstanding the tendency of pre- and postconciliar anthropological reflections within the Catholic Church to have decisive recourse to Christ, theologians have also recognized the importance of Mary as one who "completes," as it were, the *imago Dei* in complementarity to Christ. As early as Justin Martyr (100–165) in his work titled *Dialogue with Trypho* we see our Lady being explicitly described as the "new Eve," as is also expounded upon by Irenaeus of Lyons (130–202) in his *Against Heresies* and Tertullian in *The Flesh of Christ* (155–220). Luigi Gambero's two-part work, titled *Mary and the Fathers of the Church: The Blessed Virgin Mary in Patristic Thought* and *Mary in the Middle Ages: The Blessed Virgin Mary in the Thought of Medieval Latin Theologians*, captures well the church's constant ruminations throughout history on our Lady, which spring from a doxological/liturgical context always in relation to both

13. Rowland, "Theological Anthropology," 12; referring to Vallin, "Filo rosso antropologico"; emphasis in original.

14. Rowland, "Theological Anthropology," 19–20.

15. Catholic Church, *Catechism*, §§1699–1748.

Christ and the church. Such an extensive survey reveals how Mariological ruminations created space, among other things, to consider *how* our Lady both enacts and sums up what it means to be human in the light of what is culminated in Christ—and so the possibility of always thinking through this relation in complementarity rather than competition—by thinking about pastoral and moral implications in view of Mary's being and actions in salvific history. The nineteenth and early twentieth centuries saw a continued increase in both Catholic Marian devotion and theological reflections, some of which was spurred on by questions concerning the possibility of Mary's sinlessness from conception, and subsequently in response to the dogmatic definition of her immaculate conception (i.e., John Henry Newman, Matthias Joseph Scheeben, etc.), as well as the possibility of her bodily assumption into heaven—all of which contained implicit anthropological questions.[16]

However, a particular trend within Mariological discourse began to slowly take shape in the twentieth century, in which a more *explicit* turn toward anthropological questions in view of Mary began to form. The highly speculative Eastern Orthodox theologian Sergius Bulgakov, in his work titled *The Burning Bush* (1927), identifies strongly, considering the tradition—particularly around our Lady's glorification and her iconic description as Mother with Child—that the "Divine image in humankind is disclosed and realized in the heavens as the image of two: of Christ and of His Mother. . . . And yet in the heavens there is still one human image which obviously pertains to the fullness of the human prototype, namely, the Mother of God, 'the second Eve.'"[17] For Bulgakov, Christ "expresses the fullness *of the image* of human nature only together with the Mother of God."[18]

The formal Lutheran turned Catholic (French Oratorian) theologian Louis Bouyer wrote extensively before the Second Vatican Council,

16. Donald H. Calloway offers a brief summary of some of the salient events that occurred in the nineteenth century that helped to spur on Marian devotion and reflection. "In the 19th century, an explosion of extraordinary Marian-themed events took place in the Church: 1842, the discovery of the lost Marian writings of St. Louis de Montfort: in 1854, the proclamation of the dogma of the Immaculate Conception; in 1858, the apparitions in Lourdes, France; from 1878–1903, the intense Marian papacy of Leo XIII (He wrote 11 encyclicals on the Rosary!); and, in 1873, Blessed Bartolo Longo began his Rosary apostolate in Pompeii, Italy. These events helped prepare for the numerous Marian saints and movements of the 20th century" (foreword to *Mother Thrice Admirable*, 5).

17. Bulgakov, *Burning Bush*, 80.

18. Bulgakov, *Burning Bush*, 83; emphasis in original.

including on Mary's significance for what he called "supernatural anthropology." Bouyer argues that "Christ was perfectly man, yet so perfectly, in so divine a way, that he was not, strictly speaking, *a* man, a human person, but God made man. That is why," he goes on to say, "we hold it to be so important to reflect upon that wholly human person who was placed, by the Incarnation, in an absolutely unique relation with the Son of God himself."[19] All this has the effect, for Bouyer, of offering a Mariologically informed anthropology with a particular eschatological slant—an "eschatological humanism," as he puts it. Thus, as he articulates, "she is, as it were, the living image, present within time, of what will be brought about in us all only at the end of time. Though unique and pre-eminent, she is yet the image of what we have to become."[20] As Michael Heintz notes, "Mary personally instantiates Bouyer's eschatological humanism in that she manifests, from her Immaculate Conception to her glorious Assumption, all the possibilities of a redeemed humanity, of just what it might look like for a human person to be configured fully to Christ, her Son."[21]

In anticipation of many of the anthropological questions and issues that would continue to arise in the twentieth century, Fr. Joseph Kentenich initiated a Marian apostolate called the Schoenstatt movement (1914) to educate and disciple people to become "Marian" people. One of Fr. Kentenich's enduring legacies was his articulation of our Lady as *causa exemplaris*, such that she is the "Catholic image of the human person."[22] His entire apostolate was founded on the principle that Mary is indeed the perfect realization of what it means to be human by virtue of *her* relation to the God-man Jesus her Son, and thus the pattern in which one is to be shaped.

In the second half of the twentieth century, the Second Vatican Council, in chapter 8 of *Lumen Gentium* (*LG*), expressed the mind of the

19. Bouyer, *Woman and Man*, vii; emphasis in original.

20. Bouyer, *Meaning of Monastic Life*, 129.

21. Heintz, "Mariology as Theological Anthropology," 211.

22. Kentenich, *Katholische Menschenbild*, 120. Also consider the later Pope Paul VI's encyclical *Marialis Cultus*: "First, the Virgin Mary has always been proposed to the faithful by the Church as an example to be imitated, not precisely in the type of life she led, and much less for the socio-cultural background in which she lived and which today scarcely exists anywhere. She is held up as an example to the faithful rather for the way in which, in her own particular life, she fully and responsibly accepted the will of God (cf. Lk. 1:38), because she heard the word of God and acted on it, and because charity and a spirit of service were the driving force of her actions. She is worthy of imitation because she was the first and the most perfect of Christ's disciples. All of this has a permanent and universal exemplary value" (§35).

church regarding our Lady's person and mission within God's economy and in relation to both Christ and his church. And since the council, continued meditations on the anthropological significance of our Lady are being offered by a variety of thinkers. The Pontifical International Marian Academy authored a work titled *The Mother of the Lord: Memory, Presence, Hope* (2007), which contains not only "themes and current questions related to the mystery of the mother of the Lord" but also various anthropological considerations in light of her. Other recent works such as Donald Calloway's *The Virgin Mary and Theology of the Body* (2005) and "The Virgin Mary and Theological Anthropology" (2018) offer a range of essays reflecting on our Lady's significance for deeper anthropological insights. And on March 25, 1988, the Congregation for Catholic Education in Rome promulgated a document titled "The Virgin Mary in Intellectual and Spiritual Formation" emphasizing the relation between Mariology and anthropological studies:

> Post-conciliar Mariology has given renewed attention to anthropology. The Popes have repeatedly presented Mary of Nazareth as the supreme expression of human freedom in the cooperation of man with God. . . . In the convergence of the data of faith and the data of the anthropological sciences, when these turn their attention to Mary of Nazareth, one understands more clearly that the Virgin is both the highest historical realization of the Gospel and the woman who, through her self-control, her sense of responsibility, her openness to others and to the spirit of service, her strength and her love, is the most completely realized on the human level.[23]

In addition to these developments, for example, a recently published essay titled "A 'New Creation in Christ' (2 Cor 5:17): Mary, the Immaculata, as Anthropological Model" by M. Isabell Naumann, ISSM, makes the argument that "the *Immaculata*, as the fully redeemed person, is significant for the view of human identity and Christian personality."[24] And in the Eastern Orthodox camp, few have come close to the sustained reflections offered by the late Alexander Schmemann on how modern "anthropological heresies" are overcome through Mary as the archetype of humanity.[25]

23. Congregation for Catholic Education, "Virgin Mary," §15.

24. Naumann, "New Creation in Christ," 171.

25. Schmemann, *Virgin Mary*, 47.

## RESEARCH PROBLEM

As we have seen above, a significant amount of research has been done on various theological anthropologies, with a not-insignificant quantity of this research pursuing questions concerning Mary's substantial relevance to anthropology. These studies have recognized both the possibility and rationale for locating anthropological insights derivative of our Lady, especially given her place in the divine economy. As observed, some Mariologically informed anthropologies have examined in a general manner ways in which Mary offers an archetypal and paradigmatic response (typically via a pastoral mode) to contemporary issues, while other research has tended to elaborate on how various dogmatic truths of our Lady (i.e., divine maternity, immaculate conception, etc.) provide specific insights into the human condition, as well as anthropological correlates discernible in the life of grace. However, these studies have tended to focus either on certain aspects of Mary in relation to anthropology or on a general appraisal of anthropological insights observable given her place in the divine economy. As a result, the existing literature does not offer (1) a robust *metaphysically* informed theo-philosophical anthropology that draws out the enduring significance Mary has *for* anthropology; (2) a full-bodied Mariological anthropology that considers *simultaneously all* the dogmatic truths of our Lady, especially in the light of perennial questions concerning human origin, identity, vocation, and destiny; (3) a Mariologically informed anthropology that recognizes the significant role both theology *and* philosophy have in exploring the ways in which Mary mutually *illumines* (grace/faith/theology) and *illustrates* (nature/reason/philosophy) anthropology. Consequently, the current research effectively leaves absent an overall robust Marian theo-philosophical anthropology, situating current Mariological considerations of anthropology as somewhat fragmented, and worse, a bit myopic.

## RESEARCH AIMS, OBJECTIVES, AND QUESTIONS

Given the lack of research on discerning a robust Mariologically informed anthropology that simultaneously includes all the dogmatic truths of our Lady in view of various perennially salient queries, with respect to both theological and philosophical analysis, this research will investigate how Mariology, understood through the four Marian dogmas of the church, provides a deep and enriching theo-philosophical anthropology. My thesis is as follows: Mary, in concert with her Son, both *enacts* and *recapitulates* what it means to be human *theo-philosophically*. My research objectives are as follows: (1) to identify a metaphysical basis for situating anthropological reflections under Mariology; (2) to identify how both theological and philosophical consideration of our Lady in view of anthropology is justified given the metaphysical basis aforementioned; (3) to identify how the four dogmatic truths of Mary address questions concerning human origin, identity, vocation, and destiny; and (4) to explore the various ways in which a theo-philosophical anthropology predicated on Mariology reveals Mary, in synergistic partnership with her Son, to be the *theoanthropocosmic synthesis* as a *mere* human. Thus, my research questions are as follows: (1) What is the metaphysical basis for having recourse to Mary in view of anthropological questions? (2) What is the metaphysical justification for the use of both theology and philosophy in investigating Mary in view of anthropological considerations? (3) How do the four dogmatic truths of our Lady effectively address questions concerning anthropological origin, identity, vocation, and destiny? (4) What are some of the ways in which a Marian theo-philosophical anthropology reveals Mary to be the theoanthropocosmic synthesis as a mere human being?

## THE SIGNIFICANCE

Pope John Paul II expresses the critical importance of Mary for rightly seeing the human being when he says, "The 'woman' [in light of Mary] is the representative and the archetype of the whole human race: she *represents the humanity* which belongs to all human beings, both men and women."[26] Mary, then, is the key, together with her Son, to opening up the mystery of anthropos. This study will contribute to the body of knowledge on Mariologically informed anthropology by investigating how the four Marian dogmas of the church, through a theological and philosophical perspective,[27] allows for the construction of a robust

26. John Paul II, *Mulieris Dignitatem* 4; emphasis in original.

27. John Paul II argues that philosophy and theology ought not to be isolated but be allowed to encounter each other in a mutually edifying manner to bring to bear the full scope of what is being investigated. "The relationship between theology and philosophy is best construed as a circle. Theology's source and starting-point must always be the word of God revealed in history, while its final goal will be an understanding of that word which increases with each passing generation. Yet, since God's word is Truth (cf. *Jn* 17:17), the human search for truth—philosophy, pursued in keeping with its

anthropology that addresses the perennial questions of human origin, identity, vocation, and destiny. This will allow us to bring together various theological research into a Mariological informed anthropology, together with further investigations into the interconnecting realities of the dogmatic truths concerning our Lady, to offer a robust anthropology, theo-philosophically construed, as a model for future studies into the nature of the human being. By systematizing the dogmatic truths of Mary in view of anthropological considerations, and by doing so within the dual methodological approaches of theology and philosophy, this study will offer a framework by which we can adjudicate distinct and sometimes dispersive insights into the nature of anthropos that can be brought together under a meta-anthropology illumined by the content of revelation (via theology) and explicated (via philosophy). This will, in turn, help the current shortage of research in this area by (1) offering a metaphysical basis for grounding anthropological studies in a Mariological frame that complements Christ (ch. 1); (2) simultaneously considering Mary from the perspective of nature and grace (and thus, reason and faith, philosophy and theology) and so offering a theo-philosophical anthropology (ch. 1; see chs. 2–5 with respect to each dogmatic truth of our Lady); and (3) concurrently investigating the interconnective relations among the four Marian dogmas in view of anthropology, particularly in relation to the perennial questions that galvanize anthropological reflections (chs. 2–5).

Other reasons for the significance of this project are as follows: (1) Mariology safeguards an anthropology that is informed by a *mere* human being and person, thus the creaturely reception and response to the person of Christ, external to Christ's human nature, yet inclusive of it (ch. 1). (2) Mariology reveals the preeminent expression of a human hypostasis in the economy of grace (chs. 1–5). Thus (3) Mariology unveils decisive "modes" in which the human being and person relates to God in complementarity to Christ the God-anthropos, thus the synergistic partnering that comes from one who is not a divine hypostasis, which

own rules—can only help to understand God's word better. It is not just a question of theological discourse using this or that concept or element of a philosophical construct; what matters most is that the believer's reason use its powers of reflection in the search for truth which moves from the word of God towards a better understanding of it. It is as if, moving between the twin poles of God's word and a better understanding of it, reason is offered guidance and is warned against paths which would lead it to stray from revealed Truth and to stray in the end from the truth pure and simple. Instead, reason is stirred to explore paths which of itself it would not even have suspected it could take. This circular relationship with the word of God leaves philosophy enriched, because reason discovers new and unsuspected horizons" (*Fides et Ratio*, 73).

allows for the expression of faith and other virtues from the side of human hypostasis as manifestations of divine grace (chs. 2–5; ch. 1 for *just* a Mariological consideration). (4) Mariology "fleshes out," if you will, the unity ingredient to the one Lord Jesus the Christ, thus sustaining the inherent logic of the hypostatic union of the dual natures of Christ and so safeguards the hominization of God and the deification of anthropos, while also grounding the complementarity of the new Adam and the new Eve (ch. 1). Absent the above, an impoverished anthropology will ensue, thus leading theological and philosophical anthropology astray. All this has the effect of showing how, through Mary, we see what each person is called to in Christ, as is the church, distinct from Christ and yet united insofar as he reveals anthropos ever only as the Second Person of the Trinity, our Lady doing so too but as a human person.

Without a Mariologically informed theo-philosophical anthropology, there remains a lacuna that otherwise accommodates, whether willingly or not, a less-than-satisfactory anthropology, which, ultimately, can metastasize into a variety of less than adequate theologies that are anxiously determined by a Christomonistic approach. This is so because anthropology shapes the contours of so much of what is in fact revealed, since the fullness of what is revealed is saliently given in the anthropos who is God! In other words, how we think Christianly about God, the world, and humanity is determined a priori by *the* human being who is God enfleshed. Nevertheless—and this can be so only since the two are truly inseparable—by taking seriously the decisive role our Lady has in revealing anthropos as a *mere* creature, we are afforded an exemplary, archetypal image of a human hypostasis perfectly coordinated with the divine hypostasis that, no doubt, shares the same humanity but is nevertheless an *other* that is not the God-anthropos: the new Eve *inseparably united* with the new Adam (Gen 1:27). In short, Mary is pivotal if we are to see the total Christ, and thus contemplate the whole truth about anthropology.

While orthodoxy safeguards the full and authentic humanity of Jesus, Jesus is nevertheless God *as* human, and so no human hypostasis could be attributed to the Son. This does not detract from the humanity of Christ; nevertheless, what we have in the Son, then, is an inexhaustible mystery preserved in the Chalcedonian formula, albeit articulable with respect to delineating where and in what manner this mystery is demarcated, and so in "Christ alone" we do not have the complementarity that can be offered only by *another*; nor do we possess the intrinsic relatedness between Christ's humanity and the one whose fiat, body, and entire being are *his* cause as anthropos. In addition, in the absence of Mary we are not given an archetypal expression of the theological virtues of neither faith, for example, since Christ did not possess it,[28] nor of hope;[29] nor are we given the architectonic expression of the human hypostasis in relation to the Trinity (and so a human being who is *not* one of the Trinity), uniquely revealing the Trinitarian ontology within an analogical metaphysics that substantiates the *mere* creatureliness as such: God above, within, and upon the human hypostasis (ch. 1). Christ ("alone") does not reveal this as God, as divine hypostasis enfleshed, albeit he indeed does reveal this truth *as God* (but only *in* and *by* his Mother) and not as a created hypostasis. And while it is true that Christ embodies, if you will, the necessarily synergistic companionship between human volition and the divine will (within the hypostatic union), we come to see this even more clearly in and through our Lady who, again, stands as *other* in an I-Thou relation to God-anthropos. This effectively solidifies the decisive importance of human participation (as *other* to God) in the divine economy.

What this, then, means—as we shall begin to explore in our first chapter—is that our Lady is essential for showing how the human being is called to enact a theoanthropocosmic synthesis, which Mary perfectly enacts and recapitulates as a mere creature, complementing her Son who is such a synthesis as God. In other words, Mary unveils the immeasurably high dignity of the human being as a human hypostasis since she uniquely shows that the human being *as a mere creature* is a mysterious theoanthropocosmic synthesis *interiorly-exteriorly* (ch. 1 for the metaphysical details; see chs. 2–5 for how this is expressed via human identity, vocation, origin, and ending). This, in turn, preserves the full humanity of Christ insofar as his humanity is from *this* human hypostasis, Mary, whose yes brought about his being into the world as anthropos. All predications to Christ are to the God-anthropos who is indeed truly God and man, united (without confusion) *in* the divine hypostasis. Mary, though, perfectly mirrors her Son but ever only as a human hypostasis—the perfect image of *the* image of the invisible God (Col 1:15), who is the reflection of God's glory and the exact imprint of his very being (Heb 1:3), and so does this as a mere creature "outside," yet united "interiorly" to him. Thus, the Son, *internal* to the Mother, yet *other* to her, united with her as

28. *ST* III, q. 7, a. 3.

29. *ST* III, q. 7, a. 4.

another, and, yet still, always transcending her as the eternal Son—thus she *in* him, *by* him, and *through* him. This perichoretic relation between Mother and Son is analogous to the relational distance found between each human being and God, as we will explore throughout our project. All this would be utterly lost if a theo-philosophical anthropology were not situated under our Lady. Mary is the *necessary* bridge between Christ and the cosmos (allowing for both descent and ascent); thus, she is the perfect image of the *church* and so of each human hypostasis (fully realized *in Christ*). Therefore, getting a Mariologically informed anthropology correct fully safeguards Christology, ecclesiology, sacramental theology, and the vast array of dogmatic theology. Insofar as Christ is the Alpha and the Omega, Mary is such as *the* human hypostasis in, through, and by *him* who is such in, through, and by *her*.

## THE LIMITATIONS

This study is situated in the field of philosophical theology and is focused primarily on anthropology, both philosophical and theological. The scope of this study is limited to a theo-philosophical investigation of our Lady in view of anthropological considerations. It will broadly include an investigation into the four dogmas of the church concerning Mary with the goal to examine and explicate the ways in which the Mother of God both *illumes* and *illustrates* anthropological truths. By using the four Marian dogmas, this study presupposes the inner unity of the church's teaching about Mary and thus will use these dogmatic claims as anchoring points to explore a general theo-philosophical anthropology. By using the magisterial teachings of the church, her dogmatic proclamations regarding Mary, along with the teachings of the church's fathers and doctors, the theological and philosophical nature of this research project is unapologetically Catholic in scope.[30]

Insofar as this research is not a historical theology, this study will not survey the dogmatic developments of the church for its own sake (except for when doing so helps to elucidate a theological point). Instead, we will use the dogmatic teachings of the church about Mary as they stand, without recourse to the historical context that brought about the

30. The International Theological Commission highlights fifteen general principles that undergird theological investigations in order for it to be considered Catholic ("Unity of the Faith"). It is in this regard that this project is considered Catholic in scope.

dogmatic truths. Neither will this project seek to investigate other proposed theological or philosophical anthropologies in relation to Mary for their own sake, but rather always in view of the larger questions pertinent to this study. Thus, this is not a study on Mariology *as such* but rather on a theological and philosophical anthropology exclusively predicated upon Mary in the light of her position in the economy of grace and nature. Therefore, this study will not include a historical survey of such anthropological considerations. In addition, explicit questions about the role of gender and other socio-politico-cultural items are not the focus of this study.

The methodological approach of this investigation is qualitative and constructive. It seeks to retrieve both theological and philosophical sources of various kind (i.e., magisterial, phenomenological, metaphysical, Christological, etc.) for the construction of a robust Marian theo-philosophical anthropology. It is important to note here that this project, in its very methodology, seeks to embody the Catholic spirit—that is, the universal, integrative, and inclusive nature of Catholic thought, which refuses the constriction of any single school while embracing the richness that each tradition offers. The diversity of sources engaged—ranging from post-Tridentine theology to the *ressourcement* movement, from the metaphysical rigor of Scholasticism to the existential intensity of French phenomenology—mirrors the breadth and depth of the church's intellectual patrimony. I take Catholic theology not to be an isolated monologue but a symphonic dialogue, where speculative theology, mystical insight, and historical retrieval coalesce without contradiction. By drawing from this vast array of thinkers and traditions, this work aims to reflect a truly Catholic mind, one that discerns the unity beneath the plurality, the common inheritance beneath the distinctions, and the coherence that arises precisely from difference. For just as Mary's own being mediates between the divine and the creaturely, uniting them without confusion, so too does this project seek to enact a similar mediation—holding in dynamic tension the manifold insights of tradition, allowing each to illuminate the other within the unity of the church's thought.

Some of the philosophical influences within this project are Przywara, Blondel, Chrétien, Michel Henry, Falque, Marion, and Merleau-Ponty. In addition, some of the theological influences found are Aquinas, Maximus, Balthasar, Bulgakov, Ratzinger, Laurentin, Scheeben, Nichols, Hauke, Hugon, Behr, Milbank, Chardon, Schmemann, Bouyer, and Rowan Williams, to name just a few. And while this study seeks to construct an anthropology predicated on Mary, it does not exclude the role of Christ in anthropological considerations but rather necessitates his inclusion as part of the larger metaphysical basis for such an endeavor.

As a constructive study we will also proceed without the illusion that a totalizing system is in fact possible, based on Mary or otherwise. Rather, this "full" construction will include aporias and paradoxes, which are ingredient to such investigations into the very mystery of being and revelation since what is *revealed* transcends any potentially exhaustive account.[31]

## THE STRUCTURE

In chapter 1, the metaphysical foundation for a Marian theo-philosophical anthropology will be articulated. A Mariological anthropology will be shown to be possible because Mary is the expressed concretization of Przywara's "God in-and-beyond creature" and thus is the existential icon of a creaturely metaphysics (via a Trinitarian ontology). Given this, I will also argue that Mary inimitably reveals in a personified manner the dynamic, undivided relationship between nature and grace—and so, coextensively, faith and reason, theology and philosophy, and God and creation.

In chapter 2, a general outline of the dogmatic truths about Mary, coordinated with the four perennial questions concerning anthropological origin, identity, vocation, and destiny, will be offered. In addition, explicit focus on Mary's divine maternity in view of anthropological identity will be investigated in order to show how our Lady reveals human identity theo-philosophically.

In chapter 3, the project will proceed by examining how Mary's perpetual virginity enacts and recapitulates human vocation theo-philosophically. Attention will be given to exploring the relationship between our Lady's divine maternity and eschatological end—her assumption—within the temporal/eternal dynamic—*pneumatic time*—constitutive of her being. Thus, it will be shown that her perpetual virginity reveals the decisive shape of human vocation as such theo-philosophically.

31. "Unity and plurality in the expression of the Faith have their ultimate basis in the very mystery of Christ that, while being at the same time a mystery of universal fulfillment and reconciliation (Eph 2:11–22), goes beyond the possibilities of expression of any given age and thus eludes exhaustive systematization (Eph 3:8–10)" (International Theological Commission, "Unity of the Faith," §1).

In chapter 4, the project will advance by exploring how Mary's immaculate conception enacts and recapitulates human origin as a graced beginning theo-philosophically. Continued reflections on the temporal dynamics involved will be offered.

In chapter 5, it will be argued the assumption of our Lady enacts and recapitulates human ending as an eschatologically deferred being.

The conclusion will summarize the key findings of the study and explicitly answer the research questions. A discussion of the study's main contributions along with its limitations will be offered. Finally, recommendations for future research will be provided.

*Virgin Mother, daughter of thy Son, humble and exalted more than any creature, fixed goal of the eternal counsel.*

~ Dante Alighieri

*Between Creator and creature no similitude can be expressed without implying an even greater dissimilitude.*

~ Fourth Lateran Council

*The truth is that only in the mystery of the incarnate Word does the mystery of man take on light.*

~ Gaudium et Spes

# I

# The Trinity and Analogy of Being as the Grammar of Theotokion Anthropology

THE ARGUMENTS ARTICULATED IN this chapter are decisive for grounding my project in theo-philosophical anthropology. Before embarking on a journey to excavate the deep anthropological insights offered to us in and through Mary the Mother of God, mediated, as we shall see, specifically to us by the church's four Marian dogmas, we must first discern *metaphysically* Mary's place and role in God's economy. This will help us to adjudicate both how and why she is crucially important in discerning a robust anthropology that simultaneously reveals how grace perfects human nature—revealing the telos of the human as such—while also observing how her very being and work, as a mere human person, uncover anthropological insight in a descriptive and illustrative fashion.

One might ask from the onset, however, why anthropology ought to be considered in view of our Lady. Are not anthropological considerations best situated in Christ *alone*, who fully reveals both God and the anthropos? While the theo-philosophical metaphysics explored in this chapter will help to fully elucidate the importance of our Lady in this regard, we can offer an initial response to this important question: as I already noted in the introduction, in the absence of Mary, anthropology is in danger of degenerating from a robust Christocentric approach to a myopic *Christomonistic* style. This style is typically driven by an anxious grasping of the centrality of Christ to the exclusion of the full dynamism of the Trinitarian economy in and through *mere* creatureliness for, perhaps, fear of competition or pantheism. However, this inevitably leads to theopanism, which ironically loses sight of both the biblical God, who upholds creaturely integrity in its freedom, and the human being as such, since God here is viewed dialectically over and against human nature and human cooperation. In the incarnation, though, Mary's fiat was truly free and hers; if not, then there was rape (there was enfleshment without consent) and, in a metaphysical register, Christ remains an "alien force," decisively divorced from creation and human creatureliness. This would tear asunder the hypostatic union of Christ for such a union is predicated on the integral wholeness of creatureliness, and thus on Mary's free consent as a person. Thus, a robust theo-philosophical anthropology requires the *archetypal pair*, the new Adam *and* new Eve—Jesus *and* Mary. Such an anthropology is thus safeguarded and expanded in the following way: (1) Mariology safeguards an anthropology that is informed by a *mere* human being and person, thus the creaturely reception and response to the person of Christ, external to Christ's human nature, yet inclusive of it; (2) Mariology reveals the preeminent expression of a human hypostasis in the economy of grace; thus (3) Mariology unveils decisive "modes" in which the human being and person relates to God in complementarity to Christ the God-anthropos, thus the synergistic partnering that comes from one who is not a divine hypostasis, which allows for the expression of faith and other virtues from the side of human hypostasis as manifestations of divine grace; and (4) Mariology "fleshes out" the unity ingredient to the one Lord Jesus the Christ, thus sustaining the inherent logic of the hypostatic union of the dual natures of Christ and so safeguards the hominization of God and the deification of anthropos, while also grounding the complementarity of the new Adam and the new Eve. Each of these four notes will be explored throughout this project.

In beholding Mary's *intrinsic* relation to the divine economy in the hypostatic order and the order of grace—for while she is our Mother in the order of grace, she is truly the Mother of God by way of the enfleshment of God—a profound theoanthropocosmic synthesis arises.[1] This, we will observe, is necessarily ingredient in the cultivation of a robust anthropology. A proper reading of the metaphysics unveiled in and through our Lady's existential involvement in the divine economy

1. I am indebted to Keith Lemna's use of the term "theoanthropocentric synthesis" in *Apocalypse of Wisdom*. By this term I mean the unity of God, humanity, and creation enacted in embodied personhood. This term conveys the reality that such a union is indeed a meta-anthropology that reveals the full meaning, ground, and scope of the human being as such.

situates the Theotokos, in a noncompetitive way with Christ her Son, as *the* archetypal human. I will argue that all this can be perceived only by first discerning the metaphysical context, a discerning of *being* and *reality*, by a reception of the gift of revelation. In short, the revelation of God's economy in and through Mary unveils the Trinitarian ontology that grounds, suspends, penetrates, and illumines in a transcendent way those questions implicit in anthropology. In addition, by virtue of her unique place in God's economy, we shall observe that the Mother of God possesses an exceptional role in revealing the dynamic, decentering, rhythmic, and nonfoundational *creaturely metaphysics* as a construal of the (Catholic) metaphysics, analogy of being, expressed in the Fourth Lateran Council. The Jesuit philosopher and theologian Erich Przywara is decisive in offering an elucidation of this metaphysics in his work *Analogia Entis*.[2]

This creaturely metaphysics situated in a Trinitarian ontology is important to observe because it displaces any nominalist hold that unfortunately construes reality and its accompanying causes along competing lines, collapsing all effects into the offspring of merely material and efficient causal forces. This, of course, renders God one being among many as a stubbornly competing agent, the resulting fruit of which is simply a failure in accounting for a vigorous metaphysics that is already illumined in revelation, but which is also concomitantly present in seed form and in a partially proleptic manner in both Platonic and Aristotelian thought. This impoverished metaphysical concoction inevitably leads to nihilism. Without accounting for all four causes in *addition* to ontological causality as participatory ontology, Theotokion anthropology will be unable to attain the categorical positioning necessary not only for a theo-philosophical anthropology that is a theoanthropocosmic synthesis but will also bifurcate God's economy and the person of Mary. Anthropology will dissolve into nothingness. Therefore, given Mary's intrinsic relation to the Trinitarian hypostasis, establishing a Theotokion anthropology will require an investigation into the metaphysics of Mary, *a* human creature who *is* the Mother of God. And since, I will argue, if any metaphysics does not presuppose a *Trinitarian* ontology,[3] not only will it be scarcely

2. This 2014 publication is comprised of two sections, the original *Analogia Entis* (1932) and a series of essays based on the original German edition (1962).

3. Bishop Klaus Hemmerle's work *Theses Towards a Trinitarian Ontology*, written as a birthday greeting to Hans Urs von Balthasar, is instructive in understanding the decisive importance of a *trinitarian* ontology not only for theology, but for philosophy

Christian (ceding, as it would, to some other "higher" or "deeper" category apart from the Trinitarian God), it would also utterly fail in obtaining an understanding of who Mary is and how she *enacts* and *recapitulates*, in a noncompetitive but rather complementary way with her Son, the human being in an archetypal mode. In brief, Mary reveals through an iconic fashion the rhythmic dynamism of the analogy of being *precisely* because she is the Mother of God *as* creature—an utterly unique role in God's economy—and thus renders to us a theoanthropocosmic synthesis that is the deep grammar of a theo-philosophical anthropology. She, as daughter of the Father, Mother of the Son, and spouse of the Holy Spirit, is the decisive expression of the human *being* and *vocation*, which is that creature called to be the humble, open, fruitful, motherly, and spousal correlate to God in Christ, unveiling *all* by way of this union. The intelligibility of this depends on a proper metaphysical reading of Mary.

Thus, this chapter will proceed in the following way: First, we will trace the Trinitarian contours in the person and work of Mary. This will help to clarify how Mary is *uniquely* a concrete expression of an analogical metaphysics. We will do this by initially investigating what Thomas Aquinas and Fr. Matthias Joseph Scheeben note about Mary's role in the incarnation. This will position us to argue how Mary, because of her intrinsic relation to the Trinitarian hypostasis as Theotokos, is the expressed concretization of Przywara's "God beyond-and-in the creature"[4] and thus is the visceral and existential icon of creaturely metaphysics, making the *analogy of being* described by Przywara a deep and abiding manifestation of Mariological metaphysics.[5] This will allow us to further argue that, because she is a perfect manifestation of a creaturely metaphysics, she recapitulates and reveals what it *means* to be creature and, along with Christ her Son, an authentic human being.

In order to deepen our investigation into the intrinsic relation between Mary and her Son, Maximus the Confessor will also be explored, which will grant us an anthropological vision that reveals a cosmic dimension, for insofar as the eternal Logos was *enfleshed* in Mary, the

as well.

4. Przywara, *Analogia Entis*, 160. This is an important section of Przywara's writing insofar as he explains the dynamism of creaturely being. See also 189–91.

5. In a letter written to Eduard Thurneysen, Karl Barth recounts his admiration of Erich Przywara in light of his encounter with him and says the following about Przywara's understanding of the analogy of being: "In response to my question he confirmed that instead of *analogia entis* one could possibly . . . say Mary!" (Barth and Thurneysen, *1921 to 1930*; as cited in Przywara, *Analogia Entis*, 22).

Theotokos is indeed the home of God's intelligibility—her very womb the site of the luminous matrix of the deep and abiding meaning and purpose of creation—and thus the archetypal space of creature *as* intelligible manifestation of the eternal Logos. This is so, as Scheeben himself states, because "by virtue of this relation to the Logos, Mary is in a special manner the 'mirror' and 'image of God,' because she is in the Logos illuminated through the radiation of the light of the godhead and permeated with the essential dew of the strength of God."[6] Maximus will help us discern that Mary, then, is the theoanthropocosmic synthesis as *mere creature* (while Christ her Son is such as both human and divine), thus complementing each other, Mother and Son, in the full expression of this anthropological truth, so that we behold with fresh eyes what Maximus describes in his Ambigua to Thomas, that "the Logos of God (who is God) wills always and in all things to accomplish the mystery of His embodiment."[7] Mary's very personhood in the order of the Trinitarian economy discloses, then, in a manifestly external way what Christ enacts in a deeply abiding and mysterious mode via the hypostatic union. Therefore, in arguing for the Trinitarian ontology that both reveals and positions Mary as a concrete expression of the analogy of being, we will discern Maximus's anthropology in order to help elucidate the significance of the assumption of Christ's humanity in the womb of Mary, a significance that is not only salvific and revelatory, but also cosmic in scope. These arguments will help us to conclude that Mary is the existential icon of creaturely metaphysics, making the *analogy of being* described by Przywara a deep and abiding manifestation of Mariological metaphysics and so positioning Mary, along with Christ her Son, as *the* human being.

Second, we will argue that given what we behold metaphysically in the Mother of God, Mary inimitably reveals in a personified manner the dynamic, non-reductive relationship between nature and grace, and so coextensively faith and reason, theology and philosophy, and God and creation. Gazing upon these coincident relations within the person of Mary in the economy of God showcases how anthropos is indeed the site of what at first appears to be dispersive, differentiated, and segregated fissures of reality, but in fact are, in the final analysis—without mixture or confusion—unified. Mary *is* this union insofar as she expressly articulates, as mere creature, what is already given in Christ her Son. This

6. Scheeben, *Mariology*, 1:167.

7. Maximos the Confessor, *On Difficulties*, 1:107.

union between nature and grace, along with those coextensive relations that parallel, can be perceived in the Trinitarian events of her conception, vocation, motherhood, and discipleship, culminating in her assumption. Mary is like a prism that refracts the white light of the hypostatic union between divinity and humanity, grace and nature, unveiling in an existentially articulated way, through the God who is in and beyond her, what is fully and mysteriously present in the ineffable union in Christ her Son. Fascinatingly, the hypostatic union is already coextensive *with* Mary's involvement. As Scheeben states, "By virtue of this intention of God, the entire existence of her person has grown together with her relation to the divine person of her Son, in a manner analogous to the existence of the flesh of Christ with His hypostatic union."[8]

Finally, by virtue of what is stated above, I will argue that Mary simultaneously *illuminates* anthropology *as* Theotokos, the theological (Mariology) illuminating the philosophical (mere creature), while she also *illustrates* anthropological truths as a mere human person, the philosophical explicating the theological, showing us, together with Christ, what it means to be human.

To summarize: this chapter serves as the *metaphysical foundation* for the present anthropological project in order to discern how and why Mary, along with her Son, is the archetypal human. This will unfold in three parts: (1) Mary *is* the existential icon of a creaturely metaphysics because she is the expressed concretization of Przywara's "God in-and-beyond creature" due to her *intrinsic* relation to the Trinitarian hypostasis; therefore, she recapitulates and reveals, conjointly with her Son, what it means to be human. (2) Given this, Mary reveals in a personified manner the *dynamic, undivided relationship* between nature and grace, faith and reason, and theology and philosophy; therefore, Mary, as *mere* creature, is the privileged manifestation of the *non-reductive* meaning of the human hypostasis (while her Son is such as divine hypostasis). (3) Therefore, Mary both *illuminates* anthropology as Theotokos and *illustrates* anthropological truths as a human person.

8. Scheeben, *Mariology*, 1:167.

## MARY IN THE PERICHORETIC DANCE OF THE TRINITY IN ANALOGICAL RHYTHM

The resplendent glory of Mary is the manifest expression of the gift of her Son given to her by the providential love of the Father, conceived in utero by the Spirit who is the unity of the Father and Son. The paradoxical union between the eternal, unconditioned Son and the temporally conditioned Mother is so close that neither of them can be fully seen or understood without the other. This is the decisive reason for the antiphonal expression in the older Roman liturgy, "Rejoice, Mary the Virgin, who alone have destroyed all the heresies in the whole world."[9] For as Christ, and, because of this, God, is inconceivable without the incarnation predicated upon Mary's yes, so too Mary remains a puzzling mystery without Christ her Son, for even her immaculate conception is, as it is dogmatically defined by Pope Pius IX, a gift "by a singular grace and privilege granted by Almighty God, in view of the merits of Jesus Christ" given for the sake of her vocation as Mother of God.[10]

In the economy of time, the moving image of the triune eternity, the mutual interpenetrative meaning of both Jesus and his blessed Mother is analogous to the transcendent, eternal, interpenetrative relationship between God the Father and his Logos in the unity of the Holy Spirit. For while the eternal Son can ever only be *Son* in relation to the Father, as the Father can ever only be *Father* in relation to the eternally begotten Son in and through the unity of the Holy Spirit, so too, originating in time but stretching out to eternity, can Mary only ever be the Theotokos in relation to her only begotten Son who is eternally begotten of the Father. Therefore, there is a deep correlation between the eternal begetting of the Logos from the Father and the temporal begetting of the Logos from Mary, as Scheeben notes:

> Christ's temporal production by the mother must not be in contradiction to His eternal production, but must be a perfect reflection of it. This temporal production can be such a reflection only if it is effected by a holy and purely spiritual power from a single principle. In other words, as the Son of God by Himself is brought forth as "light of light," here His bodily production must

9. Within the tract of the Mass *Salve Sancta Parens* (MMMO Database, "Gaude Maria Virgo cunctas haereses sola").

10. Pius IX, *Ineffabilis Deus*, s.vv. "The Definition."

> also be actualized, not through the mixing of material elements, but through a heavenly influence on the earthly element.[11]

Thus, as Thomas explains, the one Lord Jesus Christ possesses two births given the hypostatic union of two natures, divine and human. Christ is the Son of the Father and of his Mother, who is merely a human creature, although "since there is only one subject there, the eternal subject, the only sonship that really exists in that subject is his eternal sonship."[12] This does not negate the authentic motherhood of Mary, however, for Thomas is careful to parse out the distinctions by stating the following:

> Christ is truly and really the Son of the Virgin Mother; because a son is so called in relation to his mother, by reason of the relation of motherhood which is really in the mother herself. . . .
>
> Temporal nativity would cause a real temporal filiation in Christ if there were in Him a subject capable of such filiation. But this cannot be; since the eternal suppositum cannot be receptive of a temporal relation.[13]

Therefore, Thomas can say, "Since therefore it was a divine person who took human nature to himself at the very instant of Christ's conception, we can truly say that God was conceived and born of the virgin, and hence that Mary is truly the mother of God."[14]

We begin to see the unfolding of this mystery as through a dark glass in the annunciation. This biblical scene, as Balthasar notes, is the first revelation of the triune God in and through Mary.

> The angel's initial salutation, which calls Mary the one full of grace par excellence, brings her the greeting of the "Lord," Yahweh, the Father, whom she knows as a Jewish believer. As she ponders what this greeting might mean, the angel responds with a second speech that reveals that she will give birth to the "Son of the Most High," who will at the same time be the Messiah for the house of Jacob. And when she asks what is expected of her in all this, the angel offers a third explanation in which he reveals to her that the Holy Spirit will overshadow her, the

11. Scheeben, *Mariology*, 1:70–71.

12. *ST* III, q. 35, a. 5, ad 3. Thomas states, "Although Christ is born twice, He is not therefore two sons, but one only; because filiation properly belongs to the person, not to the nature." See also the corpus: "Filiation is a personal property, and therefore it cannot be multiplied in Christ, since there is only one person."

13. *ST* III, q. 35, a. 4; q. 35, a. 5, ad 1.

14. *ST* III, q. 35, a. 4.

> handmaid. *The divine Trinity must be made known when the Son becomes man*, but not by means of a merely verbal statement, as, for example, God's laws were promulgated on Sinai. *It must also be enacted existentially in a human being possessing perfect, archetypal faith.*[15]

The faith of Mary, which is no doubt a gift received and therefore most properly her own, is the wellspring that completes the initial revelation of the Trinity in time. In the annunciation is an echo of *creatio ex nihilo* as a Trinitarian act—the Father speaking forth the Word in the overshadowing power of the Spirit—and so John of the Cross was keen to pen these poetic words:

> Then he called
> The Archangel Gabriel
> And sent him to
> The Virgin Mary,
> At whose consent
> The mystery was wrought,
> In whom the Trinity
> Clothed the word with flesh. And though Three work this,
> It is wrought in the One:
> And the Word lived in-carnate
> In the womb of Mary.[16]

The mystery of Mary and her Son are mutually illuminated conjointly in the creational dynamic of the Trinity, and the mystery of the triune God is brought to the fore in such a way that reveals God *as* Trinity *as* infinite love, the One who upholds and honors the integral freedom of Mary's fiat. As such, Mary's motherhood is properly understood as divine without negating but fulfilling her free, integral creatureliness.

Upon reflecting on Thomas's mature thought on the mystery of the incarnation, Aidan Nichols summarizes this well by noting that Mary's motherhood is an intrinsic relation to the eternal Logos in the mode of human birthing, although this "befalls her rather than" constituting her very being, since she is merely a creature.[17] By way of this intrinsic relation-

15. Balthasar, in Balthasar and Ratzinger, *Mary*, 106–7; emphasis added.

16. See John of the Cross, *Collected Works*, romance 8.

17. Nichols states the following: "Mary's motherhood is throughout divine. It is a real and immediate relation to the Word in his divine subsistence, albeit in the modality of human birthing. Though her motherhood is a created relation, and one, moreover, which befalls her rather than constitutes her personal being for what it is, nevertheless it has as its immediate term the person of the Son of God. For evermore, Mary

ship, the divine motherhood of Mary is irrevocable to the extent that the human sonship assumed by the eternal Logos is irreversible. Therefore, Mary is truly the Theotokos since "*the divine motherhood resembles the hypostatic union*, since it is a union with a divine person, which embraces the mother's entire and most intimate being."[18] Thus, "by virtue of this intention of God, the entire existence of her person has grown together with her relation to the divine person of her Son, in a manner analogous to the existence of the flesh of Christ with His hypostatic union."[19] Here we begin to see that in Mary we behold in a *manifestly external* way through her interpenetrative encounter with the Trinity what occurs in the hidden and ineffable hypostatic union. In other words, in Mary as in her Son but in a different register, we behold the eternal God made flesh. In addition, her very being, which is immaculately conceived and after "having completed the course of her earthly life, was assumed body and soul into heaven by glory,"[20] is, then, the very mirror of the Trinity, for *in* her, *through* her, and *by* her we behold the Trinity via a profoundly unique Trinitarian engagement with mere creatureliness.

In a coextensively yet concave way, through Jesus, we gaze upon Mary, who is the highest of God's creation (after Christ's humanity), who is also the *inherent* source and meaning of the sacred humanity of the eternal Logos. Creatureliness as such, which includes both Mary and the sacred humanity of Christ, is thus deified. All of this is possible only in the great condescension: the immovable moving, the eternal temporalizing, the infinite finitizing, enacted in the incarnation. As Maximus imaginatively explains to Mary via the voice of the archangel Gabriel,

> And immediately your immortal bridegroom and son, *who is the power of the Most High, will overshadow you*, for Christ is

is essentially or inherently related to the divine person who subsists in the humanity formed in her womb" (*There Is No Rose*, 42).

18. Scheeben, *Mariology*, 1:166; emphasis added.

19. Scheeben, *Mariology*, 1:167. Scheeben continues: "The analogy between the relation of Mary and the humanity of Christ to the Logos, expressed in the 'marriage with the Logos,' is particularly revealed in this, that Mary is characterized in a signal manner in the language of the Church as 'house and seat of the godhead' or the eternal Wisdom. She is as a house and seat in which in the real meaning of the word, the fullness of the divinity, is so infused as to dwell bodily therein. The eternal Wisdom is so implanted and deeply rooted in her that she seems to have grown together with Him. This, too, is the deeper meaning of the representation of Mary in the Apocalypse: the woman clothed with the sun."

20. From Pius XII, *Munificentissimus Deus* (1950), which dogmatically defined the assumption of Mary.

> the power of God and the wisdom of God. He will overshadow you himself and will build within you the temple of his all-holy body. And the immaterial and bodiless one will put on from you bodily and material flesh. The power and brilliance of the Father will overshadow you in essence, and the Word of the Father will become incarnate from you.[21]

Thus, through its deification via the hypostatic union enacted by this incarnation, the body formed in Mary's womb as passible flesh—limited, transient, oriented toward death—is, paradoxically, the locus of both God's salvific work and revelation. Therefore, even passible flesh—which comes from Mary—which is properly ordered within the human constitution as subject to the soul, has a decisive role in the divine economy fulfilling God's will to be embodied. Mary is the heart and center of this mysterious, ineffable exchange.

However, it is important to note that this does not mean that the power of the incarnation is somehow initiated and rooted in the generative "seed" of Adam via Mary even while Christ's body is derived from Adam in bodily substance. This would effectively render human nature implicitly capable of the efficient cause of the conception of the Son of God rather than the Holy Spirit. As Thomas is careful to parse out the distinctions:

> By saying that Christ derived from Adam in bodily substance we don't mean that Christ's bodily substance existed materially in Adam, but that the matter taken from the virgin was actively prepared for the conception of Christ by the generative power of Adam and his descendants. *But it was not fashioned into Christ's body by that power, and so we say Christ originated from Adam in bodily substance but not through the power of a male seed.*[22]

However, as Thomas notes, this is not to mean that the body of Christ formed from the stock of humanity was somehow formed prior to the enfleshment of the eternal Logos. That would mean that "in the mystery of the incarnation a creature, i.e. the human matter conceived independently if miraculously in Mary's womb, was subsequently raised to the dignity of union with the Word."[23] Aidan Nichols captures the logic of Thomas's thought here by identifying that Mary did not "conceive the

21. Maximus the Confessor, *Life of the Virgin*, 54; emphasis in original.

22. *ST* III, q. 31, a. 1, ad 3. ; emphasis added.

23. Nichols, *There Is No Rose*, 41.

Word mediately" but rather "immediately" because the eternal Logos himself made the birthing process his own.[24] Therefore, Thomas can say, "We are to conceive of the divine fullness descending into his human nature, rather than of a pre-existent human nature growing toward God."[25] This is fleshed out in his following explication:

> If what was conceived was to be the Son of God himself, as we profess in the creed, then the body had to be taken on by the Word of God at the moment of conception; this he did through Christ's soul, and the soul through its spirituality as mind, so from the first instant of conception Christ's body must have been animated by a rational soul. What Christ and other men have in common is the breathing into their body of a human soul just as soon as the body was formed and disposed to receive it. The difference is that Christ's body was perfectly formed earlier in the process than ours is. Christ is a natural son of man because he has a genuine human nature, even though he received it in a miraculous way. A blind person's restored sight is natural even if miraculously received.[26]

Truly, then, *God as human* is fully and substantially present in and through the womb of Mary from the first moment of conception, such that he "had the fullness of grace and holiness and known truth."[27] All of this is unintelligible without the coextensive relationship between the Mother and her Son by the power of the Spirit articulated in the divine economy.

For Thomas, the entire Trinity is involved in this process, such that Mary can be rightly observed as the site of the Trinitarian God within the economy of time. Under the providential guidance of the Father, the incarnation is decisively brought about through a special working of the Holy Spirit. Thomas even enumerates three reasons for the specific role of the Spirit in this event: (1) the Spirit is the love between the Father and Son and, therefore, it is fitting that the Spirit is the "source" of the incarnation in God; (2) the source of the incarnation in humanity can come only by way of grace, which comes forth from the Spirit; and (3) the telos of the incarnation, which is the enfleshment of the holy Son of God, comes through that Spirit which makes humans holy and children

24. Nichols, *There Is No Rose*, 41.
25. *ST* III, q. 2, a. 6; cf. q. 3, a. 1; q. 4, a. 2.
26. *ST* III, q. 32, a. 2; cf. q. 33, a. 2.
27. *ST* III, q. 7, a. 1; cf. qq. 9-12.

of God by adoption.[28] Therefore, the Holy Spirit within the undivided Trinity perichoretically is, for Thomas, the galvanizing reason for the incarnation as the manifest expression of the love between Father and Son, as an unmerited gift, bringing about a holy conception, which is the fruit of Mary's womb. And this is truly the fruit of Mary's womb, for the union between the divine operation by the Spirit and the maternal process in Mary is such that the marriage between the two indeed brings about the incarnation. As Scheeben notes,

> The Holy Ghost formed Christ's flesh of the Virgin Mary, and in such a way that Christ according to His humanity is truly produced and born of her. Hence the supernatural action of the Holy Ghost *did not exclude the cooperation of a maternal process in producing the humanity of Christ, or Christ himself, but rather explicitly intended it and directly brought it about.*[29]

Thus, "Mary is a principle of Christ's humanity, or of Christ Himself according to His humanity—a principle subservient to the Holy Ghost, influenced by Him, and working in union with Him."[30] We can then recognize the following truth: Christ's humanity is the highest elevation of a created *nature* since it is hypostatically united to divinity, while Mary is "the highest conceivable elevation of a created *person*,"[31] positioning her as an archetypal person in unity with Christ her Son.

Thus, we can see that Mary and Christ are inextricably bound together in such a way that the mutual mystery of the two is illumined only by their intrinsically corresponding relationship as Mother and Son in the Trinity. The entire Trinity is perichoretically present in the event of the incarnation in, through, and even by the coextensive maternal process of Mary. She, then, is truly Theotokos while remaining a mere creature, and so is elevated positionally to the highest status as a *human person*. Mother and Son are inseparable only because God willed that *this person* would become his Mother according to the humanity of God. Through her we can speak of God as a zygote, embryo, fetus, child, son of Adam, and so on, for she is the door to the *communicatio idiomatum* ever only possible by this ineffable union between the uncreated and created.

28. *ST* III, q. 32, a. 1.

29. Scheeben, *Mariology*, 1:61; emphasis added.

30. Scheeben, *Mariology*, 1:62.

31. Scheeben, *Mariology*, 1:67–68; emphasis added.

## The Trinitarian Union Between Mary and Jesus in Maximus

To explicate further the significance of the humanity of God via Mary and the divine maternity via Christ, I turn to Maximus the Confessor. Maximus offers a richly textured account of anthropology that signifies the depth of the enfleshment of God in Mary.

Ambiguum 7—typically perceived as a piece in which Maximus is merely arrayed against Origen but is in fact based on Origen's own style and format—can be partially seen as a treatise on theo-philosophical anthropology via his doctrine of the logoi in response to the enigmatic passage from Gregory's "On Love for the Poor."[32] In order to elucidate Gregory's words Maximus first unpacks the arguments that "they say," followed by offering his own two points of view, one regarding the Logos/logoi and the other showing that Gregory was not attempting to explain the metaphysics of human origins but rather the problem of the existential tension derived by the issue of human passibility. It is in the first point of view offered that Maximus engages the anthropological question, situating it within his participatory ontology of the logoi.

As the fulcrum of all things, both particulars and universals, the ineffable Logos is the one in whom all things subsist via their logoi, which is one with the Logos, undivided, coterminous, eternal. These logoi, for Maximus, are ontological—and hence the epistemic ground of all. Thus, the nature of each thing, their deepest reality, *is* their logoi, eternally united to the Logos; all things are by virtue of their participation in the Logos via their corresponding logoi. Therefore, the essential nature of reality in all its multiplied diversity is fundamentally singular, united to God by way of participation. "For by virtue of the fact that all things have their being from God, they participate in God in a manner appropriate and proportionate to each."[33] This, of course, is true of human nature as well, thus humanity eternally subsists via its logoi, as Maximus states, "A logos of human beings likewise preceded their creation."[34] Here we see the integrity of the human being, eternally subsisting in the logoi, not as preexisting souls but as the eternal logoi of God, a "portion of God."

After grounding the human being (and all reality) eternally in the logoi/Logos, Maximus addresses the composite nature of the human

32. Maximos the Confessor, *On Difficulties*, 1:75.

33. Maximos the Confessor, *On Difficulties*, 1:97.

34. Maximos the Confessor, *On Difficulties*, 1:97.

being, which, in its unity, is a single form. This form is not accidental but essential to anthropology.

> Therefore, insofar as soul and body are parts of man, it is not possible for either the soul or body to exist before the other, or indeed to exist after the other in time, otherwise what is known as the principal of reciprocal relation would be destroyed.[35]

For Maximus, the body is as essential as the soul in comprising the *form* of the human being, both parts being fundamental to human nature and, thus, the articulation (in time) of the ontological cause that is logoi/Logos, even though each part possesses distinct material and efficient causes.[36] As we will see below, Maximus's anthropology will maintain and amplify the dignity of this composite unity, the human being, through the enfleshment of the Logos in time and space, via Mary, followed by eschatological fulfillment.

The ascetical dimension of Maximus's thought operates *within* the inherent logic of this unity, whereas the soul, by the cultivation of virtues, ought to serve the body by leading it toward the end of God's eschatological embodiment, fulfilling Adam's squandered but recovered (and heightened) mediatory role vis-à-vis his somatic reality:

> The aim is that "what God is to the soul, the soul might become to the body," and that the Creator of all might be proven to be One, and through humanity might come to reside in all beings in a manner appropriate to each, so that the many, though separated from each other in nature, might be drawn together into unity as they converge around the one human nature.[37]

Through the ascetic, virtuous life—a life that is in concert with the abiding, anchoring logoi—the human being returns, transcendently so, to his vocation—a vocation that is discernible within the placement of humanity in, for Maximus, the Genesis narrative:

35. Maximos the Confessor, *On Difficulties*, 1:137.

36. Maximos highlights this distinction by stating the following: "The soul does not originate from underlying matter, as bodies do, but by the will of God, through the *vital inbreathing* in a manner which is ineffable and hidden, known only to the soul's creator. Receiving its existence at the moment of conception simultaneously with the body, the soul contributes to the completion of a single human being, whereas the body is created from the underlying matter of another body at the moment of conception, and is synthesized together with the soul into a single form with it" (*On Difficulties*, 1:140–41). Here we begin to see the significance of Mary's contribution via *her* body.

37. Maximos the Confessor, *On Difficulties*, 1:121.

> This is why man was introduced last among beings—like a kind of natural bond mediating between the universal extremes through his parts, and unifying through himself things that by nature are separated from each other by a great distance—so that, by making of his own division a beginning of the unity which gathers up all things to God their Author, and proceeding by order and rank through the mean terms, he might reach the limit of the sublime ascent that comes about through the union of all things in God.[38]

Here we behold a theoanthropocosmic vision of the human being, one that is completed in Christ but only ever through his Mother, who, by *her* virtues given her in cooperation with grace, *inaugurates* this great synthesis. As Maximus states,

> For she was completely unfamiliar not only with the affairs of marriage but also with the desire of lust, as she was trained from the beginning in complete holiness and purity of soul and body. And no desire of passion at all had come into her heart and mind, and in this regard she was greater and more exalted than all human nature. That is why her beauty was pleasing to the king and creator of all things (cf. Ps 44.12), who sees thoughts and *who scrutinizes hearts and reins* (Ps 7.10). And he made his dwelling place holy, and he saw fit to dwell in her and be clothed in our nature from her.[39]

For Maximus, her "soul was filled with all humility, meekness, and fear of God, and that is why God her Savior had regard for her," bringing about the incarnation, for "this reason he saw fit to dwell in her, and from her he took on a human body and came to seek the lost."[40] As Andrew of Crete states in a homily on the nativity,

> When the Redeemer of the race, as I said, decided to show a new birth and formation [of a female] in place of the former one, just as he formerly took mud from virgin, untouched earth and fashioned the first Adam, so now, acting himself on her own flesh instead of another [piece of] earth, as we might say, he selected this pure and supremely unblemished virgin from the whole of nature and made new in her, out of our [substance], that which is ours; so the Fashioner of Adam was called a New

38. Maximos the Confessor, *On Difficulties*, 2:105.
39. Maximus the Confessor, *Life of the Virgin*, 54.
40. Maximus the Confessor, *Life of the Virgin*, 57.

> Adam in order that the One who is recent and who transcends time might rescue the old [Adam].[41]

This is possible only given how Mary is the superadded expression of grace, which profoundly frees and ennobles her volitional integrity and dignity.

It is important to note that, for Maximus, human vocation, especially Mary's unique call, springs forth from the ontic ground as a composite creature, the logoi of humanity, as well as man's placement as "last among beings." Therefore, the body has a central role, coterminous with the soul, to bring together sensible and intelligible reality into unity, recapitulating all things in and as God's *embodiment*. Special dignity, then, is afforded to the human body by Maximus, especially as passible flesh, not only because of the integral wholeness of the form of human nature—thus not choosing to disregard the body by virtue of its passibility—but also, as we shall see below, because of the enfleshment of the eternal Logos into the very structures of passibility via the creatureliness of Mary, temporally conditioned, and thus, paradoxically, eternal life mediated through death.

Church fathers like Maximus do not possess a blind allegiance to Greek metaphysics, which, under the preconditions of paradigmatic strictures, subsume, transmute, and rearrange the content of revelation. Instead, they, in fact, surrender to revelation's content—regardless of its counterintuitive appearance to a Greek metaphysical disposition—allowing the content of revelation to transfigure Greek metaphysics and its intuitions. That impassibility, for example, would become passible, without change, such that the divine hypostasis is now passible via a human Mother, non-competitively transfigures classical metaphysics under the grammar of revelation. The hominization of the eternal Logos, for Maximus, reveals that "in this new mystery, He truly and without change became whole man, being Himself the hypostasis of two natures, uncreated and created, impassible and passible, for He accepted without exception all the attributes of human nature."[42] Thus Mary becomes the Mother of God because the Word "became the *seed* of His own *flesh*, and being thus compounded by means of his ineffable conception, He became the hypostasis of the flesh that He assumed."[43]

41. As found in M. Cunningham, *Wider Than Heaven*, 79.

42. Maximos the Confessor, *On Difficulties*, 1:13.

43. Maximos the Confessor, *On Difficulties*, 1:13; emphasis in original.

For Maximus God truly possesses passible flesh, uniting himself to the flesh of humanity by way of Mary. While there is a human tendency to perceive the body and its situatedness as fetters that need to be thrown off for the sake of transcendence of some kind, Maximus, in concert with the fathers and doctors of the church, sees the body and its density as essential in fulfilling human vocation as cosmic mediator, a density that, though transfigured eschatologically, remains substantive and fundamentally crucial to the human constitution. This is a profound mystery that is, fascinatingly, not exhausted by God's enfleshment but is in fact heightened. For Maximus, there is an interesting dialectic between mystery and revelation that is granted by way of the incarnation—and, subsequently, passible flesh—which spills over even into the nature of that flesh, which we can see in the following passage:

> "He who eternally transcends being is no less overflowing with transcendent being," for in becoming man He was not subjugated to human nature, but on the contrary He elevated nature to Himself, making nature itself another mystery, while He Himself remained entirely beyond comprehension, showing that His own Incarnation, which was granted a birth beyond being, was more incomprehensible than every mystery. As much as He became comprehensible through the fact of His birth by so much more do we now know Him to be incomprehensible precisely because of that birth.[44]

Notice how Mary as Theotokos is at the heart of this dialectical dance between apophatic mystery and revelation, for while the Son "became comprehensible through the fact of His birth," this heightens to an infinite pitch the Son's incomprehensibility because this is *God* who is being born. Mary becomes the paradoxical fulcrum, simultaneously revealing the incomprehensible God as man, expressed in the asymmetric non-competitive union of the hypostasis, the one Lord Jesus Christ, who "performs the activities proper to each nature as a single subject, and in all His activities He reveals the energy of His own flesh, united inseparably to His divine power,"[45] which was made possible only in her humanity and through her fiat. This union is mediated by human nature being assumed in its fullness, though without change, and "without confusion to the divine nature, is completely penetrated by it, with absolutely no part of it remaining separate from the divinity to which it was united,

44. Maximos the Confessor, *On Difficulties*, 1:37.

45. Maximos the Confessor, *On Difficulties*, 1:43.

having been assumed according to hypostasis."[46] Passible flesh and bodily contingency are completely shot through with divinity without suffering change on either front. This, of course, could be understood only as a noncompetitive union, possible only for the One who is "beyond being" and is simultaneously its ground. Thus, given this profound union, Maximus can state the following:

> As God, He was the motivating principle of His own humanity, and as man He was the revelatory principle of His own divinity. One could say, then that He experienced suffering in a divine way, since it was voluntary (and He was not mere man); and that He worked miracles in a human way, since they were accomplished through the flesh (for He was not naked God). Therefore His sufferings are wondrous, for they have been renewed by the natural divine power of the one who suffered. So too are His wonders wedded to passibility, for they were completed by the naturally passible power of the flesh of the one who worked them.[47]

Consequently, Maximus maintains the integrity of passible flesh throughout his reflections on the somatic reality of Christ as a critical medium, given by Mary, through which God works his salvation by union with it, and through which God is seen.[48] As Andrew of Crete exclaims, "O, what a miracle! She mediates between the height of divinity and the humility of the flesh, and becomes Mother of the Creator."[49] All of this is substantiated by a deep Trinitarian ontology revealed in the interpenetrative dance between God and Mary, unveiling a decisively unique theoanthropocosmic unity in Mary as mere creature. The continued exploration and subsequent discoveries found within the hypostatic union unceasingly elevate the dignity and glory of Mary, clarifying the perfection of her creatureliness through her asymptotic proximity to divinity in Christ via the providential love of the Father enacted and completed in the unity of the Holy Spirit. Thus, as John of Damascus states in a homily,

46. Maximos the Confessor, *On Difficulties*, 1:45.

47. Maximos the Confessor, *On Difficulties*, 1:49.

48. The keeping of human integrity via the incarnation is most forcibly stated by Maximus when he writes that "He made human nature His very own—literally, really, and truly—uniting it to Himself according to hypostasis without change, alteration, diminishment, or division, and maintaining it unaltered in accordance with its essential principle and definition" (Maximos the Confessor, *On Difficulties*, 2:133).

49. M. Cunningham, *Wider Than Heaven*, 73.

> Truly you became more precious than the whole of creation. For from you alone the Maker received a share, [that is,] the first-fruit of our dough. For his flesh is from your flesh, and his blood is from your blood, and God suckled milk from your breasts, and your lips were united with the lips of God. O incomprehensible and ineffable matters! The God of all things, having known in advance your worth, loved you; and because of this love, he predestined you, and "at the end of times" (1 Peter 1.20) he brought you into being and revealed you as Theotokos, Mother, and Nurse of his own Son and Word.[50]

As creature of God, Mary is constituted by a Trinitarian grammar in such a way that illumines the Trinitarian grammar that inscribes and thus is instantiated in all of creation. Out of nothing, creation, rooted in its multivalently corresponding logoi, is sustained by its proleptic consummation by the Father, through the Son the eternal Logos, in the unity of the Spirit. In a certain way, Mary's intrinsic relation to the Trinitarian hypostasis allows us to see that she is a microcosmic, "externalized" expression of this mysteriously inward, abounding truth which pervades all of reality. We can see this because she *is* the Theotokos, the Mother of the eternal Logos. But in a general sense, every human soul (which, as Maximus explained for us above, is inseparable from the body to make the *form* of the human being) is an icon of this metaphysical truth. It is our Lady, however, together with her Son, that expresses this to the highest degree possible.

Upon reflecting on the Trinitarian image of the soul by way of Gregory of Nyssa and Augustine, David Bentley Hart helps us to observe the rhythmic dynamic of an "analogical ontology" that is the direct expression of the Trinitarian unfolding of eternity *in* creation, and most wonderfully, *in* the human person:

> I am an openness whose depth does not belong to me, but to the boundless light that creates me, and whose identity is then given me as other. And as the otherness of God is the soul's true depth, she can possess no identity apart from the otherness of the neighbor; and both the soul's otherness from God and the otherness of each soul from every other reflect the mystery of God's act of "othering" himself within his infinite unity.[51]

50. John of Damascus, "Nativity of Holy Theotokos," 63.

51. Hart, *Hidden and Manifest*, 134.

While this is the case for every soul irrespective of recognition, this is especially the case for our Lady, and not just her soul, but also in the interior-exteriorized relations[52] (expressed *in time* in the incarnation, gestation, birth, and subsequent earthly life of Jesus, but *consummated* in eternity) of the Theotokos and the Trinity, such that in her depth (womb) is simultaneously her otherness—which is "God's act of 'othering' himself within his infinite unity," who is also the "othering" as communal relation, Mother and Son—and, by extension, the church, the body of her Son, of which she too is the preeminent member. Mary becomes pregnant with the Logos who is united in a coextensive manner to the logoi of her humanity by the providence of the Father in the infinite unity of the Spirit. Thus, as John of Damascus articulates,

> Her whole being is the bridal chamber of the Spirit; her whole being is a city of the living God which "the flowings of the river gladden" (Ps 45[46].5); [that is] floods of the gifts of the Holy Spirit. She is "all fair," entirely the "companion" of God (cf. Song 4.7; 5.16). For she who was raised above the cherubim and the seraphim, as a transcendent being, was called "companion of God."[53]

In Mary, in a unique and unrepeatable way, human logoi *contain* the Logos in the divine economy, thus human logoi become the home of the eternal Logos that is united to the logoi of all of creation, making the human logoi the *site of all reality*, paradoxically.[54] And while it is true that, according to Maximus, all logoi are united to the Logos and thus, in their respective instantiations, reveal the Logos in proportion to their capacity, our Lady really and truly becomes the *living tabernacle* of the Logos in time, thus revealing in an utterly unique way this One who upholds all creatureliness in being, indeed revealing the One who is *born* of her and,

52. I try to express in the use of the term "interior-exteriorized" the interpenetrative relation between the triune God and Mary—that is, the God "above her" is the God "in her" womb in the unity of the Spirit who is the God "overshadowing her."

53. John of Damascus, "Nativity of Holy Theotokos," 67. In the same homily and on the same page, he also states the following: "A womb in which the Uncontained dwelt and breasts of milk from which God, the little child Jesus, was nourished! Ever-virginal gateway of God! Hands which carried God and knees, a throne that is higher than the cherubim, through which "weak hands and feeble knees" (Isa 35.3) were strengthened!"

54. As we have seen above, Maximus's anthropology is cosmic in scope, which, in his reading, is gestured toward in the Genesis narrative but fully and finally revealed in the incarnation. Mary, in a different metaphysical register, complements this as the creaturely source and center of this theoanthropocosmic synthesis.

by her own flesh, tabernacles among us! In this way Mary enacts and recapitulates the telos of mere creatureliness—most specifically the human being—actualizing the purpose and goal of all of creation, which is to be embodied in an utterly mysterious way by God. Considering this, the following metaphysical description of each person (and of creation overall) by Hart can be aptly expressed as a glorious description of the Trinitarian grammar of Mary, not only *as* human but most abundantly and uniquely as Theotokos in the salvific economy of the holy Trinity:

> Our participation in the being that flows from God is an imparted splendor, always seizing us from nothingness, drawing us into the infinite depth of God's essential simplicity and Trinitarian diversity, into his knowledge and love of his own beauty, but always only insofar as we comprise within our "essence" an interval of incommensurability that is the created likeness of the infinite ontological interval between God and us.[55]

In time, the triune God in a unique and unrepeatable manner "imparted splendor" to Mary, "drawing" her "into the infinite depth of God's essential simplicity and Trinitarian diversity, into his knowledge and love of his own beauty" via the annunciation, incarnation, and finally her assumption. And so, in her "essence"—that is, her womb, the locus and wellspring of her motherhood—she possessed "an interval of incommensurability that is the created likeness of the infinite ontological interval between God and us." It is in this that Mary recapitulates in an interior-exteriorized way—that is, in her unique, existential participation in *the* Trinitarian event of salvific history—coextensively with Christ her Son, the inherent, deep structure of reality, *as well as* the determinative meaning and vocation of the human being. This is so, as Philip Gonzales rightly identifies, because Mary's receptive yes to God images what all of creation is called to do and thus be, and so therefore "the *analogia entis* is in its heart deeply Marian."[56]

## Mary as the Concretization of Przywara's "God in-and-Beyond Creation"

In his enlightening essay, Gonzales offers a programmatic and constructive sketch by "creatively rethinking the Mariological potential of

55. Hart, *Hidden and Manifest*, 135.

56. Gonzales, "Towards an Analogical Mariology," 121.

Przywara's interpretation of the *analogia entis*" for the sake of Christian thought considering contemporary challenges that seek to thwart it, and so offer an "analogical Mariology which would integrate metaphysics, systematic theology and spirituality."[57] He does this by first identifying Przywara's interpretation of *analogia entis* as a creaturely metaphysics that simultaneously situates creaturely being, especially the human being, in a decentering and rhythmic dynamic ("essence in-and-beyond existence"), such that "the creaturely being is seen as ecstatically and eschatologically open-ended and provisional" and so is not in possession of its own being.[58] Gonzales does this while also identifying that, over against critics like Karl Barth, *analogia entis* is not a kind of bridge that connects or collapses the distinction between God and creation but rather guards such a difference which "simultaneously affirms the ever-greater mystery of God" ("God in-and-beyond existence").[59] As Przywara notes, "In this respect, the *analogia entis* shows itself to be—in the strongest sense—a 'creaturely principle' and, thus, as consisting in the illimitable openness of the movement of becoming."[60] This clears a path for Gonzales to showcase Mary, a creature, as a profoundly concrete expression of the analogy of being by pinpointing Mary (because she is *mere* creature) as *the* analogical difference via her life and her relation to grace, and thus through her a revelation of the perichoretic dance of the Trinity. Under

57. Gonzales, "Towards an Analogical Mariology," 113, 121.

58. Gonzales, "Towards an Analogical Mariology," 119.

59. Gonzales, "Towards an Analogical Mariology," 118. See also Przywara, *Analogia Entis*, 190.

60. Przywara, *Analogia Entis*, 310. It is important to note that as a "creaturely principle" it in no way "comprehends" the totality of the mystery of being and God but rather preserves the mystery, and thus even articulates the right ordering of theological-philosophical metaphysics. The following lengthy quote from Przywara is decisive in this regard: "It is not a principle that makes the creaturely comprehensible and thus manipulable, but one in which the creaturely oscillates unhindered in its utter potentiality. It is the principle of metaphysics that measures out the 'all' of the creaturely: not because this metaphysics deduces the all from this principle, but because it opens itself to the all in this principle. It is the principle of a metaphysics that sees the all as ordered to God as its origin and defining end: not because it takes this principle to comprehend the all from the vantage of God, but because its openness allows it to experience the all as pointing through and beyond itself to God. It is, finally, the principle of a philosophical-theological metaphysics: not because it is a metaphysics that can deduce even the mysteries of theology from this principle, nor even because it can resolve them by reducing them to this principle, but because the depth of this principle is the very *potential oboedientialis* that stands in immediate relation to the God of supernature (*in potential ad ill aquae supra naturam Deus in eo potest facere*)" (*Analogia Entis*, 310–11).

the Trinitarian grammar described above this makes sense, and so Mary's intrinsic relation to the divine hypostasis uniquely positions her to be the cipher of all of creation's origin, vocation, and eschatological orientation. It is worth quoting Gonzales's reading of why Mary decisively reveals a creaturely metaphysics in an archetypal way:

> Mary is seen as the humble consummation of the meaning, end and fullness of created being. This consummation, meaning, end, and fullness are revealed and testified to through the single truth of Mary's life and election—a life and election which is the summit (ground in the profoundly humble act of self-differentiation) of the receptive readiness, of the active-potency of Mary's openness to receive the gift of grace from her ever-greater God. Indeed, Mary shows the always already intended co-belonging of being and grace in a harmonious analogical unity-in-difference of *being as graced*. Mary's *fiat* shows that being is a response to the address of the double donation of being and grace given by the infinitely free ever-greater God of creation and grace. Mary's life (and Mary's response), indeed, manifest that being cannot be thought apart from grace. Or, that our being is always already a response to grace . . . in a word, created being's end is a life of total abandon, a doxological life of sacrifice and service offered up in love for the greater glory of the living Trinitarian God.[61]

Mary is this by virtue of her Trinitarian engagement with God, for God is in and beyond her precisely through a proper reading of the Trinitarian grammar in and through her being and life: the undivided Trinity is *in* her (the Son) *and* (the Spirit) *beyond* her (the Father) effected and established in an irrevocable and infinitely unified way by the Spirit. And the Son is always *in* her, so to speak, by way of the irreversible enfleshment of the Logos. Thus, in Mary we behold the analogical interval of God in and beyond creation in time. In addition, and because of this, Mary as the immaculate Theotokos reveals the creaturely dynamic of essence in and beyond existence. She, unlike any other as mere creature, possesses pure integrity, and so *is who she truly is* (in response to the invitation to "become what you are") without fracture, duplicity, or division, thus imaging God perfectly *as mere creature*. Through her immaculate conception (which we will explore later in this project) and her grace-filled fiat, she signifies the rhythmic middle (and is an archetypal image of the suspended middle) between pantheism (for Mary is not divine but mere

61. Gonzales, "Towards an Analogical Mariology," 126.

creature) and theopanism (for Mary's yes was truly free and, thus, hers). In this, Mary, as a human hypostasis, reveals what Christ *enacts* in the hypostatic union as *God*.

It must be stressed that Mary's role in revealing this analogical interval in no way stands in competition with, let alone in contradistinction to, her Son. Rather, it is *in* and *through* her Son that she unfolds in an illuminative fashion the way a prism reveals what is already present—the full spectrum of visible light—as does Eve with Adam. We can say that Mary images her Son in a way that parallels the Son's image of the Father. To see the Son is to see the Father, and to see the Mother is to see her Son (as Elizabeth bears witness to in the visitation, along with John the Baptist in utero), while the Mother is also beheld clearly and most distinctly ever only in and through the Son (as is also observed in the visitation, for Elizabeth calls her "blessed among women"). Therefore Christ, who is the true image of God eternally *and* in time in the economy of his own life and flesh, grants to Mary a share in the hypostatic order so that, in the final analysis, she reflects as in a mirror the perfect union, without mixture, division, confusion, between God and creature, enacting in an *interior-exteriorized* manner the ineffable union *internal* to the Son. Mary, then, safeguards Christology, as the church in her battle with christological heresies in history already bears witness to. The Theotokos parses out, so to speak, only ever as a simple creature of God—a human person—the unspeakable union of God and humanity in Christ. She *is* this symphonic and harmonious interval found between creation and the uncreated, *as mere creature*. The dynamic encounter between the Trinity and Mary, in her body and being, through her faith and fiat, by her love and humility, fleshes out what occurs in the filial relation between Father and Son in the unity of the Spirit *in time*. While Christ *is* this union as *God* (for only God could ever be this union in the fullest sense),[62] she *is* this union as a human hypostasis, as a creaturely correlate to the divine hypostasis; she enacts this union in the unity of her being and actions in the domain of creaturehood *alone*. While Christ is love personified *as God made human* (incarnation), Mary is love personified *as human made God* (theosis). Christ is the embodiment of the *analogia entis* as God, for in him is unity in difference, the apophatic marriage between

62. As Przywara states, "It [*analogia entis*] is a 'principle' insofar as He alone is called *principium et finis*, i.e., the principle from whom and to whom are all things: *idem Deus*. This 'insofar' is its measure: the nothing before the Creator out of nothing" (*Analogia Entis*, 314).

divinity and humanity. With every likeness and similarity between God and creature we gaze upon in Christ, there is an ever-greater unlikeness and dissimilarity, perfectly revealed in his cross,[63] unveiling the ultimate apophatic ground that is *no* ground, height that is *no* height, being that is *no* being. Yet, Mary *is* the embodiment of this analogical interval as *mere* creature, for in her, by her, and through her is unity in difference in this unique, interpenetrative encounter with the undivided Trinity. Thus, a beautifully full revelation is given via the archetypal pair of the new Adam and new Eve.

In his concluding chapter in *Christ: The Heart of Creation*, Rowan Williams reveals how Christ embodies Przywara's vision and thus is the "heart of creation."[64] Echoing the Jesuit theologian and philosopher, Williams states that only God perfectly mediates the coincident relations of material and immateriality, transcendence and imminence, similarity and alterity, insofar as "God is that *in* which everything finds coherence and *on* which all acts converge (material or immaterial), in the sense of working towards their fullest level of intelligible connectedness and their place in a consistent universal structure."[65] Christ is the heart of creation as *God incarnate*. Thus, he is the perfect actualization of God in and beyond creation *in time*, and so "holds finite reality as one" as he who is "revealed in the historical mediator . . . who 'appears as *the* reality of the way in which God-the-middle takes up the All: as the "infinity that assumes" (*infinita virtus assumentis*) he is the unifying head of everything from the invisible to the visible.'"[66] It is worth quoting Rowan at length here in order to listen carefully to the profundity of this thought:

> It is as the unfree, the mortal, the failing and suffering, that God realizes the centrality, the focal and magnetic significance of the divine in the created world. Only in the incarnate Word as revealed in the crucified Christ is it possible to have both direct openness to infinite activity and an unarguable sign of the fact that God is that which is "always greater," *semper maior*. This, Przywara affirms, is the heart of the doctrine of analogy—no similarity without an always greater difference; so the Christ

63. "Here too the deeper form of analogy—which is the mystery of the Cross—holds sway: to ascend into the 'similarity, however great' only falls into the 'ever greater dissimilarity,' though it is in just this way that one first comes to participate in the majesty of God" (Przywara, *Analogia Entis*, 352; see also 368–69).

64. Williams, *Christ*, 219–54.

65. Williams, *Christ*, 224; emphasis in original.

66. Williams, *Christ*, 225; quoting Przywara, *Analogia Entis*; emphasis in original.

> who reveals what the analogical relation of finite and infinite actually and abidingly is must be "man wholly circumscribed in his humanity, in whose humanity there is nothing visible, audible, scrutable, or tangible, that would immediately suggest divinity." Revelation means that we are enabled to recognize not only that God in general terms is the focus, the ground of the "rhythm," of finite reality, but that this is realizable only when God acts in *and as* the unequivocally finite, not in some sort of exalted and insulated finitude that "looks more like" divine liberty as we might be tempted to imagine it.[67]

Like a laser, Christ is the focused expression of the luminous content revealed in all of creation as God in and beyond being. This is ever more the case given that God the Son *possesses a creaturely Mother* according to his humanity. In fact, only in and through Mary is this "unequivocally finite" one, who is paradoxically God, can ever be the concretization of the rhythmic middle expressed in time. And while Christ is the "logic and heart of creation," revealed existentially in the hypostatic union, displaying the transcendent, unconditioned, infinite, eternal God through *his* imminent, conditioned, limited, temporal flesh—and thus actualizing the truth of creation as God in and beyond being—Mary, I submit, is *also* the "logic and heart of creation" but as mere creature, complementing her Son in every way but as a human hypostasis, revealed in the interpenetrative dynamism of the Trinity with her. While it is true that the Logos shows himself as the "non-*duality* of God and the world and the non-*identity* of God and the world" because the Son is "informing, subtending, permeating the finite"[68] as the Son of the Father in a "non-duality and non-identity" relationship, it is also true that Mary *articulates* this in her perfect humanity as a free human agent in the divine economy. As mere creature, she is created, called, sustained, and eschatologically consummated in the God who is in and beyond her in a way that is paralleled in a complementary fashion in the blessed humanity of God. Therefore, insofar as Christ is the heart and soul of creation as its apex and middle, then Christ is *the* heart and soul of Mary, her immaculate heart and her soul, which was pierced as Simeon prophesied. She is this because as Theotokos she enacts and recapitulates the nature and vocation of creatureliness as that which contains God inwardly (unity/similarity/imminence) in her womb and through her flesh, who is uncontainable in

67. Williams, *Christ*, 225.

68. Williams, *Christ*, 227; emphasis in original.

an ever-greater register (alterity/difference/transcendence) all of which is enacted and recapitulated in her creaturely yes to God. She perfectly images God *as* self-gift, for while God *is* the nonidentity *and* non-duality as Trinity, Mary embodies this analogical interval not only in her intelligibility and specificity as creature, but in a far more gloriously unique way as *Theotokos* such that she is indeed the "seat of wisdom," the "mirror of the Trinity," the perfection of God's creation as mere creature. Mary is the melodic scale of the incarnation, her life the symphonic rhythm of the unspeakable union of God and humanity, and the unity in difference that is already the Trinity. She is, then, the theoanthropocosmic synthesis that both telescopically and microscopically manifests what Augustine beautifully describes by stating that God, who is higher than our highest self, is also more inward to us than our innermost self. Therefore, we can look to her, like her Son but in a different register, to behold what it means to be human theo-philosophically, for in her she enacts and recapitulates the origin, vocation, and consummate end of the human person.

## MARY AS THE MATRIX OF NATURE AND GRACE AS MERE CREATURE

The metaphysics described above ineluctably leads us to seeing Mary as one who exceptionally reveals in a personified manner the dynamic, undivided relationship between nature and grace, and so coextensively faith and reason, and theology and philosophy.[69] This means that Mary, as mere creature, is the privileged manifestation of the *non-reductive* meaning of the human as such. In her, we perceive the kenotic movement of grace, which always presupposes, without destroying, nature.[70] It

69. This is so because she is the concrete manifestation of the *analogia entis* as *mere* creature, as argued above.

70. Since she is a creature uniquely positioned, and given the Thomistic axiom, this is the case (*De Ver.* q. 14, a. 10, ad. 9; *ST* I, q. 1, a. 8, ad 2; q. 2, a. 2, ad 1). Also note the following from Przywara: "As much as the actually existing creature first appears in its actual 'final form' within the mystery of the supernatural participation in God and supernatural redemption, it is nevertheless the case that both this participation and this redemption are given to it precisely as creaturely endowments, which, as such, neither stand in 'contradiction' to the 'nature' of creatureliness, nor 'negate' it, but rather presuppose 'certain similarities' within it and therefore, 'in fact complete' it. Moreover, in keeping with this ontological relation, even God's revelation speaks in a creaturely way, indeed 'in likenesses taken from the data of the senses,' and precisely for this reason faith 'presupposes natural knowledge, as does grace nature, and perfection that which is perfected.' Thus the ultimate and conclusive view of the matter is that of the

is because Mary is the peaceful interval and rhythmic beat of the Trinitarian unity in difference as *mere* creature that she reveals, in unity with her Son in and by his humanity received from her, what grace can do with nature, and what nature is called to in grace. In her as in her Child, we see how grace is in and beyond nature, how theology is in and beyond philosophy, and how faith is in and beyond reason, for their undivided relational dynamic, as Przywara notes throughout his work, is also construed along an analogical interval such that theology does not destroy philosophy, faith does not undo reason, nor does grace negate nature.[71] Therefore philosophy, reason, and nature—the creaturely correlates to Mary as mere creature—are elevated in a theophanic pitch that not only maintains their creaturely integrity but perfects it, as we see in the Theotokos.

This is how Mary as mere creature is the archetypal expression of the suspended middle complementing Christ who is that expression as God. Without artificially separating, mixing, confusing—and so destroying—the coterminous relations, we can ever only discover that nature is indeed already graced as *gift*, reason is already suspended on the *presuppositions* of faith, and philosophy is ever always *beholden* to theology (good or bad). The theological, for instance, *illumines* the philosophical, and the philosophical in turn explicates and *illustrates* the theological as the philosophical remains grounded in (orthodox) theological presuppositions.[72] The same could be said of faith and reason, and grace and nature.

ontically and noetically '*completed nature*' of the '*creature*': because the whole of the creature's growth into more and more of its supernatural endowments constitutes precisely not any 'progress on God's part,' but rather a progress of the creature: certainly, it is a progress that goes beyond every 'natural' possibility or ability or claim proper to the creature, but it is still a progress that 'can' happen to the 'creature' through the 'creator' (since, in its '*potentia oboedientialis*,' precisely as a 'creature,' it is absolutely in the hands of the creator), and as such is truly a 'progress' of the creature towards 'perfection'" (*Analogia Entis*, 370; emphasis in original).

71. Przywara, *Analogia Entis*, 172–74, 189–91.

72. In thinking about the status of philosophy (as a creaturely correlate) in relation to faith/grace/theology, Przywara states the following: "Concretely existing philosophy occurs as genuine philosophy within the one concrete order of original sin and redemption to the degree that its operative principle is the Pauline 'dying, and yet we live' (2 Cor. 6:9). The either-or of concretely existing philosophy stands between 'fallen' philosophy under the sign of 'original sin' and 'redeemed' philosophy. A fallen philosophy is one that seeks to be absolute . . . , only then to succumb either to the dead absoluteness of 'pure concept' (in a 'pure logic') or to the hellish absoluteness of a 'pure critique' that rends everything apart (in a 'pure dialectic') and thus truly progresses from sin to death to hell. A 'redeemed' philosophy not only knows itself to be living before the *one* living absolute (God) in its creaturely distinction from this absolute (and hence to be

Nature, for example, is *gift* given and sustained freely by God (by virtue of *creatio ex nihilo*) and thus is already grace in a nonidentical, non-repetitive way, yet nature is truly its own and so *is* nature. Grace returns (fallen) nature to itself (or, as is the case in Christ and Mary, simply perfects nature), vouchsafing its vocation by elevating, intensifying, perfecting, and thus making it really *nature*, completing it via grace. This too with faith and reason: faith exalts, deepens, and completes reason by way of *illumination*, while reason explicates (*illustrates*) what is given in faith, while it also gestures toward what is fully and finally only given in revelation. These relations are coextensive in a manner that mutually illumines and illustrates each via the singular source that is the singularity of God's unity in difference revealed perfectly in Christ, as God, and his Mother as mere creature. And it is in this singularity that we ought never to speak or think about grace and nature, theology and philosophy, and faith and reason in such a way that divorces one from the other, granting them a false autonomy, or collapsing one into the other, resulting in a monstrous hybrid.

Just as Mary cannot be understood without her Son, and her Son without his Mother (in the hypostatic order revealed in the economy of time), so too we can never hope to arrive at a "pure" philosophy, rationality, nature. Metaphysically speaking, it is simply not possible. Neither does a "pure" theology, despite the Reformed position, exist; nor a "pure" grace, or "pure" faith, resulting in a manifestly ugly fideism or creaturely negating theopanism (a pantheistic collapse of the creature into God). No. Only in their unity in difference do they co-inhere intelligibly in an immanent mode transcendently, only because they are suspended in a decentered, exocentric fashion in a perpetually spiraling, rhythmic analogical dance. Their alterity is only ever so in their unity, and their unified harmony is only ever so in their nonidentical, non-repetitive, peaceful interval that is their real difference. Mary *is* this singularity in her creaturely personhood as is her Son as divine hypostasis.

Therefore, Mary is uniquely and vividly positioned as creature to behold *in her* the interplay of these relations, such that they find their

living within the unfettered creaturely movement of genuine 'becoming'), but also and precisely recognizes its own native tendency to fall into the death of 'pure concepts' and into the hell of 'pure critique.' . . . Thus Christian philosophy, in the proper sense, consists in Christianity's transformation of 'fallen' philosophy into 'redeemed' philosophy, redeeming it from 'philosophy as God' and *into* a 'philosophy of the creature *coram Deo*' (in the 'analogy' of 'ever greater dissimilarity' within 'a unity, however great')" (*Analogia Entis*, 404; emphasis in original).

culminating and integrated expression only ever as *this* historically positioned, materially petite, existentially bound *mere* creature, in her words, decisions, actions—in short, the totality of her life both on earth and in glory. Neither do we behold these relations accidentally in her, as if to say *despite* her creaturely personhood, but truly, really, and substantially in and through her finite, bounded, and beautiful person. It is *as* human person, *as* mere creature, she *is* the unifying matrix of reality, the theoanthropocosmic synthesis, coextensively complementing her Son who is this synthesis as God, the Synthesis of syntheses. Thus, she reveals the depth and height, the meaning and purpose, the origin and end of *anthropology*.

## THEOTOKION THEO-PHILOSOPHICAL ANTHROPOLOGY

We have thus far discovered that (1) Mary is the existential icon of creaturely metaphysics because she is the expressed concretization of Przywara's "God in-and-beyond creature" due to her intrinsic relation to the Trinitarian hypostasis; therefore, Mary recapitulates and reveals, conjointly with her Son, what it means to be human. Considering this, we have also discovered that (2) Mary, as mere creature, is the *non-reductive* manifestation of the meaning of the human as such. This is rooted in our metaphysical discernment of Mary, which allows us to perceive in her the dynamic, unmixed, and undivided relationship between the natural and the supernatural. With all this, we can now observe that Mary, as the concrete expression of the analogical ontology—Trinitarian in form—as a nonfoundational, decentering, suspended middle, like her Son though in a distinct register, *illuminates* anthropology as Theotokos, the theological (Mariology) illuminating the philosophical (creaturely being), while also *illustrating* anthropological truths as a mere human person, the philosophical explicating the theological. Therefore, this project is an exercise in *theo-philosophical* anthropology.

We can now proceed by closely examining the four Marian dogmas, each of which will be studied in its respective chapter. The anthropological significance of Mary as the *Mother of God* will be explored in chapter 2. These chapters will excavate in an exploratory fashion Theotokion anthropology that is at once theological and philosophical, unitedly differentiated and distinctly unified in a nonidentical manner, by using the tools and methods that are proper to theology *and* philosophy, in the one person of Mary, who embodies the unity in difference of theology and philosophy, faith and reason, grace and nature. Given the metaphysics of Mary as seen above, which almost mysteriously turns out to be metaphysics *as* Mariology, it becomes evident how the Theotokos is uniquely positioned in God's economy, as mere creature, such that she is the revealed cipher to the deepest meaning of the human person. Therefore, by examining the *anthropological* significance of each of the Marian dogmas, we will have the basis to argue the following: Mary both *enacts* and *recapitulates* the true meaning of the human being. This will be seen in the bidirectional, rhythmic manner by examining how the theological truths of the Theotokos illuminate the philosophical nature of humanity, while also observing how a philosophical examination of Mary illustrates in an explicative mode the theological already discernible in revelation. Theology is the science of grace, though never to the exclusion of nature, but instead always in and through nature as its presupposition. (Healthy) philosophy is the science of nature but never as "pure nature," but instead always in and through grace, from which it springs forth and in which it is sustained. Therefore, David Bentley Hart's invitation ought to be kept in mind as we proceed:

> I would say that the Christian philosopher should proceed in obedience to such a "transcending" phenomenology: an initial trust in being's goodness and veracity, a surrender of self to the testimony of creation (embraced, naturally, within and consummated by an essential faith in God revealed in Christ).[73]

73. Hart, *Hidden and Manifest*, 36.

*The paradox is not a concession but a category, an ontological definition which expresses the relation between an existing cognitive spirit and the eternal truth.*

~ Søren Kierkegaard

*The finite is already transcended in the very positing of it.*

~ F. W. J. Schelling

*For after all what is man in nature? A nothing in relation to infinity, all in relation to nothing, a central point between nothing and all and infinitely far from understanding either. The ends of things and their beginning are impregnably concealed from him in an impenetrable secret. He is equally incapable of seeing the nothingness out of which he was drawn and the infinite in which he is engulfed.*

~ Blaise Pascal

# 2

# Divine Motherhood

## *The Human as Finitude Containing the Infinite*

In our last chapter, we were able to determine metaphysically Mary's position and role in God's economy. This metaphysical exposition reveals both how and why she is critically important in discerning a robust anthropology by uncovering, through her, the height, depth, and breadth of human reality in both its capacity and orientation. A proper reading of the metaphysics unveiled in and through Mary's existential involvement in the divine economy situates her, in a noncompetitive but complementary way with her Son, as the archetypal human. In other words, Mary is the unique—*intrinsic*—relation to the divine hypostasis, only ever as *mere* creature, which discloses her to be the existential icon—the perfect image as mere creature and human person—of creaturely metaphysics. And we have observed that this is so because she is the expressed concretization of Przywara's "God in-and-beyond creature" through her participation in and through and with the Trinity in an *interior-exteriorized* way. As we have seen, this means that Mary "parses out," so to speak, as a simple creature of God, the unspeakable union of divinity and humanity in her Son. She is this symphonic and harmonious interval found between creation and the uncreated, as mere creature. While her Son is this union as God through the hypostatic union between humanity and divinity, she is this union as a human person; she enacts this union in the unity of her being and action in the domain of creaturehood *alone*. Therefore, Mary recapitulates and reveals, like her Son but in a different metaphysical register and so conjointly with him, what it means to be human.

Appropriating this metaphysical truth about Mary, chapter 1 also argued that she inimitably reveals in a personified manner the dynamic, non-reductive relationship between nature and grace, and so coextensively faith and reason, theology and philosophy, and God and creation. Given this, Mary, as *mere creature*, is the privileged manifestation of the *non-reductive* meaning of the human as such (while her Son is also such but as a divine hypostasis). Therefore, Mary simultaneously *illumines* anthropology as Theotokos and *illustrates* anthropological truths as a mere human person. Consequently, a *theo-philosophical* anthropology is discernible in our Lady.

In this chapter we will begin to flesh out this anthropology by focusing on the first—both chronologically and principally—of the Marian dogmas: her divine maternity. This chapter will argue that Mary as *Theotokos*, in both an illuminative (grace/faith/theology) and illustrative (nature/reason/philosophy) manner, enacts and recapitulates human *identity as maternal being*. This will unfold in four parts: (1) A general outline of the dogmatic truths about Mary will be offered, coordinating each to unveil the deep and abiding theo-philosophical anthropological significance of the four Marian dogmas. This will allow us to discover that Mary, always in concert with her Son, reveals human *identity*, *vocation*, *origin*, and *destiny*. This will be followed by (2) a theological analysis of Mary's divine maternity to establish the argument that the human being *is* the maternal being. This will be followed by an analysis of her fiat, *gestation*, *birth-giving*, and *parenting* in order to explain how she *illuminates* (grace/faith/theology) anthropological identity as such. The chapter will then proceed to argue that (3) Mary also *illustrates* (nature/reason/philosophy) anthropological identity. We will explore how, from a philosophical perspective, Mary's fiat is the source of her motherhood. By exploring the metaphysics and phenomenology of Mary's fiat, we will discover that her divine maternity is indeed an icon of human finitude paradoxically capable of and oriented toward receiving the infinite. Finally, via her fiat, we will then investigate how (4) Mary's *body/flesh* illustrates (nature/reason/philosophy) how she is the site of the exchange between the infinite and finite and so observe how the human body/flesh is this *locus of union*. A metaphysical and phenomenological analysis of Mary's body/flesh will be undertaken, exploring how philosophy can continually fund this investigation.

## MARIOLOGY AS THEO-PHILOSOPHICAL ANTHROPOLOGY

Given the aim of this project, which is to construct and present a unique approach to a theo-philosophical anthropology that positions Mary as qualitatively decisive for addressing the mystery of the human being and person, an exploratory investigation of the theological and philosophical implications of the four Marian dogmas is key. It is important to note that, in grounding anthropology in Mary *through and in light of* Christ rather than in Christ to the *exclusion* of Mary, the following are achieved: (1) an anthropology rooted in the archetypal pair—new Adam and new Eve—and thus a full, complementary articulation of anthropology; (2) an anthropology cleared (via the immaculate conception) from the obscurity due to sin for a human hypostasis; (3) an anthropology shaped and informed by *mere* creatureliness (via Mary's non-divinity); and (4) a theoanthropocosmic synthesis granted to us, because Mary, the second Eve, is the culmination of God's preparatory work of creation and Israel, receiving and embodying God himself and thus making her the apex and center of creation as *mere* creature. Absent the above, an impoverished anthropology will ensue, thus leading theological and philosophical anthropology astray.

As we have begun to see, Mary's intrinsic relation to God's economy signals, in a fundamental way, what it means to be human. Mary is a perfect model of theandric humanism—which, I submit, is the only true humanism—the human creature in synergistic harmony with the divine in both being and act, which enacts and recapitulates the human as *imago Dei*. Put differently, she sheds light upon the mystery of anthropological identity, vocation, origin, and destiny because of her unique involvement in the divine economy; she is the hermeneutical key to the questions implied in the existence of the human being. She is this because she is the one who stands before God as mere creature, as bearer of God's image. Indeed, she is graced by God and so fully human, embodying God as one who receives his Word in faith. Thus, she is pregnant with God's Word, giving birth to this Word, and, at the summation of her life, is glorified by this same Word who is God. It is precisely under these conditions that tradition has always recognized Mary and the church in a reciprocal way: Mary as the personification of the church, the body of Christ, and the church as symbol of Mary (Rev 12), who is also the model of true discipleship, the Mother of all disciples.[1] Therefore, an investigation into the dogmatic truths about Mary ought to yield fruitful insight into exactly how she uniquely images, in a revelatory manner, anthropology.

Considering this, we can observe the following: Mary's identity, vocation, origin, and eschatological end both enact and recapitulate anthropology such that the questions implied in human existence—What is the human? Why and to what end is the human being called forth? What is the (essential) origin of the human being as such? And to what ultimate end is anthropos oriented?—are addressed along four cardinal points that correspond to the four Marian dogmas of the church. This could be understood in the following way: (1) The dogmatic declaration of Mary as *Theotokos*, defined in the Council of Ephesus in 431, recognizes her *identity* in a deep and abiding way. (2) The dogmatic declaration of the *perpetual virginity* of Mary, defined at the Council of the Lateran in 649, identifies her *vocation* as the fitting extension of her identity. (3) The dogmatic declaration of her *immaculate conception*, defined in 1854 by Pope Pius IX, expresses her *origin* in relation to God's preemptive saving grace in respect to her intended identity and vocation. (4) The dogmatic declaration of the assumption, defined in 1950 by Pope Pius XII, indicates her eschatological end, her *destiny*, which is the proper telos that springs forth from her identity, vocation, and origin, while it also paradoxically informs her identity and vocation *proleptically*. Thus, the Marian dogmas coordinated with the quintessential questions implicit in anthropology together give us the following answers to those questions: the human being is definitively (1) the *maternal* being in relation to its *identity*; (2) the *virginal* being in relation to its *vocation*; (3) the *immaculate* being in relation to its primordial *origin*; and (4) the *glorified* being in relation

1. *Lumen Gentium*, a document promulgated by the Second Vatican Council, identifies as part of the deposit of faith in sacred tradition the inextricable link between our Lady and the church. Consider the following: "The blessed Virgin, through the gift and office of the divine motherhood which unites her with the Son the Redeemer, and by reason of her singular graces and gifts, is also intimately united to the church: the mother of God is the type of the church, as already St. Ambrose used to teach, that is to say, in the order of faith, charity and perfect union with Christ. For in the mystery of the church, which is also rightly called mother and virgin, the blessed virgin Mary has taken precedence, providing in a pre-eminent and singular manner the exemplar both as virgin and as mother. For by her faith and obedience she brought forth on earth the very Son of the Father, and this without sexual intercourse but under the shadow of the holy Spirit, believing like a new Eve not the ancient serpent but the messenger of God with a faith that was not adulterated by any doubt" (*Lumen Gentium* 63 [see also 64], in Tanner, *Vatican II*, 180–81).

to its *destiny*. While (2), (3), and (4) will be addressed in the subsequent chapters, this chapter will argue that anthropological *identity* is indeed *maternal* in nature.

Fascinatingly, a meditative reflection on the relationship among the four Marian dogmas yields a symmetrical pattern along a temporal axis that is shaped by an inherent eschatological tension. The Marian dogmas as revealed truths not only offer an anthropological grammar but do so within a uniquely eschatological mode. For example, reflecting on their inherent relation one can begin to see that *identity* (maternal being) is the temporal realization of that which is rooted in the predestined, eternal *origin* (immaculate being [Eph 1:4]), and so the immaculate *origin* is the foundation for what will be manifested in time, the maternal *identity* of the human being. This is inversely related to the latter two Marian dogmas: *vocation* (virginal being) is the expression *in time* of the proleptic embodying of the angelic state, which is rooted and realized in the *glorified* state in eternity (Matt 22:30).

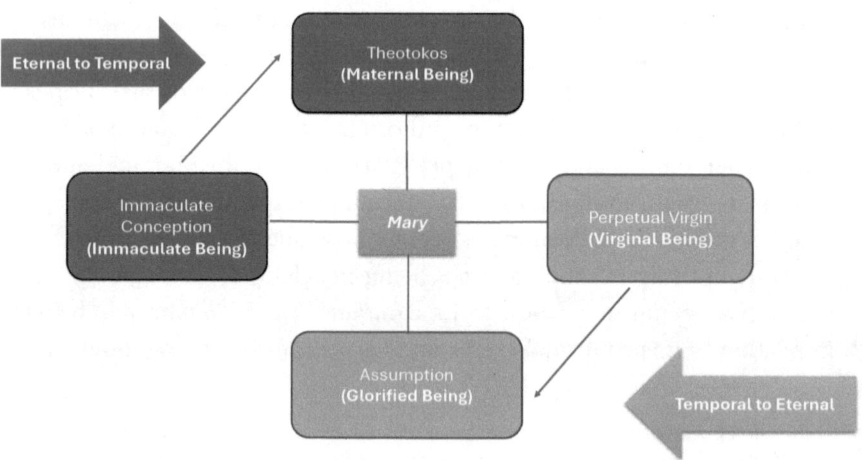


Thus, while anthropological *identity* (in time) is established in anthropological *origin* (eternal/predestined), anthropological *vocation* (in time) is eschatologically founded in anthropological *destiny*. The temporal/eternal dynamic situates the human being (as it does all of creation) within the eschatological tension between the *here* and *not yet*. This tension, which is clearly expressed in the person of Mary through the dogmatic truths of the church, reveals the mutually informing answers to the questions implied in human existence. For example, *identity* is the expressed manifestation of what is already given eternally as *origin* and so can be understood only in this light, while *vocation* can be comprehended only considering the eschatological *end* as its decisive and determinative orientation. Of course, this relationality among the different anthropological truths must be held together within the singularity of the person because each dogmatic truth about our Lady can ever only be fully revealed in the light of each other. So, while it is true that, for instance, Mary's motherhood is intrinsically connected to her immaculate conception as the condition of possibility for a divine maternity, her perpetual virginity and eschatological end, her assumption, are also the fitting outworking of both and so are meaningfully expressed in the light of each.

Thus, while Mary's identity, vocation, origin, and eschatological end enact and recapitulate anthropology such that the questions implied in human existence are addressed along four cardinal points that correspond to the four Marian dogmas of the church, we also observe that anthropology is shaped and informed determinatively by a temporal/eternal dynamic that is eschatologically construed. The human being can be understood only considering the eternal since it pervades the temporal transcendently—as its meaning and primary cause—while also sandwiching the temporally conditioned human being with the eternal as bookends. Human identity and vocation are irrevocably shaped by their predestined origin and eschatological end. Mary is the conclusive manifestation of this. This is why she enacts and sums up the meaning of anthropology; Mary is normative and exemplary for all of humanity. This is also the reason further theological and philosophical investigation of Mary ought to yield additional insights into anthropology.

Father Alexander Schmemann saw the importance of our Lady clearly, especially in light of what he called "anthropological heresy," which for him is the leading spiritual disease in the contemporary world—one that can be treated only with the balm of a proper anthropology.

> Properly understood, Mariology is thus the "locus theologicus" *par excellence* of Christian anthropology. In this unique knowledge of a unique Person, a knowledge which the Church always renews in her veneration of Mary, in communion with her and in joy about her, there can be dissolved the hopeless contradiction proper to the secular anthropology of our time: the contradiction between the "minimalistic" view of man stemming

> from science, and the "maximalistic" claims permeating our man-centered culture.[2]

But one may ask, "Why Mary? Why not Christ?" The problem, however, is that under these very questions lies a false either/or dualism, which rests upon a Christomonistic presupposition that is blind to the Catholic both/and truth. Nevertheless, Fr. Schmemann easily addresses this type of query with the following:

> Truly she is unique because unique is her human perfection and unique her relation to her Son. And yet she is one of us, she is like us: her life, her experience are fully human. But then is it not in her and in her experience that we should seek the true "measure" of our own lives, the answer to the agonizing questions about man? Where else? Where else is the end and the solution of all the dichotomies and dead ends that threaten to dehumanize our world? She gave Christ to us. *And He, who eternally remains her Son, gives her to us as the assurance that man is the image of His ineffable beauty, the object of an eternal love in an eternal Kingdom.*[3]

Again, Mary can be understood only from *within* her unique role in the divine economy, her singularly distinctive relation to *her* Son. The archetypal pair are to be held together to see the full depth and breadth of human reality, and thus all of creation. Considering this, it is Mary who reveals human destiny, which is, in differing analogical ways and degrees, to give birth to God, to achieve a chaste existence, to recover our paradisal innocence, and to gradually receive deification.[4]

In thinking about a Mariologically informed anthropology, Fr. Louis Bouyer is instructive as he addresses the question of whether situating an anthropological investigation in Mary amounts to an implicit rejection of the humanity of Christ:

> We . . . believe that Christ was perfectly man, yet so perfectly, in so divine a way, that he was not, strictly speaking, *a* man, a human person, but God made man. That is why we hold it to be so important to reflect upon that wholly human person who was placed, by the Incarnation, in an absolutely unique relation with the Son of God himself. . . . A human person, in fact, and

2. Schmemann, *Virgin Mary*, 53.

3. Schmemann, *Virgin Mary*, 55; emphasis added.

4. This turn of phrase is borrowed from Dr. John Milbank's assessment of my own thesis.

> no more than a human, became the Mother of God, the Mother of the very Son of the eternal Father. We are, therefore, entitled to see in her and in her alone, all that grace was able to make of a creature, of a human nature, while still leaving it in its order as a created being.[5]

We will now proceed to explore the anthropological significance of the first Marian dogma: *divine maternity.*

## DIVINE MATERNITY AND THE HUMAN AS MATERNAL BEING

The recognition of Mary as Theotokos, or "God Bearer," was solemnly defined at the Council of Ephesus in 431, crystallizing a truth already deeply embedded in Christian faith and devotion. In response to the Nestorian controversy, which sought to separate Christ's divinity from his humanity, the council affirmed that the one born of Mary was none other than the eternal Son of God. Saint Cyril of Alexandria, the foremost defender of this doctrine, declared, "If anyone does not confess that God is truly Emmanuel, and that on this account the Holy Virgin is the Mother of God (for according to the flesh she gave birth to the Word of God become flesh by birth), let him be anathema."[6] In defining Mary's divine maternity, the council illuminated not only her singular role in salvation history but also the way in which human nature, through her, becomes the very place where God dwells—not abstractly, but personally, historically, and irrevocably in Christ.

The unique, unrepeatable divine maternity of Mary signals the deepest meaning of human *identity*, for while it is metaphysically true that God is "closer to us than we are to ourselves," intimating, so to speak, an intimate indwelling as Other, only *in* Mary do we uniquely behold the beginning of the fulfillment of Maximus's words that "the Logos of God (who is God) wills always and in all things to accomplish the mystery of His embodiment."[7] She stands, therefore, as the concrete representation of creation's reception of its very being from the Unconditioned so it can eventually arrive at its own authentic identity: bearer of God.[8] This is true,

5. Bouyer, *Seat of Wisdom*, vii–viii; emphasis in original.
6. Denzinger, *Sources of Catholic Dogma*, no. 113.
7. Maximos the Confessor, *On Difficulties*, 1:107.
8. As articulated in ch. 1 this is to be read not in competition with her Son but as

of course, most fully for humans *as image bearers of God*, but it is indeed coextensive with all of creation to the degree that all creation reveals in varying analogical gradations those transcendental qualities that are the overflow of God's infinite plenitude by virtue of its participation *in* God, and thus God *in* all, as it were.

Mary is truly who she is meant to be while all of creation is on pilgrimage, seeking to become what it truly is. "Virgin Mother, daughter of thy Son, lowly and exalted more than any creature, fixed term of the eternal counsel."[9] Simultaneously, her emptiness and fullness, her virginity and motherhood, her poverty and richness, reveal all of creation's yawning openness, ready to be filled with the Other that always already continually sustains it in being. But it is her motherhood, her divine maternity, that captures creation's *identity* eschatologically—an identity that is indeed *already here* (by virtue of the singular event of the incarnation and its reverberations through time as church and sacraments) but *not yet* fully so. It is creation's longing to be filled with the transcendent immanently, to truly arrive and so embody the gift that is coextensive with the Giver; all of creation longs for this, yearning to fulfill its fundamental *maternal* disposition, but it can do so only when humanity follows the Theotokos in her fiat, and so allow herself (that is, creation), her very flesh to become the *interface between the infinite and the finite*. This is why Paul writes that "we know that the whole creation has been groaning in *labor pains* until now; and not only the creation, but we ourselves, who have the first fruits of the Spirit, groan inwardly while we wait for adoption, the redemption of our bodies" (Rom 8:22–23). In this, Mary's divine maternity enacts and sums up the decisively capacious and singular identity of the human: *maternal being*.

Human identity *as* maternal in no way stands in contradiction to the enactment of anthropological identity via her Son. Instead, it complements and thus images such an identity *on the side of creatureliness alone*; that is, it reveals the inherent receptacle-like character of creatureliness (for its very being is but a gift and thus remains open) while also illuminating creation and thus humanity's active rather than passive role (creation's synergistic participation in grace). Joseph Ratzinger notes well

---

the necessary synergistic union between Mother and Son. Christ's creatureliness—his humanity—is the highest expression of creation's fundamental identity by virtue of the hypostatic union, but Mary is such as mere creature and so fulfills the complementary coefficient ingredient to the mysterious union between the two.

9. Dante Alighieri, *Paradiso* (1984) 33.1–3.

the significance of Mary's role in both creation and salvation history in safeguarding the shared, robust dynamic between divinity and creation, and thus articulating the importance of creaturely participation in union with the divine. Creation, and so humanity, therefore, is not a mirage lacking substance (theopanism) but is indeed a "real player" in the drama of God's economy. Consider the following words from Joseph Cardinal Ratzinger on this score:

> Mariology expresses the heart of "salvation history," it nonetheless transcends an approach focused solely on that history. Mariology is an essential component of a hermeneutics of salvation history. Recognition of this fact brings out the true dimensions of Christology over against a falsely understood *solus Christus*. Christology must speak of a Christ who is both "head *and* body," that is, who comprises the redeemed creation in its relative subsistence. But this move simultaneously enlarges our perspective beyond the history of salvation, because it counters a false understanding of God's sole agency, highlighting the reality of the creature that God calls and enables to respond to him freely. Mariology demonstrates that the doctrine of grace does not revoke creation; rather, it is the definitive Yes to creation. In this way, Mariology guarantees the ontological independence of creation, undergirds faith in creation, and crowns the doctrine of creation, rightly understood.[10]

This is why Mary is ingredient in a vigorously generative Christology, discerning her as constitutive of a christological grammar that captures the affirmative embrace of God in and through creation, redeeming and elevating creatureliness in a theophanic pitch, transfiguring it, devoid of any notion of theopanism or lurking nihilism. Again, this is the theoanthropocosmic humanism that is presented in Mary. In this sense, Mary's fiat encapsulates creation's proper response to God's incisive invitation, a yes that was slowly being cultivated in the history of Israel, a yes that constitutes the genesis and very expression of humanity's *identity as maternal* since it embodies the fertile disposition of a creaturely womb paradoxically made for God.

> At the moment when she pronounces her Yes, Mary is Israel in person; she is the Church in person and as a person. She is the personal concretization of the Church because her *Fiat* makes her the bodily Mother of the Lord. But this biological fact is a

10. Ratzinger, in Balthasar and Ratzinger, *Mary*, 31; emphasis in original.

> theological reality, because it realizes the deepest spiritual content of the covenant that God intended to make with Israel.[11]

The anthropological significance of Mary's maternity, a motherhood that is no doubt enacted in time but transcends it in the degree that enfleshment *in her* pertains to God hypostatically, situates in a bidirectional temporal manner the disclosive nature of the communal *identity* of both Israel and church—Israel reaching toward this truth while the church lives from it—doing so as the concretized person, a Palestinian Jewish girl, that is the Theotokos. Thus, Mary reveals the true identity of Israel and church, doing so conjointly with her Son but in a different metaphysical register and so complementing Christ.[12] As stated above, her maternal identity expresses all of creation's true identity—and anthropological identity uniquely—since her divine maternity is the fruit of her humble faith, radically opened and dependent on the Other, therefore "as such, she represents the creation, which is called to respond to God, and the freedom of the creature, which does not lose its integrity in love but attains completion therein."[13]

This is why the then Cardinal Ratzinger, reflecting on Isa 55:10–11, identifies Mary as the "maternal mystery of the soil" that receives fruitfully through her all-encompassing yes the generative Word that will not return to God empty, thus "Mary, the holy soil of the Church, as the Fathers so wonderfully call her, is an essential part of Christ."[14] All of this distinguishes Mary as the apex of creation's inner longing for this

11. Ratzinger, in Balthasar and Ratzinger, *Mary*, 30.

12. This is the reason any notion of attempting to "ground" Mariology in an either/or framework between church and Christ is fallacious, simply because it fails to see the substantial, multivalent connections between Mary, Christ, and the church. Ratzinger is instructive on this point: "We cannot assign Mariology to Christology alone or to ecclesiology alone (much less dissolve it into ecclesiology as a more or less superfluous exemplification of the Church). Rather, Mariology underscores the *nexus mysteriorum*—the intrinsic interwovenness of the mysteries in their irreducible mutual otherness and their unity" (Ratzinger, in Balthasar and Ratzinger, *Mary*, 29). Fr. Schmemann also recognizes the intrinsic connection between Christ, Mary, the church, along with creation: "Here stands Mary as, indeed, the personal 'icon' of the Church, of that movement of love and adoration. There is no 'icon' of the Church except the human person that has become totally transparent to the Holy Spirit, to the 'joy and peace' of the Kingdom. If Christ is the 'icon' of the Father, Mary is the 'icon' of the new creation, the new Eve responding to the new Adam, fulfilling the mystery of love" (*Virgin Mary*, 65).

13. Ratzinger, in Balthasar and Ratzinger, *Mary*, 31.

14. Ratzinger, Balthasar and Ratzinger, *Mary*, 14.

redemptive, life-giving Word, such that her divine maternity becomes the very core of her identity, thus revealing the *true identity* of humanity.[15]

> The Fathers of the Church say that prayer, properly understood, is nothing other than becoming a longing for God. In Mary this petition has been granted: she is, as it were, the open vessel of longing, in which life becomes prayer and prayer becomes life. Saint John wonderfully conveys this process by never mentioning Mary's name in his Gospel. She no longer has any name except "the Mother of Jesus." It is as if she had handed over her personal dimension, in order now to be solely at his disposal, *and precisely thereby had become a person.*[16]

Here Ratzinger recognizes the subtle flowering that streams forth from "John the Theologian" in his Gospel by revealing the potency of what is not said about Mary—her name—to reveal her true name, as it were, which is her *identity*: Mother of Jesus the God-man. This is the wellspring of her true identity, and thus the realization of her true personhood.

Of course, one may ask whether this can actually be true for the rest of humanity. Could it ever be the case, for example, that *I* could become the "Mother of Jesus"? In what sense, in other words, can *I* "bear the Christ" who is God in flesh?

Without denying the utter uniqueness of Mary's role in God's economy, Jesus himself signifies the real importance of her humble, faith-filled fiat—and through that yes the subsequent *gestation*, *nativity*, and *motherly care*—as the quintessential pattern that indeed enacts and sums up human identity as *maternal*. Her singular fiat, gestation, birth, and parenting reveal the source and pattern by which *any* human can

15. Fr. Alexander Schmemann captures this well: "She—Mary—is the ultimate 'doxa' of creation, its response to God. She is the climax, the personification, the affirmation of the ultimate destiny of all creation: that God may finally be all in all, may fill all things with himself. The world is the 'receptacle' of his glory, and in this it is 'feminine.' And in the present 'era,' Mary is the sign, the guarantee that this is so, that in its mystical depth the world is already achieving this destiny" (*Virgin Mary*, 66). And Fr. Louis Bouyer in his important work *Seat of Wisdom* also captures well the "maternal" image coextensive with creation's responsive nature to God: "The maternal relation belongs exclusively to the creature inasmuch as it is truly active, since it is the highest expression of the kind of activity proper to created being—that is, it is essentially, a reflex activity, a secondary one. It is a real activity, but one that is exercised consequently, and so dependently, on the action of another. Motherhood implies real creativity, not, however, as the first and sovereign source of it, but as a secondary and subordinate agency, though it is much more than a mere instrumental one" (148).

16. Ratzinger, in Balthasar and Ratzinger, *Mary*, 15–16; emphasis added.

authentically enact their identity as maternal. For when praise was given about his mother, Jesus was keen to highlight the source of such praise when he said, "Blessed rather are those who hear the word of God and obey it!" (Luke 11:28). Mary indeed deserves praise but only because of her "hearing" and "obeying" that Word which became incarnate in her womb. So, while unique praise is no doubt given to Mary—for she alone is the Theotokos—she simultaneously shows us the path that leads to our deepest identity, a path that is open and available to all humans.

This is also the reason Jesus responds to the request to be seen by his family in a puzzling manner, asking, "Who is my mother?" He answers by pointing to his disciples, saying that "whoever does the will of my Father in heaven is my . . . mother" (Matt 12:48–50). Thus, again, the way is open to all. Yet is Mary not the one who performs the will of the Father so completely that she literally becomes filled by him whom the heavens themselves cannot contain and thus becomes truly *his* Mother?[17] In this we behold Mary as the *first disciple*, the first one to obey the Father in the manner of Christ her Son *before* his very arrival. Fascinatingly, her obedience is the condition of possibility for Christ's coming into this world, he whom she is called to follow. Yet, it is only because she is "full of grace"—a gift given preveniently in view of the merits of Christ's death on the cross—that she can do this, which means, paradoxically, *he too* is the condition of possibility for her fiat. All this touches upon an inexpressible mystery, one that points to the co-predestined pair who are the new Adam and new Eve;[18] nevertheless, in all this Mary enacts and sums up human identity.

Thus, the following can be said concerning how Mary *illuminates* (grace/faith/theology) human identity such that we behold its *maternal* nature: (1) Through her we see how human identity is enacted and

17. Fr. Alexander Schmemann's homily on the Mother of God identifies the connection between the church's veneration of Mary with her profound obedience as a human being, thus making her an iconic description of what humans can achieve in grace, and what they are in fact called to: "The Church's veneration of Mary has always been rooted in her obedience to God, her willing choice to accept a humanly impossible calling. The Orthodox Church has always emphasized Mary's connection to humanity and delighted in her as the best, purest, most sublime fruition of human history and of man's quest for God, for ultimate meaning, for the ultimate content of human life" (*Virgin Mary*, 22).

18. As *Lumen Gentium* states, "The Father of mercies willed that the incarnation should be preceded by the acceptance of her who was predestined to be the mother of His Son, so that just as a woman contributed to death, so also a woman should contribute to life" (*LG* 56).

summed up by *consent to divine invitation*, making human fiat to God (and thus a radical no to that which is *contra*) the *source* of anthropological identity, a source that remains unobstructed to the extent that the yes is renewed each moment in loving obedience. (2) In addition, through her we also observe how human identity is realized by *gestating* and *giving birth* to the Word, which for us translates into an authentic participation in the suffering of Christ via discipleship (the carrying of our cross) as the manifest presence of our perpetual fiat; without this fiat, the inward life would be aborted and thus terminated. (3) Finally, through Mary we behold how human identity is enacted and recapitulated by *parenting* the Word, which, in our case, paradoxically signifies human obedience to that Word (which is the expressed will of the Father in Scripture, tradition, the magisterium of the church, and our conscience). This too is coincident with that lasting fiat that finds its final realization in glory. Therefore, in Mary we uncover the deepest truth of human identity, an identity that is maternal and so whose source is that perpetual fiat to the divine life, *gestating*, *giving birth*, and *parenting* that life via human *consent*, *discipleship*, and continual *obedience* to that life-giving, life-sustaining Word. The following will be a brief theological investigation of these sources of anthropological identity.

## Fiat

The maternal identity of the human being (along with, though in varying degrees, all of creation) is *illuminated* by the Theotokos through her fiat. Her yes reverses the destructive and nihilistic trend that has shaped humanity, and with it all of creation. Through this, new life, a new mode of existence, is realized—precisely because it fulfills and thus enacts and sums up the essential nature of the human being. This yes is the sum of the fullest expression of a proper response to the source and summit of all. This, in turn, galvanizes the total structure of creatureliness because it is an affirmative embrace of the One who is the font of its very being, sustaining its integral wholeness without destruction, violent intrusion, or false identification that would deny the other as authentically *other*. Thus, this yes is creation's mother tongue as reciprocal gift, a fitting response to the Giver, filled with thanksgiving; a gift that emanates from charity and humility. It is only ever a yes to life, to love, to light, to Reality itself, that can be the genesis for new and real life, deep and abiding love, a luminosity that truly enlightens, that grounds the self via anamnesis in what is true, good, and beautiful. The antinomy of such a fiat could only bring about the opposite: death, hate and apathy, darkness, and unreality. Such a no is, in the final analysis, suicide; it is even nihilism itself, for it is a denial of Being and thus being, along with all those transcendental qualities that bubble up as creation's glorious garment and form. It is *this* fiat that is the source of Mary's motherhood—her divine maternity and thus the heart of her identity—and so reveals the form and pattern of our being as maternal, our genuinely fecund identity, as well as creation's maternal disposition.

Since Mary is the paradigmatic and archetypal expression of the human as such, she reveals in an illuminative way (grace/faith/theology) that the deepest source of humanization is an active, consensual participation in God's economy. This participation is foundationally constituted by our responsive yes to God's continual life-giving and life-fulfilling invitation. Thus, this participation is the source of a theandric humanism, the key to a synergism that is perichoretic, the fulfillment of the human being, and thus the enactment and summing up of human identity. And because it is this, such participation is not extrinsic to the total self—and, specifically, the *body*[19]—but is *intrinsically* linked to it. For while this yes to God issues forth from within the deepest part of our being, as it did our Lady, its articulation is ever only salient by means of the total self as reciprocal gift to the Giver. The body too, then, is transmogrified as it becomes the carrier and transmitter of this fiat, a transformation that is akin to the actualization of its potentiality, for the body, in concert with the entire self, is ordered toward this supernatural end. Thus, the totality of our being, including (and especially) our bodies, become the mysterious locus, the interface between the infinite and finite, as we see in Mary, because through this fiat—which is enduring—the finite becomes the abode of the infinite, the particular becomes ever more the home of the universal, the hidden, ever more seen, paradoxically.

Intriguingly, without mixture, confusion, separation, or division, the Unconditioned One and the contingent one come together in such a way that Providence is fulfilled coextensively with the fulfillment of creaturely identity in and through *love*. In other words, through this ineffable exchange between God and Mary, the maternal identity of anthropology is seen as made *for* love *by* love himself. In this, God is revealed as love,

19. As Sr. Mary Timothy Prokes states, "The privileges celebrated in Mary are grounded in her body" (*Theology of the Body*, 172).

while Mary (and all of humanity) is created to be filled and fulfilled with this love. As Paolo Prosperi notes in his essay on Nicholas Cabasilas,

> In a nutshell: by willingly making of himself the "Son of his daughter"—to paraphrase Dante's famous formula—the Creator "invents" a way to exchange with his creature not only the properties or idioms of their respective natures, as the tradition of the Church has always and rightly stressed, but even, in an analogous and yet real sense, the very incommunicable properties that define each one's role in the *creator-creature relationship itself*. On the one hand, the Maker, who is by nature the one who freely gives his creature to be, becomes here the "made one" who is *himself* "given to be" through the freedom of his creature. On the other hand, the creature, who is by nature the pure recipient of God's gift, becomes here the giver, the one who quenches God's desire to share in her life and being.[20]

This is why love is foundational in understanding the reason *for* and the structure *of* Mary's fiat, and thus our own. Such an exchange can be understood only as the revelation of love. In the incarnation, God simultaneously reveals his unspeakable love in a profoundly visceral and (supra) rational way by fulfilling the very telos of Mary. Anthropologically, we can even observe that the maternal identity of the human as such is the very condition of possibility for God *to* reveal his love to us. Prosperi captures this well in the following:

> To the question "why the annunciation?" we can answer, with Cabasilas: because this particular way of becoming man manifests in the greatest way possible (*summon modo*) the glory of God's love for mankind. The Creator does not limit himself to sharing with his creature *what is properly his own* in a general or abstract sense. Rather, he bestows upon her, in a relative and yet absolutely real way, that very power that decisively marks the disparity and difference in their mutual relation: the power to give the other to "be born" through one's *fiat*. By *freely desiring* (*agathos eros*: Dionysius) to receive his flesh as a gift from his creature, God bestows the greatest possible share in his goodness, by granting his creature the power to *bestow upon him* the most fundamental gift that she continually receives *from* him, that is, *human existence*. In Cabasilas's elegant words: "the Creator is created by the voice of a creature."[21]

20. Prosperi, "Fixed End," 213; emphasis in original.

21. Prosperi, "Fixed End," 214; emphasis in original.

Thus, the anthropological significance of Mary's fiat as the enactment and recapitulation of human identity as maternal is profound: the human is made to be the generative locus of the enfleshment—embodiment—of God. In this sense is the architectonic form of the human being love, for such a being is made for that very One who is responsible for its continued subsistence: Love himself.[22] The human is made for infinite love, Who is the Source of all: God. This is why anthropological identity can ever only be *revealed* (grace/faith/theology) since it constitutes an incomprehensible reality, a paradox really, since unaided reason could never arrive at such a truth. Thus, we can echo the closing words of Cabasilas's homily on the annunciation that at once captures not only the glorious role of our Lady, but also the anthropological significance of her fiat:

> We will conclude with the salutation of Gabriel, adorning the sum of our oration with this addition: "Rejoice, you who are full of grace, the Lord is with you." *May you prepare us to make a habitation for him within ourselves, not just in word but also in deed*, for this is conducive to this glory and to the laudation of you who gave birth to him, for unto him belongs glory unto the ages. Amen.[23]

## Gestation and Birth

In addition to Mary's fiat, the maternal identity of the human being is also *illuminated* by the Theotokos through her *gestating* and *birth giving* of the Word. This gestational period along with the subsequent birth giving is the continued actualization of that initial fiat, a fiat that, in a real sense, continues throughout the rest of her life as the source of her identity. Anthropologically, this is realized through an authentic participation in the suffering of Christ via (cruciform) discipleship as the manifest presence of our perpetual fiat; without this fiat, the inward life would be aborted and thus terminated. The maternal identity of the human is enacted by the self-denial spoken of by Christ, which is realized by taking up one's cross; and it is this that corresponds to the singular event of Mary's maternal gestation and birth giving.

22. John is profoundly instructive on this point if we but read meditatively 1 John 4:7–12.

23. Cabasilas, "Homily on the Annunciation," 398; emphasis in original.

But why think this? How do Mary's gestation and birth giving of God made man signify the maternal identity of the human being via participation in the suffering of Christ through discipleship? How, in other words, do the unique gestation and nativity that Mary underwent in bearing the God-man—which, according to tradition, was a bearing that did not manifest the experience of birth pangs typical for other women who undergo labor since she herself was immaculate[24]—signal anthropological identity through a sharing in the passion of Christ?

The key to understanding this is rooted in a reading of both Scripture and tradition that recognizes Mary's gestational period and travail not located within the immediate temporal frame of the post-annunciation period, but rather as parallel with the travails of her Son in his life, culminating at the foot of his cross.[25]

Much of Fr. John Behr's work on the apostolic fathers and Scripture discerns a proper Christian anthropology, which, he argues, is a dynamically unfolding (and thus not something merely "given") work done (in time) and eschatologically completed in Christ via his cross—such that death is defeated by death, thus transforming the tomb into a womb.[26] This realization perceives the intimate connection between discipleship as a carrying of one's cross and the formation of the human being—the finding of one's true life by means of a loss of life—through the established pattern laid down by Christ on his cross. What is instructive for us is how Mary's participation in the suffering of her Son, especially seen in John's Gospel,[27] is the way she gives birth, as it were, to his eschatological

24. Consider Gen 3:16.

25. Origen of Alexandria in his commentary on the Gospel of John insightfully paraphrases Jesus's words to his mother concerning the "beloved disciple" by saying "this is Jesus whom you bore." She, as it were, gives birth, through much travail, to her Son in the mystery of the church. In fact, she gives birth to the whole Christ—head and body—and thus the church (*Commentary on John* 1.23).

26. Fr. Behr's work *John the Theologian* is a profound reading of the Gospel of John. Through a careful exegetical exploration of key portions of the text in conversation with patristic sources and contemporary phenomenology, Fr. Behr identifies this Gospel as paschal from beginning to end and thus ought to be read as such. Some of the themes in this work are present in earlier pieces such as *Becoming Human* and *Mystery of Christ*, which are also replete with a well-worked-out anthropology derived from the early church.

27. This is so because, as Fr. Behr states, "It is not simply that the Gospel of John reports details of which the other evangelists were ignorant or had forgotten. What we have in the Gospel of John, the theological Gospel *par excellence*, is already a theological interpretation of the event of the Passion, in terms of the fertile preaching of the gospel" (*Mystery of Christ*, 128).

state via his cross such that, as the new Eve, she becomes the mother of all the living and so of the church in the order of grace. Thus the following: this is the reason much of the language used in John's Gospel and the Letters of Paul concerning the bringing about of a "new creation," that is, the realization of one's true identity—for one's self or others—are especially maternal: "born from above" (John 3:3); "we were gentle among you, like a nurse tenderly caring for her own children" (1 Thess 2:7); "my little children, for whom I am again in the pain of childbirth until Christ be formed in you" (Gal 4:19); and so on. This seems to suggest that Mary (as the symbol of the church,[28] especially seen in Rev 12 as a woman in travail, and as the archetypal figure of anthropological identity as maternal) is the locus by which we observe this first wave of "gestating" and "birth giving." Mary is the paradigmatic person that reveals the way in which the human being (that is, the one "in Christ") comes about since she was the first to offer her fiat and bear Christ, allowing him to be formed in her womb (both literally—historically—but also theologically via her participation in his suffering), and to give birth to him, again both literally (historically) and theologically through his passion and death.[29]

In light of Mary's unique vocation to reveal the maternal identity of anthropology through her fiat, gestation, and nativity, we can see that human identity is therefore realized through the use of one's freedom by freely participating in God's economy through the offering of one's fiat.[30] This, then, allows God to form in the womb of the human being, so to

28. As Adrienne von Speyr noted, "Whatever the Lord did to His Mother He did with His Church in mind" (Speyr, *Handmaid of the Lord*, 139).

29. The following description by Fr. Behr is insightful on this point: "From the beginning, the gospel of the crucified and exalted Lord was proclaimed in terms of a birth, both that of Christ and of Christians. The letters of the apostle Paul, which, it should be remembered, predate the writing of the four canonical Gospels, do not even mention the name of Mary, though they do mention that Christ 'was born of a woman, born under the law' (Gal 4.4) and that Christ is of the line of David (Rom 1.3). However, the apostle does use the language of hearing and receiving the Word, to describe the begetting of Christ, that is later used of Mary in the infancy narratives, and uses it to great effect" (*Mystery of Christ*, 115). Therefore, in a very real sense, each person who takes up the call to proclaim and thus help shape and form Christ in others, along with those who take up their own cross in following him, is enacting a Marian role.

30. As Fr. Behr notes, "Rather than thinking of the Incarnation of Christ as an event restricted to a long-gone past and a far-removed land, we should instead think of it as a possibility that is to be lived as an ever-contemporary reality, here and now in those who respond to him" (*Becoming Human*, 104). One of the decisive arguments in his work on the Gospel of John carries this insight forward, as Fr. Behr states, "The Incarnation, in brief, is not 'an episode in a biography,' an event now in the past, but the ongoing embodiment of God in those who follow Christ" (*John the Theologian*, 5).

speak, Christ through a gestating process that is brought about through participation in a "sharing in the sufferings of Christ." The further along the gestational period the human being is, the more she is identified with Christ.[31] The travailing that leads up to the birth of Christ (which, sacramentally, is enacted through our baptism and sustained by participation in his body and blood in the Eucharist) is culminated in our *dying in him*, which is really the birth of our eschatological self, a birth that is coextensive with the birth of Christ. Christ is formed in us as we are formed in him; he is born in and through us, which in turn shapes and forms our maternal identity as humans. Paradoxically, true life—*life in Christ*—is mediated through death. Just as the Holy Spirit transformed the tomb of Christ into a womb by raising him up from the dead, defeating death by death, so too the dying body of the maternal being that is the human is transformed through the Spirit into an *eschatological womb*. Through the Spirit, human participation in the sufferings of Christ and his death is the actualization of the gestating and birth-giving process, which is all initiated and sustained by fiat. As Fr. Behr notes,

> From what we have seen, we might also say that in order to be a true human being in the image of God, who is Christ the true human being, we must be born into a new existence in Christ by a birth effected through our voluntary use of our mortality—as an act of sacrifice through baptism—thereby freely choosing to exist as a human being and grounding that being and existence in an act of freedom, so living the same life of love that God himself is. The human being only comes into existence by giving their own "fiat"—"Let it be!" For every other aspect of creation, all that was needed was a simple divine "fiat"—"Let it be!" But for the human being to come into existence, required a creature able to give his or her own "fiat"! This is, of course, accomplished sacramentally, once and for all, in baptism. The life of the baptized thereafter is one of "learning to die," learning, that is, specifically to take up the Cross of Christ.[32]

Notice the slippery use of metaphors that come from Scripture. Are we ourselves being born, or are we doing the bearing and birth giving? Both! *We give birth to our true selves in Christ, which is the formation of Christ in us, through our fiat.* The overlapping of metaphors indicates the mysterious reality that is truly being communicated through this entire process.

31. Consider Paul's words in Gal 2:20.

32. Behr, *Becoming Human*, 64–66.

However, Mary is central in this for she is uniquely the Theotokos who participated in his suffering and death at the foot of his cross (as she continues to do so mystically as Mother of the Church). She is indeed the Mother of Sorrows.

Consider, for instance, the words of Ignatius of Antioch written to the Roman Christians concerning his coming martyrdom to take place in Rome. Especially note the use of metaphors regarding "death," "life," "birth," "labor pains":

> It is better for me to die in Christ Jesus than to be king over the ends of the earth. I seek him who died for our sake. I desire him who rose for us. Birth-pangs are upon me. Suffer me, my brethren; hinder me not from living, do not wish me to die. . . . Suffer me to receive the pure light; when I shall have arrived there, I will be a human being, suffer me to follow the example of the passion of my God.[33]

Ignatius's language indicates that the formation of Christ in those who offer their fiat to God in synergistic participation with his will by embracing their cross (which, for Ignatius, is his willing acceptance of martyrdom) results, also, in the formation of one's true self, one's *maternal identity*, which is here articulated as the "human being" (ἄνθρωπος). Paradoxically, to not embrace the cross is to "die"—that is, to not actualize one's maternal identity in bringing about Christ and thus one's own life. Mary, again, is the pattern for this: through her fiat, gestation, and subsequent nativity—both historically and theologically (as seen in the Gospel of John)—we discover that anthropological identity is indeed maternal. Mary, in and through her Son's incarnation and cross (which are seen inseparably in the Gospel of John), is the archetypal model for the formation of real human identity as the one who enacts and recapitulates this truth.[34]

Indeed, because of her maternal love for her Son, she suffered the pains of the cross in proportion to such love—even to the point of martyrdom (fulfilling the words given to her by the aged Simeon in the temple). It is this dying that allowed for the blossoming of her deepest identity as *maternal* since through it she gave birth not only to Christ via John (and the church), but also to herself via Christ. The seventeenth-century Dominican theologian Rev. Louis Chardon, OP, captures well Mary's death through her Son's death:

33. As quoted in Behr, *John the Theologian*, 196–97.

34. See Fr. Behr's work for the details.

> St. Peter is represented with a cross, St. Paul with a sword, St. Stephen with stones, St. Lawrence with a fiery grill, and St. Catherine with a wheel inset with knives, to show how they died. Jesus in Mary's arms was the instrument of her martyrdom, a sword of suffering piercing the soul of His Blessed Mother, as Simeon had prophesied. Jesus was indeed that adorable Word, more penetrating than any double-edged sword, separating Mary's spirit and soul.[35]

Mary shares in a profound unity with her Son his suffering and death as his Mother. As Stefano Maria Manelli, FI, articulates, "The nails and the blood, the wounds and thorns which lacerated the divine body of Jesus form a single unity with the unspeakable sufferings of His Mother . . . the mystery of the suffering of Mary forms a unity, a perfect synergy with the mystery of the suffering of Christ."[36] Thus, in dying (that is, her gestating and birth giving) in and through and with her Son, Mary's maternal identity, an identity that could ever only be *revealed/illuminated*—because of the profound paradox at the heart of this—comes to its fullest expression. Therefore, she is the form and shape of anthropological identity par excellence since in her, always in concert with her Son, real identity is enacted and recapitulated.[37]

35. Chardon, *Cross of Jesus*, 1:166. In chs. 25–30, Chardon beautifully articulates the mystical union between our Lady and her Son via the cross, which is her share.

36. Manelli, "Mary Coredemptrix," 94.

37. In an extensive passage, Joseph Cardinal Ratzinger brings together the suffering of the Son and Mother in the mode that allows for Mary's maternal identity to be completed. This suffering occurs as the perpetual fiat offered by Mary throughout Christ's earthly life. "The sword shall pierce her heart—this statement foreshadows the Son's Passion, which will become her own passion. This passion already begins with her next visit to the Temple: she must accept the precedence of Jesus' true Father and of his house, the Temple; she must learn to release the Son she has borne. She must complete the Yes to God's will that made her a mother by withdrawing into the background and letting Jesus enter upon his mission. Jesus' rebuffs during his public life and her withdrawal are an important step that will reach its goal on the Cross with the words 'behold, your son.' It is no longer Jesus but the disciple who is her son. To accept and to be available is the first step required of her; to let go and to release is the second. Only in this way does her motherhood become complete: the 'blessed is the womb that bore you' comes true only when it enters into the other beatitude: 'Blessed rather are those who hear the word of God and keep it' (Lk 11:27–28). By this means Mary is prepared for the mystery of the Cross, which does not simply end on Golgotha. Her son remains a sign of contradiction, and she is thus kept to the very end in the pain of this contradiction, in the pain of her messianic motherhood" (Ratzinger, in Balthasar and Ratzinger, *Mary*, 76).

## Parenting

Finally, through Mary we behold how human identity is enacted and recapitulated by *parenting* the Word, which curiously signifies human obedience to that Word (which is the expressed will of the Father in Scripture, tradition, the magisterium of the church, and our conscience). This, of course, is coincident with that lasting fiat that finds its final realization in glory through the cross. It is interesting that the last words of Mary recorded in the New Testament are an instruction to "do whatever he tells you" (John 2:5), words she herself put into practice when she received John as her son at the foot of the cross. Indeed, Mary (along with Joseph) *parented* Christ as he was obedient to them (Luke 2:51), but the shape of that obedience was reversed as Jesus entered his public ministry: Mary followed Jesus by listening to and obeying him. Mary's parenting was transformed into an obedience to the God-man. As Jesus states, those who do the will of his Father, hearing and obeying the Father, are indeed *his* mother (Matt 12:48–50). No doubt Mary felt the pain of the apparent disconnect as Jesus seemingly distanced himself from her (Matt 12:48; Luke 11:28; John 2:4; etc.). This suffering was in one sense unique to her, but in another sense, it is the model for all who would participate in his suffering. Nonetheless, this was to expand the maternal dimension of Mary to include the entire church, even the world. In other words, the apparent distancing enacted by Christ between him and his mother in his public ministry—a distancing that found its perfect pitch in his handing over of John to her in his stead, followed by his death—was to have Mary's maternity finally include all those who will be a part of his body so she can become the "mother of all the living" (Gen 3:20). Therefore, *parenting* for Mary took the shape of *obedience*. In this way also she enacts and recapitulates the maternal identity of the human being. Such an identity is realized when one *parents through obedience* to Christ the Word. This is the manifestation of authentic love for him, for whoever loves him will keep his commands and thus obey him (John 14:15, 21).

Given the theological analysis of Mary's fiat, *gestation*, *birth*, and *parenting* provided above, we can now proceed to explore how Mary also *illustrates* (nature/reason/philosophy) a vision of human identity. As we observed, this is possible since she is the concrete expression of the analogical ontology as a nonfoundational, decentering, suspended middle, like her Son though in a distinct register. This means that a philosophical investigation of our Lady ought to yield further insights since reason, conjoined with but not destroyed by faith, is sustained considering the creaturely metaphysics.

## MARY ILLUSTRATES ANTHROPOLOGICAL IDENTITY THROUGH HER FIAT

Mary, as mere creature, is the *non-reductive* manifestation of the meaning of the human as such. Considering the metaphysical discernment of Mary provided earlier, we behold in her the undivided relationship between the natural and the supernatural. Thus, a philosophical analysis of Mary will *illustrate* the theological truths given and explored above, insofar as philosophy remains grounded in Catholic theological presuppositions. In other words, a philosophical examination of Mary will illustrate in an explicative mode the theological already discernible in the given revelation. This will be so since philosophy, reason, and nature—the creaturely correlates to Mary as mere creature—are elevated in such a way that not only maintains their creaturely integrity but perfects them, as we see in Mary herself. Therefore, we can proceed to discern how Mary *illustrates* (nature/reason/philosophy) a vision of human identity as she does so *illuminatively* (grace/faith/theology). In order to do this, we begin with the following query: How exactly does a philosophical analysis of the Mother of Jesus illustrate anthropological identity as indeed maternal?

Our initial observation draws us to the fact that she is *a* creature. And while revelation taken up and received in faith sees her as *the* one, *the* Mother, and thus notes her *perennial* significance and scope, reason can also begin with what is merely observed and deduced: the particular in relation to the universal, such that the universal and the particular are bound together.[38] She is *a* human creature—*a* woman—within *a* given cultural and historical milieu. But by way of causality, philosophy also observes that she is the effect of multiple causes, especially that of a transcendent ground that holds all things together in being at every moment—the ontological cause both of her and of all. Thus, this one who, through faith, is beheld as cosmically significant since she becomes, in time, the abode of the infinite and eternal, is also truly conditioned as

38. Although presupposing a univocal concept of being, John Duns Scotus captures this relationality between the particular and universal in his description of contingency: "I say that contingency is not merely privation or defect of Being like the deformity . . . which is sin. Rather, contingency is a *positive mode of Being*, just as necessity is another mode" (as cited in Falque, *God, the Flesh*, 262; emphasis in original).

one among many in the economy of creatureliness, inscribed by spatio-temporality. Given the data of revelation coupled with her existential facticity, we can observe how her fecundity is the meeting of *the* limited and limitless, the stretching forth of the contingent, embraced by the all-encompassing, transcendent Being who is the very condition of her possibility, who remains finite, a creature. Her fertility, then—limited not to her body but also including her immaculate virtues given her at the first moment of her conception—allows for the transposition of divinity and humanity to occur such that, through her, humanity is divinized while divinity is humanized. This is the lush garden provided by revelation, received in faith, that reason can joyously contemplate, enjoying the fruits therein.

Clearly, revelation unveils the impossible as possible (revealing "contradiction" to be "paradox"). The inbreaking of this light illumines the given, the everyday, the "mundane" as capable of and indeed destined for much more than reason alone can ever surmise. Yet does not reason already discern a hint of this as reason reflects upon contingency? Are we not given glimpses of the eternal in the presence of every moment, for those who have eyes to see? Does not impermanence crash against any attempt at grasping at solidity, thrusting us over the precipice into either nihilism or hope? Contingency itself thrashes the foundations of hope, ever tempting one to give up on hope for the apparent purchasing power of despair; or one could strike out against this despair with hope even against hope (Rom 4:18). We either look above, reaching in faith for that which pertains to the truly glorious, or we simply cave in, believing nothing truly matters since all is decisively empty and meaningless.[39] These options are continually present within the web of our existential particularities, and, as the history of philosophy bears witness, the choice for nihilism is ubiquitous, even when it lurks hiddenly behind systems of thought that fail to reckon with their own (empty) foundations. Only faith can save reason from despair; only revelation's light given by grace chases away the dark, brooding forces that seek to steal away the inherent

39. As F. H. Jacobi wrote, "Man has this choice, however, and this alone: Nothingness or God" ("Open Letter to Fichte," 534).

beauty of nature.[40] Theology is the salvation of philosophy.[41] Faith reveals that, along with her Son, Mary is the perfect image of what it means to be human, to be rational, to be what she is—her *nature*—since she is "full of grace." In Mary we see the highest realization (after the sacred humanity of Christ) of graced nature, of reason elevated and illumined by faith, which is why, as Pope John Paul II states, "that between the vocation of the Blessed Virgin and the vocation of true philosophy there is a deep harmony."[42] This insight is provided precisely through the elevation of nature by grace because, as the philosopher Maurice Blondel stated, "the Christian religion presents itself not as a creation superimposed on nature, but as an elevation, an assumption, a transfiguration, a grace that makes use of normal faculties, fortifies them without destroying them, rests on rational foundations and perfects without suppressing."[43]

Faith reveals that Mary is the Mother of Truth incarnate. She models for all philosophers, for all pursuers of truth, what it looks like to attend to truth, to behold it, to carry and caress it, to bring it forth, and to suffer for it.[44] She learns and thus discovers that (the fullness of) truth is

40. Maurice Blondel's reckoning of the First Vatican Council identifies this relational truth between revelation/faith and reason well: "In the historical and concrete state that is ours, the [First] Vatican Council teaches that there is no separate philosophy, that the problem of religion strikes persons and peoples with an undeniable force; and, by reason of this very universal vocation of humanity, the Council declares Revelation to be necessary for reason: also necessary are the attentions Revelations calls for on our part, the examination and the adherence that should result from it" (*Philosophical Exigencies*, 7).

41. This does not mean philosophy is swallowed up by or transmuted into theology. That would not save but rather destroy philosophy. Faith, rather, heals and elevates reason. John Paul II notes, "Of itself, philosophy is . . . with the assistance of faith . . . capable of accepting the 'foolishness' of the Cross as the authentic critique of those who delude themselves that they possess the truth, when in fact they run it aground on the shoals of a system of their own devising" (*Fides et Ratio* 23).

42. John Paul II, *Fides et Ratio* 108.

43. Blondel, *Philosophical Exigencies*, 6. Blondel explains further the need for reason to be elevated by grace through faith, which is not its destruction but completion: "All of Christian religion is higher than reason, but nowhere is it contrary to reason; and reason, without transgressing on the mystery of grace, finds in it nevertheless a light in facing certain problems that it can and must raise, but that it cannot and must not resolve itself" (14).

44. In this way Mary models the vocation of a true philosophy—one radically open to what *is*—rather than seeking to manipulate reality and truth to one's own end. The Jesuit theologian David Meconi states this well: "Mary exemplifies philosophy's initial task to receive reality and not manipulate it. Unlike some Baconian mastery or Cartesian orchestration of the world, Mary symbolizes the awe of standing before a reality wholly independent of the human mind" ("Philosophari in Maria," 71).

indeed a Person; that one, in the end, ought to attend to truth with love, a love that caresses and bears, and a love that listens and follows reverently. As Cardinal Newman wrote, "Mary for thirty continuous years saw and heard him, being all through that time face to face with him, and being able to ask him any question which she wished explained, and know that the answers she received were from the Eternal God, who neither deceives nor can be deceived."[45] Her total life reflects the vocation of philosophy and the philosopher,[46] while also observing that *in and through* her we can begin to discern a philosophical anthropology that is sustained and illuminated by theology, freeing the philosophic gaze to truly explicate her glorious being and way. Thus, the question still stands: How exactly does philosophical thinking about the Mother of Jesus illustrate anthropological identity as indeed maternal?

Mary's fiat, her yes to transcendence, her self-gift to the Giver, actualizes and sums up her maternal identity as *finitude containing the infinite*. Her glorious ascent as consent is the iconic expression of the paradoxical truth that finitude's identity, its being, is a womb ready to be received and thus receive the transcendent—a transcendence that even the highest heavens cannot contain. This creaturely yes to the transcendent breaks open the immanent frame, which, in turn, is the manifestation of the fertile disposition of creatureliness, ready to receive life transcendently, which is in fact the very life creaturehood is called to embody and thus give life to. The self-enclosed, fallen state of the human being, expressed in her no, is really the surrendering to a nihilistic frame—the immanent frame, really—that results in an animating death state, zombie like, or vampiric, parasitic since innate life is denied with that enduring no to transcendence. *The* option before all is either nothingness or transcendent love—the One who desires to be all *in* all. Mary's fiat is a reckoning with this truth, and so she becomes, with the totality of her being, a temple of God, and thus her true identity as both a mere creature and human person. This enigmatic and paradoxically fecund exchange is the

45. Newman, *Mystical Rose*, 95. In another place, Newman highlights well how Mary's active participation in the economy of grace models, again, a life of true reflection as a pursuer of truth: "She does not think it enough to accept, she dwells upon it; not enough to possess, she uses it; not enough to assent, she develops it; not enough to submit the reason, she reasons upon it . . . and thus to triumph over the sophist and the innovator" (*Mary*, 188–89).

46. Sr. Prudence's essay on the relationship between Mary and the vocation of philosophers was key in helping me understand some of the connections between our Lady and philosophy: Allen, "Mary and the Vocation."

center by which anthropological identity as maternal is both enacted and summed up since it is so in Mary, who truly enacts and recapitulates this reality.

A yes or no itself symbolically reveals the inherent either/or dynamic that arises within contingency, for only a finite, contingent being's freedom is ever caught betwixt these options. Philosophy's sober gaze perceives the positive and negative forms of freedom that are available to that creature with the ability to choose. Yet, in a certain sense, certain choices are, so to speak, already "pregnant," already "maternal," since they already implicitly contain the life that will be birthed by means of the completion, the terminus, of that particular choice made. A no, however, to faith, to revelation, is in the deepest sense an abortive termination of life, a choosing that is intrinsically suicidal, since one then is left only with the bottomless pit, with the abyss, with the incurable disease of an existential sickness that is a "sickness unto death."[47] This no is really the affirmative embrace of self-enclosure, a yes to the heart closed in on itself, to an idol that is lifeless, which possesses eyes but is unable to see, ears but is unable to hear, and so on. However, a yes to the transcendent ground of all, who is at the center of all, results in the true *nativity* of the self, a child of light inbreaking into this world through that same "blood and water" that came forth from the side of Truth itself crucified. This is the fiat that at once contains the infinite, unconditioned, transcendently immanent One—for it is a yes sustained synergistically by the will of both the creature and God—while also reverberating through the spatial and temporal matrix of that creature, adapting in time the body and total being to *bear the infinite*. In reality, this fiat witnesses to the presupposition that nature itself is suspended by grace via *creatio ex nihilo* even while it is given superaddedly. In other words, the yes ever stands over against nothingness, held together and supported by transcendence as the condition of possibility, while this yes is also the generative gift of superadded grace given to nature. This is why a yes to transcendence is the mother tongue of creatureliness.

Maurice Blondel is profoundly instructive in detailing that, on the side of creatureliness alone, given the inherent dynamisms of human volition, a philosophical exploration yields the discovery of an innate insufficiency in resolving and completing the human will without recourse to the transcendent. His "method of immanence" reveals the necessity of

47. Consider God's warning to Adam that if he eats of the tree of the knowledge of good and evil, he will die (Gen 2:17).

the transcendence without doing so "from the side" of the transcendent.[48] The significance of this approach simultaneously reveals the inherent integrity of nature—particularly, of the human being as such—while also revealing how nature stands open, made ready to be completed with and for the Other. The following extensive quote from Blondel explains his reasoning behind this philosophical approach.

> We see thereby how we have to excavate within ourselves the place where the supernatural solution will come to fill the abyss. Let no one say then that it is ridiculous and useless to put so much effort into indicating such an emptiness, into proving such an abyss: the acknowledgment of this impossibility the philosopher finds himself in of completing himself, of tying thought and life into one another, is on the contrary the highest service reason can render; and the Christian spirit, which has no greater enemy than the false sufficiency of egoistic autonomy, has no better auxiliary than this sense of mystery and of humility. God, says Scripture, loves empty vases in which to pour Himself. And it is already a beautiful role to have to shape and to purify these vases of nature and of man that are to contain the divine presence.[49]

Many thinkers encountering this "abyss" within the heart of the human being seek to fill it or resolve its presence with recourse to philosophical speculation that, even while at times taking a significant cue from theology, nevertheless jettisons key theological presuppositions that would safely undergird such speculation, as is the case with Hegel. For while Hegel, for example, sought to resolve Kant's antinomy between human autonomy and transcendence in his *Phenomenology of Spirit* by thinking about transcendence as self's exit from self via a dialectical process of assimilation of the other through self's own becoming, Blondel, on the other hand, understood that the "movement of the self toward the other is not a moment in the process of the self's own becoming as the absolute source of self-determining being [but] rather, the logic of action

48. As the Jesuit philosopher Cathal Doherty, SJ, states concerning Blondel's philosophical work in providing an opening for the transcendent, "The necessity of the supernatural remains 'hypothetical' because it is the consequence of a conditional: *if* the dialectic opened up by the phenomenon of willed human action is to be resolved, then there must be a supernatural complement, whose point of heterogeneous insertion in human life is voluntary human action. . . . The highest task of philosophy, for Blondel, is to demonstrate the insufficiency of the natural order unto itself, and that is what the dialectic of *Action (1893)* achieves" (*Maurice Blondel*, 2).

49. Blondel, *Philosophical Exigencies*, 21.

brings the self to the cusp of genuine transcendence as 'other' through the religious option."[50] This move counters the temptation to cultivate a totalizing system that would seek to domesticate the other really only as a moment of the self, or against thought forms that would think of difference as pure rupture. Blondel's work in *Action* incisively dwells in the in-between space of philosophy and theology by modeling how philosophy can be done while it humbly remains attentively open to the transcendent gift as genuine *other*.[51] This is why Mary can be read as a personified description of philosophy.[52] Just as she was opened to and thus became, through her consent, filled and thus completed by transcendence while ever remaining a mere creature, so too philosophy finds its fulfillment in theology while ever remaining philosophy, paradoxically impregnated with the eternal, the transcendent, the suprarational, and thus elevated and perfected by grace.

In addition, in light of Blondel's "regressive analysis" of the will done in *Action*, his discovery of the need for the transcendent other in order to unite the polarity between the willed will (*la volonté voulue*) and willing will (*la volonté voulante*)—a disparity innate in human volition itself—can be read metaphorically as a maternal opening ingredient in the human will that contains the *other* implicitly in human action itself, that *other* in which the maternal *womb* of human identity in action finds its life and fulfillment.[53] And since "the polarity of the wills simultane-

50. Koerpel, *Maurice Blondel*, 105. The quote goes on to read that "for Blondel self-transcendence is a gift given in which the agent freely chooses to be receptive to the gift, and in choosing to be receptive to the gift is open to the genuine possibility of self-transcendence as other."

51. In remarking on Blondel's philosophy, Robert Koerpel notes, "From this perspective, one can begin to read the role of philosophy . . . as attending to the Christological rupture that takes place in the mediation of being. Philosophy's recourse to the Incarnate Word, as both fully human (reason) and fully divine (faith) is the direction in which Blondel seeks the solution to the problem of immanence and transcendence" (*Maurice Blondel*, 106). While this is true, I would add that philosophy attends to the "Mariological embrace" that, coextensively with Mary's Son, takes place in the mediation of being but in a different metaphysical register.

52. Robert Koerpel's description of Blondel's philosophy can be read as a metaphorical description of our Lady: "It has been suggested that the character of Blondel's philosophy is captured well by the twin terms 'greatness' and 'weakness.' That is, greatness in the sense that philosophy seeks a comprehensive understanding of reality, and weakness insofar as, through this process, philosophy (reason) discovers its own contingency" (*Maurice Blondel*, 109). In the womb of Mary is indeed a "comprehensive understanding of reality," yet it is her womb, her being, that is contingent and thus understands this as an ineffable gift.

53. As Koerpel notes, "God . . . is the source of unity of the wills that dwells within

ously reveals humanity's desire for transcendence and its inability to achieve symmetry between the two wills,"[54] then perhaps we can read Mary's fiat as an icon of Blondelian *action*, a metaphysics of action perfectly displayed in Mary's yes to transcendence as mere creature in need of transcendence for the proper enactment of a flourishing human being as an image bearer of God. This is also why a no to transcendence, as we have described above, will lead only to the very "Death of Action" in favor of an idol—which, in the end, is nothingness.[55] Blondel's entire philosophy of action could be read as revealing, as it were, a maternal identity inherent in the human being insofar as action always points to and thus presupposes the transcendent—that is, something ever greater than itself.[56] The possibility of human action itself is indeed *pregnant with meaning*, filled with a life that transcends itself—the very life of God, seen not only as its proper end and fulfillment, but even as its genesis and sustenance. Therefore, considering Mary, a Blondelian reading of action points *philosophically* to the maternal identity of anthropology.

For Blondel, this is why in the final analysis the religious option, the life lived in accordance with the truth of transcendence, is the only way of enacting and completing anthropological identity—an identity that is maternal: "We must all give ourselves birth by giving God birth in us, Θεοτόκος."[57] As Blondel notes,

> The gift which religious life brings him is so closely incorporated into his substance that human nature becomes capable of producing and creating in some way the One from whom it has everything, as if at one and the same time the donor wanted to have everything from the donee, and as if man, summoned

humanity, but is not of humanity. This distinction . . . derives from humanity's inability to achieve equipoise between spontaneous (free) and willed action. The argument for the insufficiency of all finite reality through human action is, in turn, an argument for the contingency of finite reality with greater force coming through the immanent aspect of finite reality" (*Maurice Blondel*, 1120.

54. Koerpel, *Maurice Blondel*, 110.

55. Blondel, *Action*, 332.

56. As Blondel himself notes in part 5 of *Action*, the will (and thus, the human being) discovers itself and truly receives itself only in God as the transcendently immanent presence in and through human action. "Hence, when we will fully, it is Him, it is His will that we will. We ask that He be, that He sustain, complete, underpin all our operations. . . . We participate freely in His necessary freedom; in accepting that He be in us what He is in Himself, we gain being ourselves what He is Himself, *Ens a se* (Being from himself)" (*Action*, 388).

57. Blondel, *Action*, 386.

> finally to satisfy the infinite excess of his willing, became, according to the expression of Saint Thomas, "the God of his God."[58]

Clearly, Blondel has in mind the image of our Lady here who, through her unique vocation as Theotokos, *illustrates* the anthropological truth of human identity, a truth that becomes even more evident philosophically after a "regressive analysis" of human will, revealing its inability to be satiated in creatureliness alone or explained solely within the domain of creaturehood. To showcase how much Mary is operative in the mind of Blondel as he parses out the religious option by describing how human identity is fulfilled through the paradigmatic pattern provided by the Mother of Jesus, consider the following extensive quote:

> In accordance with what we have to conceive and hope for, He makes Himself so small that we can hold Him, so weak that He needs us to lend Him our arms and our acts, so condescending that He hands Himself over to the ebb and flow of sensible life, so dispossessed that we have to return Him to Himself, so dead that we have to engender Him anew, as in the mysterious labor which brings forth living members from inert nourishment. It was the great temptation to become "like gods"; impossible dream. And yet man seems to have been given the ability to work a greater wonder: *to be, we must, we can bring it about that God be for us and by us.*[59]

Therefore, thinking with Blondel helps us to see how a philosophic gaze upon human action itself brings us to a profound reckoning with Mary as exemplary for anthropological identity, enacted and recapitulated in her fiat, which is the archetypal expression of "Blondelian action." The human being *is* the maternal being ready to receive, to gestate, to give birth, and to care for that Life that completes and fulfills human life as such. As Aquinas stated, "The ultimate purpose of a rational creature exceeds the capacity of its own nature."[60]

58. Blondel, *Action*, 386.

59. Blondel, *Action*, 386–87; emphasis added.

60. Aquinas, *Comp. Theol.* 1.143n82.

## MARY ILLUSTRATES ANTHROPOLOGICAL IDENTITY IN AND THROUGH HER BODY AND FLESH

Given the total involvement of Mary's being as Theotokos, we could continue our philosophic gaze upon her by asking the following: How could a philosophical investigation of Mary's *body*—and specifically, her *flesh*, as it is understood in the varying ways philosophy thinks through this term—further offer *illustrative* insights into the perennial identity of the human being? Such an analysis ought to yield further discoveries on how, like her fiat, her body and flesh illustrate how she enacts and recapitulates her maternal identity as *finitude containing the infinite*.

A phenomenological analysis of Mary's life reveals a fascinating interplay between hiddenness and manifestation, of absence and presence. Specifically, for example, in the annunciation the *hidden* is *disclosed as transcendence*, made manifest via the angel Gabriel and, most poignantly, through the overshadowing presence of the Spirit resulting in the gift of the incarnation in Mary's womb, which, through gestation, *increasingly* becomes visible in her body. The maternal identity of Mary is *disclosed synchronically with the disclosure of transcendence*, coupled with her fiat that allows for further disclosure, a greater presencing and manifestation of her as Mother of the infinite, transcendent, which, in turn, is *the disclosure in time of the eternal.* Nevertheless, the disclosure of the transcendent—the infinite and eternal—is paradoxically veiled all the more because this is a disclosure of an ineffable transcendence—God—through the womb of Mary and the flesh of humanity. What *appears* phenomenologically, however, is the generation of life by means of a call-and-response between transcendence and a woman, followed by a subsequent conception without human generation but rather enacted through the call-and-response between the invisible and visible, such that the hidden slowly becomes disclosed visibly *through* the body of this woman, resulting also in the disclosure of her maternal identity. Phenomenologically, this play of hiddenness (absence) and manifestation (presence) are but a few of the manifolds that point to the maternal identity of Mary and can, in turn, help us discern similar manifolds in the human as such.[61]

61. Concerning the critique from Dominique Janicaud that the use of phenomenology toward theological ends transgresses the phenomenological method as grounded in an immanent frame, I echo Jean-Yves Lacoste's recognition that phenomenology goes beyond such a limiting frame, that "there is no perception of the visible without a co-perception of the invisible . . . perception grasps—*Auffassung*—simultaneously the

Given the metaphysical description of Mary discussed in our first chapter, along with the theological insights regarding anthropological identity that she *illumines*, we can explore phenomenologically how she *illustrates* human identity as maternal by inquiring into how the human body/flesh points to the revealed truth of human identity.

Paradigmatically, as one whose fiat generates life, which is disclosed in her body—bearing and giving birth to transcendence made human, actualizing her motherhood from fiat to *cross* through the process of gestation, nativity, and parenting (as we have seen above)—Mary *illustrates* that the body/flesh is the *locus of union* between the hidden and the manifest, the interplay between absence and presence, for all human beings in the dynamic unfolding of transcendence immanently. In this way she enacts and sums up Paul's teaching that the body is "made for the Lord" and the "Lord is for the body" since the "body is a temple," and thus one ought to "glorify God in . . . body" (1 Cor 6:13, 19–20). The body is this *locus of union*, and so is the site of this mysterious interface between the Unconditioned and contingent reality. If Mary's body *illustrates* (nature/reason/philosophy) this anthropological truth, then we ought to see all human bodies inherently capable of this in an analogous way. Can reason detect this in the nature of the body?

A body reveals things *about* the one who is embodied as it also reveals the person herself phenomenologically, and the events that person has undergone are encoded, so to speak, into the fabric of her flesh. All bodies reveal a narrative. A body carries implicitly a story that discloses choices that were made, events that have occurred, along with certain perceivable limits and strengths. Mary's body manifests her fiat, her choice, along with the invitation given to her, an invitation to become Mother to him who is without beginning. Since her gestational body discloses conception by way of the call-and-response that occurred in time as the mode of this paradoxical union, we ought to find analogical correlations of this within all human bodies that offer a consenting response to transcendence. To put it another way, the human body as such should somehow visibly indicate this maternal identity of anthropology—or should somehow register this within the domain of "flesh," depending on how that term might be construed—especially when a positive affirmation to the transcendent invitation that stands before each person is enacted.

---

visible and the invisible" (Lacoste, "Perception, Transcendence," 5). See also Janicaud et al., *Phenomenology and "Theological Turn."*

In one sense, this can already be seen in all bodies insofar as each body, like each act of the will, is already *pregnant with possibilities* that are actualized through decisions made. The potentialities inherent within the body are actualized through volition, and so in a certain sense this could be viewed metaphorically as the body's maternal capacity to ever "embody" the will's willing. This is evidently true considering a person's yes or no to transcendence since such a decision will have reverberating repercussions for all subsequent decisions in and through the body given the gravity of such a decision made. The body, in response to a positive embrace to the transcendent invitation, will, over time, begin to visibly disclose the maternal identity of the human, of course distinct from the once-and-for-all-time event of Mary's divine maternity, but nevertheless analogous to this unique event in the way one's body changes, grows, and adapts to the indwelling presence of transcendence. This is reflected in ascetic struggle, penance, prayer, and even martyrdom—all acts done in and through the body. These are signs of love enacted in an exocentric engagement with the transcendent, just as the pregnant body of Mary is the visible illustration of the love between her and the blessed Trinity (think, too, of our Lady under the cross: her tears, her surrendering, her martyrdom). This is why it is impossible to envision (for humans) a consenting yes to transcendence in a disembodied way. As noted above, these actions done in and through the body enact the gestational, birth-giving, and parenting process; they—ascetic struggle, penance, prayer, martyrdom—are the *signs of pregnancy and maternity*. That the body is always included within the inner dynamism of decision-making, and that the body reveals, metaphorically, new signs of maternal life coextensive with those generative decisions *for* life, *for* transcendence, indicates the body's natural orientation toward a supernatural end, even though such signs seem antithetical to an abundant life—hence, Nietzsche's quip about Christianity's life-denying ethos. This is so because if the signs of maternity are ascetic struggle and self-sacrifice *as a response to* the invisible/hidden, signs that culminate in martyrdom, then the maternal body becomes itself a sign of that which transcends *this fallen "life."* In a way, this is already illustrated in a "natural" pregnancy since it entails, so to speak, an ever-increasing mode of self-denial for the sake of the other—the unborn—who is yet invisible though slowly being disclosed in the mother's body over time.

So, as the philosopher Jean-Louis Chrétien notes, through Mary we behold an illustrative example of the deep potency of the call-and-response between transcendence and the human being in such a way that "to be thus touched in one's very substance by the Word, beyond all image is . . . to listen, to listen with one's whole being . . . thanks to the gracious transfiguration accomplished by this very touch."[62] This "transfiguration," as Chrétien puts it, of the body is initiated by the "first hospitality," which is an active listening to the Word that addresses.[63] The human body registers this encounter in such a way that reveals its maternal identity, opened, ready to receive *transcendent* life, which stands in contradistinction to "life" in this world—which is no life at all, hence the paradoxical statements from Jesus about losing one's life for his sake to actually find it (Matt 10:39). This is evident in the body through self-denying, sacrificial acts of love for the *invisible other* and so are seen as antithetical to a flourishing life "in this world." Again, we see something of this in "natural" parenting. What parent does not exclaim about the finding of one's life in the event of sacrificing for the sake of their newborn? Such a *human* experience like parenting illustrates this profound truth ever only made fully known in revelation.

Interestingly, a phenomenology of life that is "hidden" from the world is worked out by Michel Henry, who, upon a close study of Christianity, reads phenomenology as historically being overly concerned with descriptive appearance of phenomena as such and so never seriously questioning the *subject* to which such appearances occur. He is careful to distinguish *flesh* from body, explaining that while "bodies" belong to the horizon of appearances "in the world," flesh is "nothing other than what *feels itself, suffers itself, undergoes itself and bears itself, and thus enjoys itself according to impressions that are always reborn.*" Thus, for Henry, to be incarnate is "not to have a body, to put oneself forward as a 'corporeal' and thus material being" but rather is "to have flesh, and, perhaps more precisely, to be flesh."[64] Henry's exploration of immanent affectivity could help us continue to discern the maternal identity of the human being since *life* is never found in the "horizon of the world" as phenomena but rather as that inward reality, the affectivity, the inward experience, the *flesh*, which is life. This immanent presence, although present to all the living and so transcending any one instantiation, is nevertheless only ever *inward* as *flesh* and so can also be read metaphorically as hinting toward the maternal identity of anthropology since life is ever inward in

62. Chrétien, *Call and Response*, 130.

63. Chrétien, *Ark of Speech*.

64. Henry, *Incarnation*, 4; emphasis in original.

the *womb of flesh* and is ever only experienced as such. Just as the "Word became flesh" through the womb of Mary, so too is Christ enfleshed in our flesh as the very life of our flesh. Mary can be read as an illustrative example of this deep anthropological truth.

Yet, as Henry notes, while "our body is only one representation among others, a sort of reflection like that seen in a mirror," the body nevertheless "draws its reality, its stunning, dynamic, and pathos-filled depths which makes of our incarnate condition what it is, from our invisible flesh . . . it is in our invisible subjectivity where our actual reality is found."[65] So while for Henry the body can never directly reveal life, it nevertheless possesses the capacity to signal what is occurring invisibly in the depth of one's flesh where true life is. This is why thinking along with Henry could help us read our flesh as the *locus of union* and thus *our* womb, illustrating anthropological identity as maternal to that extent it is understood that Christ is the inward life of our flesh. This is also why Rose Ellen Dunn reads the annunciation along with Henry to discover that it "celebrates the participation of human life in the givenness of divine life . . . that reverberates with and in the voice of the divine, and in the human life as being-in-divine-life—such that this text can suggest that in the depths of its Life, 'our flesh is God.'"[66] So, through Henry, we can observe how Mary illustrates human life as mutually co-inhering in the divine life, human life "being in divine life" since divine life is the "givenness" of our life, immanently so. That inward life that constitutes actual life is God: "Our flesh is God." Thus, *flesh* can be read as that womb by which we possess life analogously to the way Mary's maternity was constituted by that inward Life in her womb. As Dunn states in light of Henry,

> The text of the Annunciation celebrates the overflowing of divine life that reverberates in and with the life of Mary and appears in the sheer givenness of the conception of Jesus. Henry's phenomenology of life insists that each living being participates in absolute life: as a finite life experiences itself as a living being—as life—through the pathos of auto-affection, it also experiences a "surpassing itself toward" a participation in the absolute life. Each self, Henry argues, "refers back to the First Living Self"; each life "presupposes the Archi-passibility

65. Henry, *Words of Christ*, 17–18.

66. Dunn, *Finding Grace with God*, 68.

> of absolute life." Being-in-life is, for Henry, being-in-Absolute-Life: "In the Depths of its Night, our flesh is God."[67]

The womb of our flesh, as I have described above, is this locus of union where transcendence is ever immanently present as *the* life of the living ones—which points to the perfect union enacted in time in the womb of our Lady, who enacts and recapitulates human identity as such. Henry allows us to discern the flesh of the human as constitutive of anthropological identity. This, then, is why

> in Luke's narrative of the Annunciation, the divine originally arrives in and through life; life is the self-revelation of the divine and it is through this gift of life—the phenomenalization of the phenomenality of life—that there is access to the divine. The message of the angel to Mary is one of life: the life of the divine will surround you and immerse you in life itself—the life of the divine will fill you with life. Mary finds grace with God through life.[68]

This creative rereading of the annunciation via Henry expresses how *flesh* is structured in such a way that intimates anthropological identity as maternal. Like Blondel's regressive analysis of the will and Chrétien's phenomenological exploration of call-and-response, Henry's study of flesh identifies subtle—and not-so-subtle—hints, intimations, allusions that prefigure what uniquely occurs in Mary, but that all human beings in an analogous way are called to enact *as* human. And while these respective philosophers differ in their style and conceptual use of certain terms, they nevertheless could be read collectively as offering a multivalent approach to the question implied in human identity itself: maternal identity. A philosophic study of the human body and flesh, in light of what is *illumined* in Mary as Theotokos, reveals what she also *illustrates*, namely that body and flesh are made to embody the transcendent,[69] and so become forever changed by this decisive Presence, as it is for a mother with child.

In a different but complementary way the work of Maurice Merleau-Ponty could also help in revealing an implicit, inherently dynamic opening of body/flesh to what appears phenomenologically such that an enfolding, an intertwining, ensues. From this perspective, it is as if,

67. Dunn, *Finding Grace with God*, 68.

68. Dunn, *Finding Grace with God*, 67.

69. Jean-François Lavigne's essay is important, for example, in thinking about the differing ways Henry uses the term, which in turn can shape our understanding of Henry's use and thus could go further in helping us think about how Mary does indeed illustrate the maternal being as identity: Lavigne, "Paradox and Limits."

according to Merleau-Ponty's study of perception, the "intertwining" that occurs between the seen and seer, the perceived and perceiver, unveils certain aspects of philosophical anthropology that may implicitly point to the maternal identity of the human being. For if the maternal identity of the human as such is conceived of as this radical opening to the infinite, the transcendent, such that the human being is paradoxically made for the infinite—the finite *for* the infinite as this *locus of union*—then Merleau-Ponty's analysis could be read as an evocative discovery of that maternal identity, here implicitly discerned, which is only truly revealed in the light of our Lady. This fundamental openness to the world, an openness that reveals an ontological monism without collapsing the difference between the subject and object, though also not separating the two, is construed under Merleau-Ponty's term "reversibility," which is initially discussed in *Phenomenology of Perception* but is developed fully in his uncompleted work *The Visible and the Invisible*.[70] For Merleau-Ponty, reversibility communicates the idea that, at the ontological level, the self, other, and the world are inherently symbiotic and intrinsically relational, while maintaining real difference (and thus, not collapsing into solipsism). This, too, is also observed in his understanding of perception to be the mediating presence of both immanence—since phenomenon is an item in consciousness—and transcendence since that same phenomenon truly communicates the other/world simultaneously. As he states,

> There is a paradox of immanence and transcendence in perception. Immanence, because the perceived object cannot be foreign to him who perceives; transcendence, because it always contains something more than what is actually given.[71]

It is as if perception itself, then, intimates and alludes to that dynamic identity of the human as opened to the ever greater, ever more—indeed, the *transcendent*, eventually. Yet, this "ever greater" is intimately present inextricably so and is given over in the phenomenon through a dynamic interplay of presence and absence. As M. C. Dillon notes, "The paradox of immanence and transcendence is grounded in perception insomuch as perception intrinsically embodies both revelation and concealment. But there is no contradiction here; indeed, it is a condition for the givenness of a phenomenon that it withhold itself as well."[72]

70. Merleau-Ponty: *Phenomenology of Perception*, 19; *Visible and Invisible*, 133.
71. Merleau-Ponty, *Primacy of Perception*, 16.
72. Dillon, *Merleau-Ponty's Ontology*, 57.

All of this is understood through Merleau-Ponty's concept of *flesh*, which for him is "not matter . . . not mind . . . not substance" but rather "an 'element' of being."[73] This "element" of being that is flesh *is* "the intertwining, the 'crossing' after which it is named," as Orion Edgar describes.[74] Thus, all sensed things in the world to which the body belongs are of the same flesh. This interpenetrative reality within an ontological monism of flesh seems to suggest, once again, this dynamic opening that is at the heart of anthropology, this *locus of union* as *finitude containing the infinite*, the human as such ever gesturing toward a manifestation of what it truly is, only fully and finally revealed in Mary: *maternal*. As Edgar notes, "Phenomenology reaches beyond itself. That is, careful attention to the phenomena reveals that they intimate the presence of a depth that is more than they can fully reveal."[75]

Thus, by briefly surveying various philosophical perspectives—metaphysical and phenomenological—albeit not exhaustively, we can observe how Mary indeed *illustrates* anthropological identity, which is definitively revealed, *illumined*, only through revelation. This illustrative inscription witnessed in our Lady pertains to both her fiat and her body/flesh and grants us a map to discern where we are to look for signs of maternal identity in the human being. And while our exploration here was by no means exhaustive, we nevertheless ought to see how such a process funds a maternal identity for anthropology.

## CONCLUSION: ANTHROPOLOGICAL IDENTITY

Predicated on the metaphysical "structure" discovered in and through our Lady's position in the economy of grace and nature shown in our first chapter, this chapter proceeded to investigate a Marian theo-philosophical anthropology by first coordinating the four Marian dogmas with those quintessential, perennial questions that pertain to the human as such. A meditative reflection on these dogmas from an anthropological perspective allowed us to discern that each dogma elucidates how Mary enacts and recapitulates the human being such that anthropological identity is *maternal*; anthropological vocation, *virginal*; anthropological origin, *immaculate*; and anthropological telos, *glorified*. By thinking

73. Merleau-Ponty, *Visible and Invisible*, 139.

74. Edgar, *Things Seen and Unseen*, 21.

75. Edgar, *Things Seen and Unseen*, 21.

about the intrinsic relations among the Marian dogmas—and thus the anthropological insights derived from those dogmas—we observed an inherent symmetry between the *identity* and *vocation* of the human being as temporal realities rooted in their eternal and eschatological correlates—the ultimate *origin* and *end* of the human.

We then proceeded to investigate how Mary *illuminates* (grace/faith/theology) anthropological identity specifically, while also doing so in a general sense for all creation. This opened space to discern how Mary's fiat is the generative source of her divine maternity, which enabled us to perceive how human *consent to divine invitation* enacts anthropological identity. By also examining Mary's *gestation*, *birth*, and *parenting* of the eternal Word made flesh, we were also granted a vision of how anthropological identity is enacted and summed up by *participation in the suffering and death of Christ*, in and through an *obedience to him*.

Subsequently, we explored how Mary *illustratively* (nature/reason/philosophy) explicates anthropological identity—which is definitely ever only *revealed*—by showing how, through her fiat, body, and flesh, we can observe how she, and thus all, are called to be authentic instantiations of *finite beings receiving the infinite* as the *locus of union* between the Unconditioned and contingency. By considering the human being through a metaphysical and phenomenological analysis, thinking along with Blondel, Chrétien, Henry, and Merleau-Ponty, we observed how the human being ever points to this deep and abiding anthropological truth—*maternal* identity—through subtle and, perhaps, not-so-subtle ways. Thus, through Mary, we see how anthropological identity is revealed *theo-philosophically*.

We are now positioned to explore human *vocation*, which is the other anthropological truth that is articulated in the temporal dynamic of Mary's life, as the fitting expression of human *identity*. Since Mary's divine maternity precluded her from "natural relations," in our next chapter we will explore how Mary's perpetual virginity reveals the *vocational* structure of each human being as maternal, a vocation that enacts in time what will be fully realized in the eschaton.

*Who will unravel this tangle? . . . Man transcends man.*

~ Blaise Pascal

*The metaphysical nature of love lies in the supralogical over-coming of the naked self-identity "I=I" and in the going out of oneself.*

~ Pavel Florensky

# 3

# Perpetual Virginity

## *The Human as Eschatologically Oriented Exocentricity*

Our thesis is that Mary reveals a decisive response, *illuminatively* (grace/faith/theology) and *illustratively* (nature/reason/philosophy), to the perennial questions that constitute anthropology. Considering the four Marian dogmas of the church, the quintessential questions concerning the human being—questions that actually indicate a profound mystery at the heart of the human being as such—are addressed theo-philosophically. And as we observed in chapter 2 of this project, the anthropological queries can be coordinated with each dogma by considering the dogmatic truths about our Lady in view of anthropology. Questions concerning the origin and end, identity, and vocation of the human being are addressed both *illuminatively* and *illustratively* with each revealed dogmatic truth about Mary; and these insights also indicate their mutually informing relationship in the singularity of the person of Mary (always in union with her Son) along a temporal/eschatological-eternal dynamic. In other words, the origin, end, identity, and vocation of anthropos can be understood ever only in the light of each, within a temporal/eschatological-eternal context. Thus, an investigation into Mary's identity, vocation, origin, and end (revealed in light of each corresponding dogma about our Lady) substantiates a theo-philosophical anthropology, an anthropology *illumined illustratively*.

Our previous chapter explored how Mary's identity as Theotokos constitutes a decisive insight into human identity as a *maternal* being. Her divine maternity enacts and recapitulates human identity as such. By offering a theological analysis of Mary's divine maternity considering anthropology, examining her fiat, gestation, birth giving, and parenting, we were able to see how she *illumines* (grace/faith/theology) anthropological identity. In addition, a philosophical exploration of her fiat through metaphysical and phenomenological analysis, coupled with a further investigation into Mary's body/flesh, allowed us to observe how she also *illustrates* (nature/reason/philosophy) the identity of the human being.

In this chapter, our project proceeds by examining how Mary's *perpetual virginity* enacts and recapitulates human *vocation* as *virginal*, both in an *illuminative* and *illustrative* manner. In view of our Lady, the human being is maternal with respect to identity, and *virginal* with respect to vocation (identity and vocation possessing an intrinsic relation to each). The argument will unfold in the following way: First, we will briefly explore the meaning of Mary's perpetual virginity and examine its relationship to her divine maternity and eschatological end, her assumption, within the temporal/eternal dynamic that constitutes her being as described in chapter 2. Second, we will investigate how Mary's perpetual virginity *illuminates* (grace/faith/theology) anthropological vocation as *virginal* being, that one called to *proleptically embody* the "angelic state" (Matt 22:30) via a chaste mind, disposition, and body. Perpetual virginity signals, anthropologically, a radical openness to the Other, which constitutes the grammar of anthropological vocation. Special attention will be given to show how this vocation is decisively determined by the eternal proleptically arriving in time. Third and finally, further examination of Mary's perpetual virginity will allow us to observe how it *illustrates* (nature/reason/philosophy) a particular shape to anthropological vocation as *virginal*, which is *exocentric*. In this part, particular attention will be given to reveal how anthropological *vocation* is also decisively determined by the temporal "stretching out," in a manner of speaking, to the eternal (ever only as a response to the eternal), such that human vocation, which possesses the shape of exocentricity, is indeed an *eschatologically oriented exocentricity*. We will thus observe how Mary enacts and recapitulates human vocation via her perpetual virginity, concluding that human vocation *is* pilgrimage, it *is* this dynamic orientation and movement toward an eschatological beckoning; thus, human vocation *is* the exocentric life as virginal.

## THE LOGIC OF VIRGINITY: MARY'S PERPETUAL VIRGINITY WITHIN THE UNITED TEMPORAL AND ETERNAL FRAME

The perpetual virginity of our Lady, a dogmatic truth proclaimed in the Lateran Synod in the year 649 under Pope Martin I but rooted in the ancient tradition of the church, reveals and upholds the paradoxical truth that Mary of Nazareth is simultaneously Mother *and* Virgin. The synod taught the threefold nature of Mary's virginity, highlighting her virginal state before, during, and after the birth of her Son: "Holy Mary, ever-virgin and immaculate . . . conceived really and truly of the Holy Spirit, without seed . . . she gave birth to Him without corruption (to her virginity), her virginity remaining equally inviolate after his birth."[1] Mary's *divine* maternity, as the fathers of the church recognized, is uniquely expressed precisely through her *virginal* state, such that these mysteries are profoundly interconnected.[2] In addition, her Son is irrevocably linked to these twin mysteries of our Lady since *he* is the one who is enfleshed in the virginal womb. Thus, the catechism states, "The meaning of this event [the virginal birth of Christ] is accessible only to faith, which understands in it the 'connection of these mysteries with one another' in the totality of Christ's mysteries, from his incarnation to his Passover."[3] This is why every revealed truth about Mary is permanently situated in the total mystery of her Son, while the dogmatic truths about our Lady, in turn, safeguard the mystery of Christ's hypostatic union. But in addition to highlighting her divine maternity, the catechism also identifies other reasons for Mary's perpetual virginity within the divine economy, from preserving "God's absolute initiative in the Incarnation," as well as showing its fittingness given that Jesus is the "New Adam, who inaugurates

1. As quoted in Ott, *Fundamentals of Catholic Dogma*, 220. Consider the patristic witness as well in offering a typological reading of Mary's perpetual virginity. Gregory of Nyssa states in reference to the burning bush: "From this we learn also the mystery of the Virgin: the light of divinity which through birth shone from her into human life did not consume the burning bush, even as the flower of her virginity was not withered by giving birth" (*Life of Moses* 2.21).

2. In elucidating this connection, Mary B. Cunningham quotes the following short hymn (theotokion): "How should we not marvel at your Offspring, who is both God and man, all-honored one? For without knowing [a] man, O all-blameless, you gave birth in the flesh to a Son without father, begotten from the Father before the ages without mother, in no way undergoing change, or mixture or separation, but preserving intact the identity of either nature" (*Gateway of Life*, 102).

3. Catholic Church, *Catechism*, §498.

the new creation," to revealing that her virginity "is *the sign of her faith* 'unadulterated by any doubt,' and of her undivided gift of herself to God's will"; even displaying her as icon of the church: "At once virgin and mother, Mary is the symbol and the most perfect realization of the Church."[4]

As revealed in the biblical text, in response to the annunciation Mary questioned how she could become Mother while remaining Virgin. This query opened up space to reveal participation in the divine life by grace—which Mary already possessed to the full as the condition of possibility to receive more superaddedly—indicating such an event is "not of blood or of the will of the flesh or of the will of man, but of God" (John 1:13). Indeed, nature is not destroyed but is presupposed and elevated in a transcendent manner by grace. As Thomas à Kempis states, "Your birth transcends the laws of nature. Since it must repair nature itself, this birth, through a great miracle, differs from the manner in which human beings are born, and with Divine power consoles us in our laborious births."[5] There is an anthropological significance to this that is articulated in the catechism, which states that "the acceptance of this life [participation in the divine life] is *virginal* because it is entirely the Spirit's gift to man. The *spousal character of the human vocation in relation to God* is fulfilled perfectly in Mary's virginal motherhood."[6] In other words, Mary's virginity provides the condition for her divine maternity to be made manifest since, by virtue of her virginity, her maternity must be the realization of a *divine* spousal union. Her perpetual virginity coupled with her maternity signals a transcendent source. That she could become Mother while a virgin means that her virginity was and is *for God*, signifying a spousal character to her—and, by extension, all—vocation.[7] Thus, Mary's virginity enacts and recapitulates in an *illuminative* manner the spousal

4. Catholic Church, *Catechism*, §§503–7; emphasis in original.

5. Kempis, *Imitation of Mary*, 37.

6. Catholic Church, *Catechism*, §505; emphasis added. See also 2 Cor 11:2.

7. Matthias Joseph Scheeben articulates the idea that Mary offered a solemn vow to God that at once realizes and undergirds her virginity, a vow that has both a subjective and objective component in relation to herself and God. In reference to the solemn vow she made, he writes, "It included both a subjective engagement, simply accepted by God, and an objective consecration, being taken possession of by God. It is a consecration which is not consequent upon the acceptance of the vow, but which rather precedes the vow as a dedication that Mary, on her side, must accept through her vow. In other words, Mary was already a virgin consecrated to God, one whom God united to Himself in marriage. But through her vow and her own will she also entered subjectively into the relationship of the bride of God, as Eve through her consent contracted her marriage with Adam which had been decreed by God" (*Mariology*, 119).

character of anthropological *vocation*, a call to live *for* God, *in* God, *by* God's grace as the maternal being.

The virginal state of our Lady not only describes her bodily integrity, but also includes a moral dimension, as the fathers of the church indicate.[8] In this way, her perpetual virginity is the flowering *in time* of what was already given her by grace at the first moment of her life: the gift of her immaculate conception. So, while the dogmatic teaching of Mary's virginity refers primarily to our Lady's bodily integrity, it can also include, as Ludwig Ott notes, "virginity of *mind* (*virginitas mentis*), that is, a constant virginal disposition; [and] virginity of *sense* (*virginitas sensus*), that is, freedom from motions of sexual desire."[9] This, too, will bear upon anthropological considerations, revealing how Mary's *chaste* existence is the moral and existential expression of anthropological vocation.[10]

Fascinatingly, the *miraculous*—virginal—birth of her Son mirrors analogously his eternal generation. Mary Cunningham makes this point in her following observation:

> His Incarnation involved a process that was not subject to the kind of corruption—or change—that is normally associated with human procreation. There are two aspects of such "corruption": one is that human birth-giving leads inevitably to the condition of all human beings, namely death; the other is that it involves sexual passion. Finally, and perhaps most importantly, the miraculous nature of Mary's birth-giving testified to Christ's eternal nature as the Word; if he had been conceived in the

8. Consider for instance John of Damascus's homily on the Virgin's nativity: "A precious vessel of virginity who was a virgin before giving birth, a virgin during the birth-giving, and a virgin after having giving birth; she alone is virgin and ever-virgin; she alone forever remains a virgin in mind and soul and body" ("Nativity of Holy Theotokos," 59). "Hail, Mary, sweetest little daughter of Anna! . . . How shall I describe your most pious bearing, your robe, your gracious countenance! [You possessed] mature judgment in a youthful body. Your modest dress escaped all softness and delicacy. Your gait was pious and undisturbed, free from foolish ostentation. Your manner was austere, but mixed with gaiety; you were unapproachable by men—a witness to this is the fear that came over you at the unaccustomed address of the angel. [You were] docile and obedient towards your parents, while your humble mind was engaged in the highest contemplation" (69).

9. Ott, *Fundamentals of Catholic Dogma*, 220; emphasis in original. Consider also ch. 7, "Mary's Perpetual Virginity," in Scheeben, *Mariology*, 110–21.

10. We will explore in greater detail in our subsequent chapter how her immaculate conception fittingly "grounds" such a vocation, as it does her maternity and eschatological end.

> normal way, a new person would have come into existence in Mary's womb, rather than the eternal Son of God.[11]

As Fr. Scheeben states, "Christ's temporal production by the mother must not be in contradiction to His eternal production, but must be a perfect reflection of it" if it is to accord in perfect fittingness. Thus, "this temporal production can be such a reflection only if it is effected by a holy and purely spiritual power from a single principle. In other words, as the Son of God by Himself is brought forth as 'light of light,' here His bodily production must also be actualized, not through the mixing of material elements, but through a heavenly influence on the earthly element."[12]

This mirroring between the eternal generation of the Second Person of the Trinity with his temporal conception reveals how Mary's virginal motherhood is the fulcrum by which this *temporal/eternal dynamic* is expressed. In fact, because she is indeed this fulcrum, this pivot point by which the one Lord Jesus Christ is made manifest, she herself is uniquely inscribed by a temporal/eternal dynamic that is constituted by her decisive role in God's economy. This is fitting given how our Lady, as described in our first chapter, discloses in a manifestly external way what Christ enacts in a deeply abiding and mysterious mode via the hypostatic union. And as we noted in our last chapter, this dynamic is especially observable in the symmetrical relations between the four Marian dogmas. So, before turning our attention to observe exactly how Mary's perpetual virginity both *illumines* and *illustrates* the vocational structure of the human being, let us consider how this temporal/eternal dynamic shapes and informs Mary's virginal vocation. To do this, we must first examine how, in a wider context, this temporal/eternal dynamic is ingredient to the grammar of our Lady's being and person.

11. M. Cunningham, *Gateway of Life*, 103. Cunningham also offers a stunning quote from Gregory Nazianzen's work *Carminum de Virginitate* that identifies the Trinity as the "original virgin," revealing further how Mary's virginal birth analogously points to the eternal generation of Christ. Gregory states, "The original virgin is the Holy Trinity. From the unoriginated Father came Christ the Lord, not having an external origin (for he himself is the Way and the Root and the Beginning of all things), nor again being born in the way that mortals are, but as Light coming forth from Light. From the Child, then, there is no other beloved child who makes a similar boast; so that the one remains the sole Parent, while the other is the sole Son, the most Unique from the Unique; these come together into on with the great Spirit, who comes likewise from the Father, one God opening up in threefold lights. Such is the Trinity's pure nature" (104).

12. Scheeben, *Mariology*, 1:70–71.

As noted in chapter 2, a meditative reflection on the four Marian dogmas of the church reveals a relational structure that is symmetrical along a temporal axis. This symmetrical pattern discernible along this axis possesses an eschatological tension, such that the *being* (maternal) and *vocation* (virginal) of our Lady are the temporal realizations of what is already given in the *preconditioned* gift of her *origin* (immaculately conceived)—which was the predestined will for her—as well as the *proleptic appearance* of her *end*, her glory (assumption).

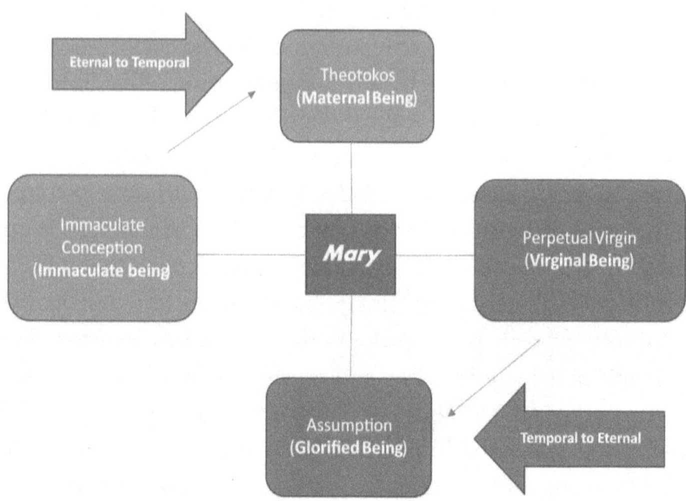


In other words, Mary's *maternal* identity and *virginal* vocation are the outworking *in time* of what is *predestined* (eternal) regarding her origin, her conception (beginning in eternity but executed in time at "the first moment of her conception"), and what is also *eschatologically realized* (eternal) in her assumption (beginning in time as a historical event but transcending it since it pertains to the eschatological as such). And while her *origin* is made manifest in her maternal *identity* and virginal *vocation* along the arrow of time, so too are both her *identity* and *vocation* the proleptic realization in time of her *eschatological end*. It is important to note that while both Mary's *origin* and *end* also occur *in* time, I read them as nevertheless rooted in the eternal/eschatological frame. So, again, her immaculate conception occurs in time at the first instant of her conception but is nevertheless an eternally determined action; and her assumption begins in time as a historical event but clearly transcends it as an eschatological event, the "future" invading the present temporal stream, not dissimilar to the resurrection.

By isolating each of the two sets of the Marian dogmas (immaculate conception—maternity | perpetual virginity—assumption) in, albeit, a somewhat arbitrary fashion, we can observe how the eternal shapes and informs the temporal stream of events, which occur both in the normal direction of time (from predestined immaculate conception to the divine maternity of Our Lady) and in a proleptic appearing in time, ultimate futurity arriving *in* time, thus in the reverse direction of the temporal flow of events (from her assumption coupled with the "angelic state" Christ speaks of in that no one is "given in marriage" [Matt 22:30] to her perpetual virginity). In this way we can read Mary's *identity* (maternal) as the temporal realization of that which is rooted in the predestined *origin* (immaculate), and so the immaculate *origin* is the foundation for what will be manifested in time via her immaculate conception and divine maternity.[13] This is inversely related to the other set of dogmas: Mary's *vocation* (virginal) is the expression *in time* of the proleptic embodying of the angelic state, rooted in her *end* (assumed body and soul into heaven).

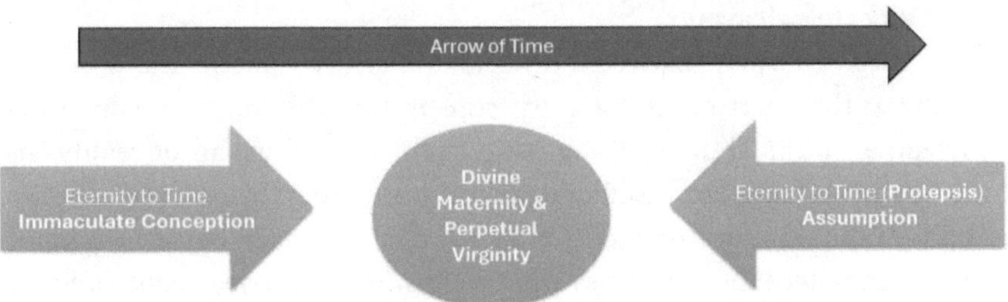


Thus, we behold in our Lady a temporal/eternal dynamic that is an eschatological tension between the *here* of temporal events and the *not yet* of the eternal/eschatological. Since it is God the Spirit who mediates this temporal and eternal dynamism as Lord of creation without collapsing either into the other, and since it is the Spirit himself who sanctified, empowered, and made fruitful the virginal womb of our Lady[14]—spouse

13. Paul writes about God's *predestined* choice for those in Christ to be "holy and blameless" (Eph 1:4), which is realized most perfectly in Mary via her preeminent salvation brought about in her immaculate conception. See also 2 Tim 1:9; Titus 1:2.

14. Catholic Church, *Catechism*, §§721–26.

of the Spirit—we can call this temporal/eternal dynamic *pneumatic time*.[15] Thus, since according to our thesis Mary's identity, vocation, origin, and end both enact and recapitulate anthropology such that the questions implied in human existence—What is the human? Why and to what end is the human being called forth? Whence does the human being come? And to what ultimate end is it oriented?—are addressed along four cardinal points that correspond to the four Marian dogmas, this *pneumatic time* observable in our Lady reveals the mutually informing answers to the questions implied in human existence. So human *identity* (maternal) is the expressed manifestation of what is already given eternally as human *origin* (immaculate)—and so can be fully understood only in this light—while human *vocation* (virginal) can only ever be fully understood in the light of its eschatological *end* (glorified) as its decisive and determinative orientation.[16] Thus, anthropology can be understood only in relation to the eternal frame since eternality pervades the temporally constituted human being transcendently—as its meaning and primary cause—while also sandwiching the temporally conditioned anthropos with the eternal as bookends. This is why, in the light of our thesis, we can observe how human identity and vocation are irrevocably shaped by its eternal origin and eschatological end.

This interplay between time and eternity—pneumatic time—is really at the heart of Christianity, constituting the frame in which the sacraments, the church, discipleship itself—and, thus, all of reality—is to be understood. For insofar as the one Lord Jesus Christ possesses two natures, human and divine, the paradoxical marriage between temporality and eternality inscribes the whole without mixing, confusing, or divorcing the two. The celebration of the Mass, the Divine Liturgy itself, for example, enacts and recapitulates this unity, this interpenetrative dance between time and eternity, such that those who participate in it are at once in the "natural" flow of time and yet are dwelling in an "eternal

15. I am coining this term to describe the unique temporal/eternal dynamic observable in our Lady and, subsequently, in the anthropos as such. What I mean by *pneumatic time* is this: our Lady (and the human being as such) is a historical being (with all the existential particularities that accompany this: risk, anticipation, change, etc.) that is nevertheless definitively shaped by an eschatological, eternal grammar.

16. The pairing of Mary's origin with her identity, coupled with the pairing of her end with her vocation, is somewhat arbitrary here, especially given that both her identity and vocation, intrinsically related as they are, are mutually related both to the eternal/eschatological frame of her origin and end. Nevertheless, this is done to highlight certain interconnecting facets between her origin and end with her identity and vocation.

moment" that transcends time.[17] The then Cardinal Joseph Ratzinger described the temporal/eternal dynamism via the mystical body of Christ in the following way:

> The relationship to that which is eternal, vis., remaining in communion with Him, is partaking in His eternity . . . Since we belong to the body of Christ, we are united to the flesh of the resurrected one, to his resurrection: "God . . . raised us up with him, and seated us with him in the heavens in Christ Jesus." Beginning with our baptism, we belong to the body of the resurrected one and are in this sense already attached to our future.[18]

Ratzinger stands within the tradition of the church in recognizing the curious interplay between time and eternity via the incarnation. In reading Paul, he notes the *proleptic* presence of the end insofar as we are "already attached to our future" through baptism, effected by the Spirit, while we nevertheless remain in the flow of temporal events. This is so because the resurrection is indeed an *eschatological* event occurring *in* time; and the one Lord Jesus Christ is the divine hypostasis who is eternal while mysteriously being temporally conditioned according to the human nature that was assumed.[19] This is the basis by which even our Lady, who

17. Consider the catechism's description of what takes place during Mass: "In the liturgy of the Church, it is principally his own Paschal mystery that Christ signifies and makes present. During his earthly life Jesus announced his Paschal mystery by his teaching and anticipated it by his actions. When his Hour comes, he lives out the unique event of history which does not pass away: Jesus dies, is buried, rises from the dead, and is seated at the right hand of the Father 'once for all.' His Paschal mystery is a real event that occurred in our history, but it is unique: all other historical events happen once, and then they pass away, swallowed up in the past. *The Paschal mystery of Christ, by contrast, cannot remain only in the past, because by his death he destroyed death, and all that Christ is—all that he did and suffered for all men—participates in the divine eternity, and so transcends all times while being made present in them all.* The event of the Cross and Resurrection *abides* and draws everything toward life" (Catholic Church, *Catechism*, §1085; emphasis added).

18. Ratzinger, *Eschatology*, xxi.

19. In articulating the temporal/eternal dynamism at play in the resurrection, Ratzinger offers an insightful analysis: "On the one hand, it [the resurrection] belongs intrinsically to the totality and ultimate greatness of this event [the crucifixion] that it is 'eschatological,' that is, that it transcends history; on the other hand, it belongs just as intrinsically to its inherent importance that it also touches upon history, that is, that this person who was dead is now no longer dead; he—really he himself and as such—is eternally alive in his individuality and uniqueness. Thus, it belongs, at the same time, to this event that it both reaches above history and is founded and anchored in history. Indeed, we could almost say that the definitive transformation that eschatology underwent by virtue of the Christian belief in the Resurrection is its transposition into

although is merely a creature, is nevertheless uniquely positioned (by virtue of her utterly unique place in the hypostatic order, as described in our first chapter) to have an anthropological grammar read in her, which *illumines* and *illustrates* the human being within this temporal/eternal dynamic, *pneumatic* time, the genesis of which is in Christ her Son.

Without succumbing to an either/or epistemology that would render time and eternity as standing in contradiction to each other, Catholic both/and thinking recognizes that while time and eternity are distinct, they are not antithetical to each other.[20] In light of this, along with the aforementioned, we can now consider in greater detail how Mary's virginal vocation is shaped by her divine maternity, her identity, as well as by her glorification, her telos, all *within* the pneumatic time described above.

By thinking about the *temporal* relation between our Lady's maternal identity with her virginal vocation, we can observe the following. First, Mary's virginity, because it is perpetual, is *coextensive* with her divine maternity. Her virginity remains before, during, and after the incarnation and birth giving.[21] Second, the simultaneity of her virginity and maternity signals an eternal intersection in time (given the seemingly contradictory but really paradoxical relation between the simultaneity of virginity and maternity)[22] through the *enfleshment* of the transcendent. The mutual presence in time of both her virginity and maternity points to a temporal/eternal dynamism at work. Third, the simultaneity of both her virginity and maternity could be read as mutually illuminating, considering the eternal transaction enacted in the incarnation: her maternal identity is revealed and *fulfilled* by the One who is signaled by Mary's virginal vocation, which in turn (her virginal vocation) points *to* and is *for*. Thus, by considering the temporal relation between Mary's

---

history. For late Judaic expectation, eschatology lay at the end of history. To believe in the Resurrection of Jesus means, on the contrary, to believe in the *eschaton in* history, in the historicity of God's eschatological action" (*Principles of Catholic Theology*, 186–87).

20. Matthew L. Lamb provides an important retrieval of patristic sources, especially Augustine, but also Aquinas, to correct erroneous notions of both time and eternity. His first four essays are particularly instructive on this: *Eternity, Time*.

21. As Pope Paul IV declared in 1555, "The Most Blessed Virgin Mary . . . always persisted in the integrity of virginity, namely, *before giving birth, in giving birth,* and perpetually *after giving birth*" (as quoted in Ott, *Fundamentals of Catholic Dogma*, 220).

22. Of course, we could consider whether "virginity" can be maintained through technological manipulation—like in vitro fertilization—but such considerations are beyond the scope of this project and are themselves a merely "horizontal" form of questioning that is devoid of the "verticality" implicit in our thesis.

maternity and virginity, space is opened for deeper consideration (and, in fact, *discovery*) of the intrinsic relationship between anthropological identity (maternal) and vocation (virginal). In essence, by reflecting on the temporal relations between her maternal identity and virginal vocation, we observe that Mary uniquely *illuminates* anthropological identity and vocation, revealing how both are oriented toward each—identity to vocation and vocation to identity—and are, in fact, mutually fulfilled by each.

That the eternal intersects time in the *enfleshment* via the womb of Mary, holding together in unison without mixing or confusing the temporal and the eternal in the incarnate One, also indicates a uniquely predestined origin of our Lady (for how could she bear the God-man with the stain of sin, either original or actual?).[23] Chapter 4 will explore in greater detail the anthropological significance of Mary's immaculate conception, but we can now consider in greater detail the eschatological presencing of her glorified end in the temporal stream of her virginity and maternity.

With respect to the eschaton, our Lady's maternity and virginity are the outworking *in time* of what *will be*, which, in a deeper and mysterious sense, already *is* (since it is eternity that is spoken of here). Divine maternity and perpetual virginity are the proleptic expression of what is to come eschatologically for all. This is to be understood in two ways. First, Mary's maternal identity is the realization *in time* of what all of creation is destined for: to become the "home," so to speak, of God, such that he will be "all *in* all" (1 Cor 15:28), as Maximus states: "The Logos of God (who is God) wills always and in all things to accomplish the mystery of His embodiment."[24] Second, Mary's virginal vocation is the realization *in time* of what is also to come in the eschaton: no one will marry or be given in marriage, but rather all will be like the angels in heaven

23. René Laurentin identifies the importance of grounding his Mariological study in "the most objective way," which is to "follow the order in which the life of Mary unfolded." Laurentin explains how Mary's predestination is to be understood in the light of the temporal flow of her life, which also keeps Mariology from being divorced from the wider scope of God's economy, the outcome of which would be a "closed Mariology." His description is instructive for our study: "Mary's predestination assuredly is the governing element, but it cannot constitute a 'chapter' in this plan founded on the history of salvation, for predestination is only a *moment* in this temporal development; it is a reality not only before the beginning of Mary's destiny, but before and *during* each of the instants of time whose free unfolding it gives rise to transcendentally from outside the bounds of time" (*Treatise on Virgin Mary*, 177n19; emphasis in original).

24. Maximos the Confessor, *On Difficulties*, 1:107.

(Mark 12:25). When Jesus teaches this he is referring specifically to the general resurrection and not the intermediate state proceeding it. Thus, Mary's eschatological end, her assumption, which occurs in time at the end of her life while simultaneously transcending it, reveals the proleptic ground in which her virginity is anchored. And while this would still be the case even if she were not assumed, it is all the more fitting that it is so since she was indeed assumed body and soul into heaven, which, in turn, points to her bodily and moral integrity in time articulated in her perpetual virginity. Thus, Mary's perpetual virginity is the proleptic embodying of the angelic state spoken of by Jesus.

By considering the pneumatic time that constitutes our Lady's being and person, we are now positioned to examine in greater detail how Mary's perpetual virginity both *illuminates* (grace/faith/theology) and *illustrates* (nature/reason/philosophy) anthropological vocation. In the following two sections we will explore this in the following way: First, Mary's perpetual virginity *illumines* human vocation as the proleptic embodying of the angelic state, thus eternity decisively shaping time. Second, her virginity also *illustrates* human vocation as an eschatologically *oriented* exocentricity, thus time is oriented toward the eternal (and thus, in a certain sense, the eternal is temporally construed within the very structure of human vocation itself).

## MARY'S PERPETUAL VIRGINITY ILLUMINATES ANTHROPOLOGICAL VOCATION

As stated above, Mary's virginity enacts and recapitulates in an *illuminative* manner the spousal character of anthropological *vocation*, a call to live *for* God, *in* God, *by* God's grace as the maternal being. This is coincident with the truth that her perpetual virginity, under the pneumatic time aforementioned, is the proleptic embodying of that angelic state which, for our Lady, was fully and finally realized in her assumption. So, while her perpetual virginity lived out in her earthly existence was a continual sign of her consecration to God,[25] a sign of living *for*, *in*, and *by*

25. Reflections on "consecration" usually invite further thinking about the role of the *will* in the act of giving over oneself to the Other. Within the tradition, this raised questions about whether Mary had a "plan of virginity" from the onset. While this is already implicitly present within the work of the Protoevangelium of James, Gregory of Nyssa and Augustine explicitly articulate the belief that Mary indeed had the intention to remain a virgin and thus consecrated herself as such. As Manfred Hauke notes,

him, it does so ever while realizing *in time* the eternal state that no one is indeed "given in marriage" since the eternal state actualizes the *spousal* character of human vocation: an irrevocable marriage to God alone. This means that our Lady's perpetual virginity as her vocation is the arrival in time of a future reality—the eschatological marriage supper of the Lamb—as the inherent grammar of her spousal consecration to God as a maternal being, the one who, while ever under God, is nevertheless *for* God as both creature and Mother. In this we observe that her perpetual virginity illumines (grace/faith/theology) the horizon of the temporal/eternal dynamic that constitutes the spousal character of human vocation. Thus, Mary's vocation as Virgin *reveals* anthropologically the vocational structure of each human being, every person who is de facto an image bearer of God. Before examining how this is decisive for human vocation as such, let us further consider the meaning of Mary's vocation as perpetual Virgin.

How exactly does our Lady's virginity reveal the spousal character of *her* vocation (which, of course, will extend to all, given our thesis)? By expanding what was stated above, we can see that she does so in two ways: First, her virginal integrity is a sign signifying a *consecration* to the Other. It is a sign of remaining totally free *for* God *by* the grace of God, which is made present as one abiding *in* God. It reveals a total claim of the transcendent One upon the creaturely will, elevating the creaturely volition to a higher freedom. This is why René Laurentin notes the following concerning our Lady's virginal integrity:

> The ancient conviction of the Church is that the virginal consecration of Mary was sealed and animated in her heart by the Holy Spirit. From within she understood what St. Paul had understood in Jesus Christ (1 Cor. 7:8), what he counseled and "prescribed" even with insistence (7:18) to Christians of the mid-first century, for the perfection of their "undivided attention to the Lord" (7:35) and their freedom in God, that is, "that each one should continue as he was when God's call reached him" (7:17—an aphorism repeated in vv. 19 and 24; cf. also v. 39). Mary

by the Middle Ages the church universally accepted the belief that Mary did indeed have a plan of virginity, albeit debate was held regarding whether "the vow was already absolute before the betrothal (the Franciscan view) or conditional before the betrothal and absolute only afterward (the Dominican view, following Aquinas)" (*Introduction to Mariology*, 198–99).

> remained "such as she was when God's call reached her," that is, in the state of virginity of the Annunciation (Lk. 1:27, 34).[26]

In this way, then, Mary's vocation is archetypal for all disciples who follow in the way of Christ (and thus *all* humans by means of a universal vocation whether or not it is ever realized *in time*); her vocation recapitulates the *specific* vocational structure of the virginal bride that is the church, while also doing so *generally* for all of humanity. Thus, "she is for always the type or icon of virginity, that is, of the eschatological life (1 Cor. 7:29–31) lived already here below, or, in other words, of the total and direct gift of self to God."[27] Again here we see, through Laurentin's reading, the eschatological inbreaking of what will be fully realized at the end, revealing how the eternal is decisive for the temporal stream of events, and how, specifically, eternality's proleptic "appearing" in time is the offspring of the pneumatic time that constitutes the grammar of her—and thus all—human vocation.

This leads us to the second way in which her virginity points to the spousal character of her vocation: the outcome of her virginal union with God *is* the birth of God made man. That her total gift of self to God results in the fruit of her womb—God enfleshed—uniquely manifests in time what is destined at the end of time for all who remain true to the strictures of anthropological vocation: the *embodiment* of God; God being all *in all*. As stated above, our Lady's virginal *vocation* corresponds to her maternal *identity*. In this, her maternal identity is ever more actualized in a continually increasing degree to the extent in which her virginal vocation is honored. In turn, her virginal vocation is increasingly fulfilled to the degree that her maternal identity is actualized, hence her *perpetual* virginity.[28]

That Mary's virginity remains as it was before the incarnation after the event of her birth giving is indeed important for the revelation that it

26. Laurentin, *Treatise on Virgin Mary*, 318–19.

27. Laurentin, *Treatise on Virgin Mary*, 319.

28. This is why Manfred Hauke notes concerning how our Lady is simultaneously the archetypal expression of virginity and motherhood, "Mary is the prototype of virgins, but with her maternity it becomes clear that virginity is not identified with the *single* life, through the fact that she is open to God for the 'generation' of Christ in the church. At the same time, Mary is prototype of the mother whose maternity is not limited to the biological contribution, but has to transcend itself in openness to God. In this way, Mary, as virgin and mother, makes concrete the convergence of these two states in the church, consecrated virginity and matrimony, even to the bodily dimension" (*Introduction to Mariology*, 201–2).

is *God* who is both enfleshed and born.[29] It is also crucial for connecting the singularity of this event with the total nature of the church and each respective disciple. Consider, again, Laurentin's thinking in the following lengthy quote:

> For the Fathers it [that is, her perpetual virginal integrity] is less a privilege of Mary than an appanage of Christ's birth. They were penetrated with the symbolic and dogmatic unity that linked the three births of the Word to one another: he is born of the Father from all eternity, born of the Virgin Mary in time, and born of every Christian soul by faith and baptism. The second birth has the value of sign in relation to the other two: it is the temporal attestation and replica of the first, the pledge and exemplar of the last. Therefore, God made this bodily birth participate in the supernatural and spiritual condition of the other two births, by exempting it in certain respects from the disabilities and limitations of the flesh. This exemption is manifest at the beginning in the miracle of the virginal conception (*ex fide et Spiritu Sancto*), and at the end in the virginal child-birth. The birth of Christ attests that the Son born of Mary in human nature is the Son of God from all eternity. It attests that the fallen creation is taken up again from the beginning. It announces that the triumph of the redeeming Incarnation extends into the realm of the flesh.[30]

Thus, our Lady's virginity reveals the spousal character of her vocation as (1) a sign signifying a spousal consecration to the Other, which in turn results in (2) conception and birth giving of the God-man. The intrinsic connection between Mary's *maternal* being and *virginal* vocation is clearly seen, and it is to be understood, too, against the horizon of the temporal/eternal dynamism, pneumatic time, at play: virginal vocation and maternal identity are the realization *in time* of what will be in the *eschatological age*; thus, our Lady's vocation and identity are both the proleptic appearances of what is indeed to come, as they also reveal the predestined ground from which her virginal maternity springs forth from; that is, her origin *and* end.[31]

29. As Thomas Aquinas notes, "To show that His body was real, He was born of a woman. But in order to manifest His Godhead, He was born of a Virgin" (*ST* III, q. 28, a. 2, ad 2).

30. Laurentin, *Treatise on Virgin Mary*, 331–32.

31. Consider the connection Laurentin discerns between Mary's virginity and both her immaculate conception and assumption: "*The miracle of the virginal birth manifests the fulness of the mystery of the Immaculate Conception and is a prelude to the eschatological mystery of the Assumption.* The preserving grace that exempted Mary from

Thus, it becomes ever clearer how Mary's perpetual virginity *illuminates* (grace/faith/theology) the horizon of pneumatic time that constitutes the spousal character of human vocation as such; how Mary's vocation as Virgin reveals the vocational structure of each human being anthropologically. While taking up what we have discovered in chapter 2 concerning in what manner our Lady's divine maternity reveals the maternal *being* of anthropos, along with the metaphysical legitimacy of such a reading discerned in our first chapter, coupled with what is stated above, we can observe that Mary's perpetual virginity enacts and recapitulates human *vocation*, shedding light in a unique manner on the very structure of this universal call upon all human beings. How so? Insofar as Mary's virginal integrity points to and is fulfilled by her maternal identity, so it is the case for each person as such. Since the human being is the *maternal* being (illuminated by the Theotokos in concert with her Son, as we have seen in our previous chapter), we can see how virginal *vocation* is the precondition for *as well as* the fulfillment of such a being. Such a vocation is the necessary ground that allows for the flourishing of human identity *as* maternal. Paradoxically, however, the maternal being is also the necessary ground and basis for human vocation *as* virginal if virginity is to be a sign of consecration to God for the sake of God's embodiment *by* and *in* the maternal being. In other words, virginal *vocation* is the necessary accompaniment to the maternal *being*—it is, so to speak, the *only* possible vocation for such a being if *God* is to be understood as the center by which this being (as maternal) is animated, sustained, and oriented toward for the sake of its fulfillment—while simultaneously the maternal being is the necessary ground and fulfillment of this virginal vocation, if virginity here is to be understood as *for* the transcendent Other who desires to be "all *in* all." Put another way, both the maternal *being* and virginal *vocation* are necessarily intrinsic to each other if either is to be truly

original sin freed her likewise from its principle personal consequences, not only in soul *(concupiscentia)* but in body as well. Mary, the New Eve, the point of departure for the new creation, incurred neither original sin nor the pains promised of the first Eve (Gen. 3): the servitude of libido (3:16b), the pains of labor (3:16a), the corruption of the tomb (3:19). If she remains subjected to the exterior servitude of the world of sin wherein she is born (the crib at Bethlehem witnesses thereto), she is freed from that other kind of servitude which the after-effects of sin cause to spring up from within. *The sign of the virginal birth corresponds to the design that appeared in the conception by the Holy Spirit and was to culminate in the Assumption, that is, the triumph of the Redeemer who saves and transfigures not only souls but bodies.* That is what the Church Fathers understood in the notion of incorruptibility, a notion at once moral and physical" (*Treatise on Virgin Mary*, 333; emphasis added).

*for God.* This is what our Lady reveals concerning the complementary nature of both the being and vocation of anthropos.

This is fitting given that the maternal being and virginal vocation are both the proleptic appearance of what is to come eschatologically, as they are also both the *contingent* realities realized in time according to the *predestined* will of God, enacted in time via the immaculate conception—uniquely for our Lady—but done so for the church via the sacrament of baptism as the birth of her members in time.[32] That the predestined eschaton—that is, the ultimate *origin* and *end*—is the basis for both the maternal structure of the human *being* and the virginal shape of human *vocation*, we can then (continue to) infer the intrinsic relation of each to the other given the singularity of the eternal ground "rooted" in God—who is his own eternality—as the fulfillment *in time* of both the maternal being and virginal vocation via the incarnation (for our Lady), which analogously occurs in all humans who actively live out both their virginal vocation and maternal being in time.[33] We see intimations of this given that God is *already* the eternal "center/ground" in which we "live, move, and have our being" (Acts 17:28); the One in whom all things co-inhere. That God is present in all things, as Thomas Aquinas notes, in presence, power, and essence,[34] *gestures*, metaphysically, to the singular anchor of both anthropological being and vocation, albeit in differing degrees and modes, which is finally *revealed* (in the datum of revelation) as coextensive with the predestined and eschatological ground.

But how exactly is anthropological vocation enacted analogously for the human being as such? In what way is the universal call to live *virginally* realized for the human being, especially for those whose vocation is not to the consecrated life?

Since we have discovered the intrinsic relation between human identity and vocation in light of our Lady, a partial answer has already been given in the preceding chapter where we observed how the maternal being of the human is realized in her fiat, gestation, birth giving, and parenting of the Word, which are analogous to the uniquely singular

32. The subsequent chapter will explore in greater detail how Mary's immaculate conception enacts and recapitulates human *origin* both illuminatively and illustratively.

33. See ch. 2 for the details concerning how this is analogously expressed in the *maternal* being.

34. "God is in all things by his power, inasmuch as all things are subject to his power; he is by his presence in all things, inasmuch as all things are bare and open to his eyes; he is in all things by his essence, inasmuch as he is present to all as the cause of their being" (*ST* I, q. 8, a. 3).

maternal events of Mary's life. And since our Lady's maternity is both the condition for and the fulfillment of her perpetual virginity, we can discern how human fiat to God's will, realized in the conception of the Word in the womb of the heart via faith, followed by the subsequent gestation and birth giving via participation in the sufferings of Christ, and the parenting of that eternal Word by obedience to him (as described in the preceding chapter) are necessarily ingredient to the virginal *vocation* of each human being. Thus, the virginal vocation of the human being is enacted to the degree that the maternal identity is itself made manifest.

However, on the side of *vocation* as such, we can also say that this is expressed by way of a *chaste existence*, which is the analogical correlate to Mary's virginal disposition, *virginitas mentis*.[35] Thus, to the extent by which a person *as maternal being* maintains and grows in a virginal disposition analogous to Mary's inner chaste existence (which, for the human as such, is also a metaphorical realization of Mary's bodily integrity as perpetual virgin), which would entail a growth in virtues, especially theological—faith, hope, and love[36]—is the extent by which one lives out one's *virginal* vocation—the general call to live *for* God as the proleptic embodying of the angelic state. A *chaste* existence, in imitation of our Lady, is a life that is lived from "tomorrow," *from* the eschatologically eternal frame (via faith, hope, and love) *in time*. A chaste existence, analogously construed, signals a radical openness to the eternal *in* time,

35. The catechism teaches that "all the baptized are called to chastity," recognizing Christ as the principal model "for all chastity" (Catholic Church, *Catechism*, §2348). This, of course, can be extended to Mary, who also embodies this perfectly. "All Christ's faithful are called to lead a chaste life in keeping with their particular state of life. At the moment of this Baptism, the Christian is pledged to lead his affective life in chastity." In addition, the catechism defines chastity as "the successful integration of sexuality within the person and thus the inner unity of man in his bodily and spiritual being" (§2337). Therefore, "the chaste person maintains the integrity of the powers of life and love placed in him. This integrity ensures the unity of the person; it is opposed to any behavior that would impair it. It tolerates neither a double life nor duplicity in speech" (§2338). This is why "chastity includes an *apprenticeship in self-mastery* which is a training in human freedom" (§2339; emphasis in original). In relation to love which "is the *form* of all the virtues," chastity "appears as a school of the gift of the person. Self-mastery is ordered to the gift of self" (§2346; emphasis in original).

36. The catechism's description of the theological virtues is insightful here since it describes how they are ordered toward God while they are gifts given by him in order to participate *in* him: "The human virtues are rooted in the theological virtues, which adapt man's faculties for participation in the divine nature: for the theological virtues relate directly to God. They dispose Christians to live in a relationship with the Holy Trinity. They have the One and Triune God for their origin, motive, and object" (Catholic Church, *Catechism*, §1812).

resulting with a no with one's whole being and body to this "world" for the greater yes to the eternal "tomorrow," which is already present as the eternal "in" time, thus "new creation," (2 Cor 5:17) eternity definitively shaping time itself, from the inside out.

We now see with greater clarity how Mary *illumines* (grace/faith/theology) anthropological vocation, which is a call to proleptically embody the angelic state by means of living *for* the transcendently *eternal* Other. We can now proceed to examine how our Lady also *illustrates* (nature/reason/philosophy) this perennial vocation as a mere—yet decisively important—creature, a person, in the order of creatureliness. As noted in our previous chapters, a philosophical exploration of Mary, the ever virgin, should grant us additional insights from the side of creatureliness as a theological examination offers us from the side of grace. This follows since (Catholic) reason, which is conjoined to faith and thus healed and elevated transcendently, is altogether situated in and sustained by that creaturely metaphysics gifted to us by our Lady's unique role in the hypostatic order as mere creature, as we noted in our first chapter.

## MARY'S PERPETUAL VIRGINITY ILLUSTRATES ANTHROPOLOGICAL VOCATION

As stated earlier, Mary is the non-reductive manifestation of the meaning of anthropos. In her we behold the undivided—without mixture or confusion—relationship between the natural and the supernatural, uniquely so, in an analogous manner to her Son. Thus, a philosophical analysis of Mary's vocation will *illustrate* the theological truths given and explored above from the side of creatureliness insofar as philosophy remains grounded in Catholic theological presuppositions. Stated differently, a philosophical examination of Mary's vocation as Virgin will illustrate in an explicative mode the theology already discernible in the given revelation. Therefore, we can proceed to discern how Mary *illustrates* (nature/reason/philosophy) a vision of human vocation as she does so *illuminatively* (grace/faith/theology).

A philosophical consideration of Mary as *ever* virgin, allows us to behold her as a creature uniquely circumscribed by a capacious grace that elevates her creatureliness since what is observed is a virginity that is perpetual *despite* conception and birth giving. This means that such a philosophic beholding of Mary—one that takes her contingency and finitude seriously yet is open to the fullness of reality since it chooses not to foreclose dogmatically the possibility of transcendence—is irreversibly enlightened by grace through faith, transfiguring without destroying philosophical query into the nature of human vocation. If philosophy were to refuse any admittance of the possibility of transcendence, and thus grace, for example, then what is presumed is that philosophical inquiry ought to be concerned only with "pure nature."[37] This would mean that any philosophical examination of the perpetuity of Mary's virginal state despite the coextensive presence of conception and birth giving would presume, at the very least, a hermeneutical posture of doubt and suspicion, for this is seen, from this perspective, as impossible tout court. The issue with this *natura pura* that funds such a hermeneutical position is that nature as "pure nature" (as posited by ontological naturalism) is fictional since it would result in ontological suicide, and thus it is self-defeating.[38] This is why a proper understanding of the relationship between nature and grace, reason and faith, the natural and the supernatural, is vital. As Conor Cunningham notes,

> Faith and reason make each other possible, just as the supernatural makes the natural possible: "The term *supernatural* does not refer to a new order of being added to nature but to the means for attaining the one final end for which the power of nature alone does not suffice." The fact that it does not suffice signals a natural call or desire for that which lies beyond, and for that very reason such a call is in some way indigenous: "*The ultimate purpose of a rational creature exceeds the capacity of its own nature.*" Indeed, man is in this world a sort of microcosm, uniting in himself all that which is below him and offering it to that which is above him. Nature and grace form a union analogous to a seamless robe, which was not to be ripped asunder and sold off.[39]

Thus, observing reality "in Christ"—which is also to say "in Mary" though in a different metaphysical register—furnishes us with the tools to observe the relationship between nature and grace (since Christ is the hypostatic union between divinity and humanity, which Mary enacts as

37. The problem with this is succinctly stated by Conor Cunningham in the following way: "In short, if there were such a thing as pure nature, there would be nothing at all, for only the abyss would obtain (and not even that)" ("*Natura Pura*," 244).

38. C. Cunningham, "*Natura Pura*," 245.

39. C. Cunningham, "*Natura Pura*," 250; referring to Dupré, *Passage to Modernity*, 171; and Aquinas, *Comp. Theol.* 1.143n82; emphasis in original.

the *interior-exteriorized* union that is internal to her Son, as we saw in our first chapter), perceiving that "the natural is not transformed into the supernatural, just as sacraments are not magic pills, religious ones at that, no, rather it is the transformation of the old into the new; more, it is the revelation of the new in the old, the old was always meant for the new."[40] Thus, a philosophical consideration of Mary's virginal vocation is indeed possible without it being destroyed by the presence of grace, faith, and theology. Philosophy, in fact, is elevated and completed by such a *gratuitous* presence, as it is also paradoxically ordered to it.

A philosophy that is opened to the full breadth and depth of reality observes something remarkable about our Lady: Mary's virginal vocation results in the fruitful exchange between her—a temporal, contingent agent—and the eternal, transcendent One without resulting in the loss of physical integrity but in fact fulfilling it transcendently as a *sign* via a seal *for* the Other. This then means that a philosophical anthropology predicated on Mary discerns a particular shape to human vocation, a shape that can best be described as *exocentric*. That the maternal *being* of Mary finds its foundation and fulfillment in her virginal *vocation*, as her virginal *vocation* is both the beginning and culmination of her maternal *being*, means that anthropological vocation—that is, the perennial *call* of each human being—is determinatively shaped by a "living for" the transcendent *Other* (*ek* as "out") as the *heart* (*centric* as "center") of the temporally construed contingent one, the human being. Put differently, in light of Mary, philosophical anthropology observes the inherent structure of human vocation in which the human being is called to pursue "outwardly," so to speak, an ever greater Other, namely, God—the One who is higher than my highest and deeper than my deepest—so that this One can finally become the "center." The center, one's center, then, is always ever "beyond" in the transcendent Other.[41] If this is so, it then makes sense, as we saw above, why an intentional, existential engagement of this vocation would result in living a *chaste* life, since this would enact a lifestyle that signals the "center" of such a life *as* the transcendent Other (since chastity, here construed, recognizes a higher and deeper order that is not of this world). Living a *chaste* life is the way one enacts

40. C. Cunningham, "*Natura Pura*," 253.

41. This is why, for example, Augustine will speak about his restless heart outside of the true rest ever only afforded by God, or why Kierkegaard will identify the final stage in life's way as the religious as ever only bringing to rest the either/or dialectic that constitutes so much of the restless engagement with all outside of God.

and recapitulates the virginal *vocation* of one's maternal *being*. Chastity, then, is the existential fulfillment of the exocentric (virginal) vocation of anthropos.

In addition, since this transcendent Other is also his own eternality, and since Mary's end is her assumption—an eschatological event that philosophical reasoning elevated by grace will observe and thus accept as part of the datum of reality perceived—then a philosophic gaze upon the ever-virgin Theotokos in view of anthropological vocation discerns that fuller and more complete shape of human vocation as an *eschatologically oriented exocentricity*. This means that while revelation illumines (vis-à-vis Mary's unique place in the hypostatic order) human vocation as decisively determined by the eternal intersecting time through both the incarnation and the proleptic appearance of the angelic state, a philosophical consideration of our Lady's virginal vocation suggests that the eternal is in fact *temporally* construed *within* the very structure of human vocation itself. In other words, the structure of human vocation is the *stretching forth toward* the eternal as the grammar of eschatological *arrival in time* (proleptically) such that temporality is reordered in light of the eternal without losing its integrity but is instead, paradoxically, transfigured. Time, then, is no longer lived forward but, so to speak, backward—*from* futurity always in light *of* that eschatological end. This is the philosophical reckoning in light of grace, a grace that reveals proleptically the end in the midst of time, as grace also reveals the eternal transacting time without confusing or separating time and eternity, which is seen in both Christ and, analogously, in his Mother, despite the metaphysical difference between the two. Thus, the call of every human in view of our Lady is to live *for* the *eternal*, the Other, *within* time, which is done through a *chaste* life. This is why Bonhoeffer—though doing so specifically in the light of Christ and his resurrection—identifies Christians as knowing and living *from* the end:

> The Church of Christ bears witness to the end of all things. *It lives from the end, it thinks from the end, it acts from the end, it proclaims its message from the end.* "Remember not the former things, nor consider the things of old. Behold, I am doing a new thing" (Isa. 43:18–19). The new is the real end of the old; Christ is the new. Christ is the end of the old. He is not a continuation of the old; he is not its aiming point, nor is he a consummation upon the line of the old; he is the end and therefore the new.[42]

42. Bonhoeffer, *Creation and Fall*, 9; emphasis added.

Bonhoeffer is right in identifying the radicality of the eschatological inbreaking through Christ, which positions the church—the redeemed humanity who enact anthropological vocation—as living "from the end." We would add, of course, that this is ever more affirmed by having recourse to our Lady's unique, privileging role in further elucidating anthropology. Through her, in concert with her Son, we see how the shape of human vocation is *eschatologically oriented exocentricity*.

If this eschatological inbreaking—through both the incarnation and the resurrection/assumption—is crucial for a proper understanding of true human vocation, how, then, is this expressed? What, in other words, are the *effects* of living a *chaste* existence that would distinguish the one who is authentically enacting human vocation from those who fail to do so?

The philosopher Emmanuel Falque identifies how time, along with its characteristics that pertain to a finite existence, is experienced differently for those who live in light of the eschaton. If philosophical investigation is truly open to the datum of all reality, then it will consider how even the experience of time, hitherto perhaps understood only in light of the conditions of creaturely finitude, is now changed for those whose lives are lived according to the contours of eschatologically oriented exocentricity. The following lengthy quote offers some insight into the way time is experienced differently considering this eschatological inbreaking, an experiential shift that pertains to those who enact a *chaste* existence as a response to their virginal vocation:

> Past and future, memory and anticipation are all radically changed. Not that the Christian would be able to satisfy himself or herself solely with the joy of the moment (*carpe diem*) but in that the "burden of the past" (Freud) and the "anxiety for the future" (Heidegger) take on, from God himself in his metamorphosis, a mode of being that liberates them from their promethean load. The apostle Luke gives witness of this in exemplary fashion. It is as though the *reception we give to the moment of salvation* were to become our sole authority, among all those other moments that might seem to deflect it from its path. To the disciple wishing "first of all" to bury his father (burden of the past), Jesus replies: "Let the dead bury their own dead; but as for you, go and proclaim the kingdom of God" (Luke 9:60). To the man who wants to build bigger barns to store the harvest ("anxiety for the future"), God replies: "You fool! This very night your life is being demanded of you. And the things you have

> prepared, whose will they be?" (Luke 12:20). While to the good thief, and only to him, because he asks for pardon *now* [the moment of God], Christ on the cross replies: "Today you will be with me in paradise" (Luke 23:43). God speaks paradoxically, in the present, of the future of his presence ("*Today* you *will* be" [the moment of eternity]), while the man weighs up his past life (the burden), or anticipates in the unforeseen of his future existence (the anxiety). Such is the *temporal metamorphosis* that the resurrection produces.[43]

Falque, here, offers an incisive phenomenological description of the experience of time considering the past and the potential future for those who, by their *chaste* existence, live in light of the eternal. By recognizing one's virginal vocation and choosing, then, to live in view of the eternal *within* time, one is freed from the typical angst that comes from living before an unknown future (or living in the light of *knowing* that their earthly future will end), as well as from the burdens that come from past events. Anthropological vocation is no longer bound by the temporal conditions that set the stage for the inevitable rise of both past burdens and future anxieties since these conditions, which spring forth from finitude itself, are changed—"temporal metamorphosis"—in the light of the resurrection and assumption. This could even be read, philosophically, in such a way that given the resulting anxieties and burdens that accompany the experience of time as a conditioned creature, it is fitting that human vocation is transfigured according to an eternal frame so that real human flourishing can occur. It is as if the temporal presence of anxiety with respect to the future and the burdened past announces a need *for* transcendence (the *eternal now*) for the one whose contingency, ever inscribed within a temporal frame, binds. It is as if finitude gestures toward the infinite—as time signals the eternal—not only as contingent realities requiring non-contingency for their existence (metaphysically speaking), but also so that the modality of the experience of both finitude and temporality are healed and elevated (though never negated), allowing for the flourishing of the human being—the *maternal* being—to take place by entering into the eternal present of God's time.

By recognizing the shape of anthropological vocation—eschatologically oriented exocentricity—and thus the true call upon the human being (to live in the light of the eternal, transcendent Other), the experience of time becomes new to the degree a *chaste* existence is enacted. However,

43. Falque, *Metamorphosis of Finitude*, 115; emphasis in original.

as Falque notes, "it is not then *another time* that the metamorphosis produces," but, rather, a real change in the experience of time (for those who live in response to the eternal). This is so because "it opens up on the contrary to *eternity*—that is to say, onto *another way to live the same time*, just as the communion of saints is another way to live the same world."[44] Elaborating on this point, Falque goes on to state the following:

> In life as in death, the Christian, though a participant in the eternal, does not leave time. Christians simply live a *certain time*—that is to say, according to a time limit that they accept as what has been granted to them (a time that is *certain*) and according to a specification that renders the time limit recognizable (a *certain manner of being in time* as welcomed by God in every moment of time). The Christian's time is no longer *the* time; it is the *time of God*, as *metamorphosis of all time in a moment.*[45]

This can be read as an underlying phenomenological description of the eschatologically oriented exocentricity that inscribes the virginal vocation of the human being. A *chaste* life is a response to God, who is "in every moment of time" as the eternal Other, as the proleptic appearance *in time* of the eschatological end that is ever "*in*" this eternal Other, God. Thus, we can ask, as Augustine did, "Who will hold the heart of man, that it may stand still and see how eternity, always standing still, utters past and future times, but is itself neither past nor future?"[46] Through her unique role in the hypostatic order, philosophy, hand in hand with theology, can answer "Mary," as she in a certain sense does this within an anthropological mode. This is possible given her distinctive relation to the eternal *Other* via her virginal *vocation* and maternal *being*, this Other who "precede[s] all times past by the excellency of an ever-present eternity" and "outlast[s] all future times, because they are future, and when they have come, they shall be past."[47] In a profoundly beautiful way, Mary shows us this in both her being and actions, as a mere creature.

Fascinatingly, a philosophical musing about time in the light of God's eternality, as is done by Augustine, uncovers a *presentism* that perhaps gestures toward an eternal reckoning of time since, for God, "today

44. Falque, *Metamorphosis of Finitude*, 115; emphasis in original.

45. Falque, *Metamorphosis of Finitude*, 115–16; emphasis in original.

46. Augustine, *Confessions*, 252.

47. Augustine, *Confessions*, 252.

is eternity"[48]—that is, the present moment is infused and thus upheld by God's own eternality. This would mean, then, that implicit to the way one experiences both the past through memory and the future through expectation (both experienced in the *present*, as Augustine notes)[49] is already a hinting toward an utterly *new* experience of time. In other words, since both expectations and memories are experiences in the *present moment*, this could be read as a sign of, a pointer toward a higher temporal reality that is a temporal/eternal dynamic (pneumatic time) that the human being is *called* to enact in one's own life, showing forth the temporal/eternal structure inherent in human vocation as an eschatologically oriented exocentricity. Since the future through expectation and the past through memory are experienced only as a *present* reality, and since the *present* is, in a certain way, coextensive with the *eternal*, this could be read, philosophically, as implying a deeper mode of time that humans are called to experience and live out of, a mode of time that is "entered into" by way of the eternal *Other* that is *present to every moment*.[50] Philosophy can observe this implicit structure within experienced time, which is *then* illumined through revelation by means of the eschatological inbreaking, through both the incarnation and the proleptic appearance of the end by way of Jesus's resurrection and Mary's assumption. While it is beyond the scope of this current project, we can imagine that future studies into experienced time in light of the aforementioned anthropological insights, could, for example, consider in greater detail the work of Henri Bergson and his concept of *duration* (*la durée*),[51] especially in light of

48. Augustine, *Confessions*, 253.

49. Augustine states, "Yet possibly it might be properly said, 'There are three times: a present of things past, a present of things present, and a present of future things.' For these three do somehow exist in the mind, for otherwise I do not see them; there is present of things past, memory; present of things present, sight; present of things future, expectation" (*Confessions*, 259).

50. This could even be considered in the light of various religious practices that invoke differing styles of meditative and contemplative engagement, especially as seen in the East. Inherent in much of these "schools" is a deep sense of the eternal "in" time that is accessible via a proper practice. This would seem to suggest that these "schools" are themselves bearing witness to a deeper anthropological call, which is fulfilled and fully realized in Christianity.

51. According to Matthew W. Maguire, Bergson's first exploration of this notion in relation to time and free will can be found in his essay "Time and Free Will: An Essay on the Immediate Data of Consciousness." Maguire recounts a description of duration offered by Bergson: "He compares *durée* to the experience of hearing a melody: the melody can be experienced or understood neither as individual notes, nor as a succession of notes regardless of their temporal duration; its power and its reality as a melody

Charles Péguy given that he offers important theological qualifications to the Bergsonion notion in such a way that, as John Milbank notes, allows him to "overcome Bergson's concerns about embracing a merely immanentist vitalism [which limits his notion of duration]. For it permits one to conceive a teleology that is eschatologized: for which the final end is not unambiguously pre-given at the outset . . . but rather is superadded from above and is continuously superadded as gift."[52] This could potentially have further implications for a philosophical anthropology that recognizes human vocation as *eschatologically oriented exocentricity*.

So, what we have here are implicit signs of a higher temporal order in the fabric of experienced time, which are then illumined and fulfilled by the eternal Other, revealed within the virginal maternity of our Lady. Philosophy can indeed discern this as it remains open to the full scope of what *is*. It is Mary's perpetual virginity, coincident with her divine maternity, that allows for the clarification of the philosophical puzzles concerning experienced time in relation to certain anthropological questions. This in turn gives greater space for further philosophical investigation into the nature of anthropological vocation and its relation to time. Philosophy, in partnership with theology, can pursue ever more deeply the great mystery of human vocation and its temporal/eternal dynamics as it learns from our Lady, seat of wisdom.

## CONCLUSION: ANTHROPOLOGICAL VOCATION

Like the layout of our previous chapter, this chapter proceeded to examine how Mary uniquely *illumines* and *illustrates* a particular aspect of anthropology—namely, vocation. We first considered the dogmatic truth about Mary's perpetual virginity, reflecting on its meaning and intrinsic

---

depend upon its duration as a whole, its inescapably temporal flow, in which the past must be distinct yet continuous with the present for the melody to act upon us" (*Carnal Spirit*, 53).

52. Milbank, foreword, xx–xxi. Milbank also observes a connection between Péguy and Maurice Blondel, since Péguy's theological correction and expansion of Bergson's notion of duration recognizes that "there is no horizontal natural freedom without vertical supernatural grace," thus, for both Blondel and Péguy "the inherent unfinishedness of the human action and its excess over any rational grasp implies precisely a constitutively existential search for something beyond given nature in order to complete it—the supernatural as 'over natural,' not as 'extra natural,' as he [Péguy] puts it" (xx). This could be investigated further in future studies considering the theo-philosophical anthropology given in our Lady.

relation to our Lady's divine maternity. Recognizing the inherent inseparability between her maternal identity and virginal vocation, we were able to explore in greater detail how their coextensive relations mutually inform each other.

Subsequently, by considering how our Lady's virginal motherhood analogously mirrors the eternal generation of the Son from the Father while also signaling the divine presence *in* time via the incarnation (hence *virginal motherhood*), we were able to examine how Mary is the fulcrum of (while she is herself constituted by) a temporal/eternal dynamic—pneumatic time. This invited us to return to our previous consideration of how the four dogmatic truths about Mary—which are coordinated to the four cardinal anthropological questions—help us to observe a particular temporal dynamism along eschatological lines.

We then considered specifically how Mary's maternal being and virginal vocation are shaped by a predestined/eschatological frame given in her conception and assumption. This positioned us to further consider what is revealed in the *temporal* relationship between her maternity and virginity, namely, that the eternal *intersects* time, so to speak, via the incarnation, as well as revealing how both maternal identity and virginal vocation are ordered toward each as both foundation and fulfillment. We also considered the *eschatological* relationship between her assumption and both her maternity and virginity, observing how they are the outworking *in time* of the proleptic appearance of the angelic state in the eschatological end, her assumption.

We then proceeded to investigate how Mary *illuminates* (grace/faith/theology) anthropological vocation specifically by showing how the human being as maternal is called to live *for* God, *in* God, *by* God, revealing the spousal character of human vocation as such, realizing in time (proleptically) what will be fully actualized in the eschaton: marriage to God alone. That this virginal vocation results in the conception and birth of *God* further signifies the spousal character of Mary's, and thus by extension all, human vocation. In considering how this is enacted for the human being, we observed that the *chaste* life is the existential mode by which this is done.

Finally, we proceeded to examine how Mary *illustrates* (nature/reason/philosophy) anthropological vocation by observing how a philosophical exploration of the structure of human vocation in the light of revelation shows an exocentric shape, which, considering the temporal/eternal dynamic at work, is actually an *eschatologically oriented exocentricity*. We observed how this, in turn, is hinted toward in experienced time, and how those who enact human vocation through an existential choice for a *chaste* life recognize what is already implicit in experienced time. Therefore, the human being is that (maternal) being which is dynamically oriented toward an eschatological beckoning, which is the source and completion of human vocation as such, the exocentric life. This is how Mary both enacts and recapitulates anthropological *vocation* both illuminatively and illustratively within a theo-philosophical manner.

As we continue to meditate upon the privileged role our Lady has in elucidating, with her Son, various anthropological truths, we now turn our gaze toward the question of human *origin*. The question of origins is ubiquitous to the study of anthropology, but ours is a theo-philosophical investigation. We will thus explore how Mary's immaculate conception *illuminates illustratively* the origin of the human being.

*Before I formed you in the womb I knew you,*
*Before you were born I set you apart.*

~ Jer 1:5

*Nature and the supernatural are thus united, without in any sense being confused. "The end of rational nature is the highest good, which is above nature." The spiritual creature does not find its end in itself, but in God.*

~ Henri de Lubac

# 4

# Immaculate Conception

## *The Human as Graced Personhood*

WITH THE STEADY UNFOLDING of our exploratory investigation into our Lady's significance for discerning a robust theo-philosophical anthropology, we continue to uncover how Mary is the answer to the perennial questions implied in human existence. Given the metaphysical basis for such a Marian reading of anthropology as we have examined in our first chapter, we have been able to observe how Mary as Theotokos reveals both theologically and philosophically anthropological *identity* as *maternal*, which was accomplished in our second chapter. Subsequently, in our third chapter we observed how Mary as ever virgin also unveils for us the decisive shape of anthropological vocation as *virginal* both theologically and philosophically. Thus, our Lady enacts and recapitulates human *identity* and *vocation* in an *illuminative* (grace/faith/theology) and *illustrative* (nature/reason/philosophy) manner.

By way of this exploratory investigation, coordinating the four Marian dogmas with the four perennial questions concerning the origin, end, identity, and vocation of anthropos, we have also discovered the temporal/eternal dynamic along eschatological lines—what we have termed pneumatic time—that decisively shape and inform the human being as it is revealed in our Lady, the theo-philosophical model of the anthropos. By considering Mary's virginal vocation in the light of its *temporal* relation to her maternal identity, and the *eschatological* relation between her virginity and her assumption and conception, we discovered in what manner the temporal/eternal dynamic is constitutive of our Lady's person and being, and thus the human being in general by extension. As begun in our previous chapters, we will continue to investigate theo-philosophically this dynamic.

In this chapter, our project advances by exploring how Mary's immaculate conception enacts and recapitulates human *origin* as a *graced being*, both *illuminatively* and *illustratively*. The argument will proceed in the following manner: First, we will briefly explore the meaning of Mary's immaculate conception and examine how it, coincident with her Son, situates Mary as the perfect *icon* of the human being, over against any temptation to render her an *idol*. Thus, Mary's immaculate conception reaffirms our thesis: we can look to her for a theo-philosophical anthropology. Second, we will investigate how pneumatic time is constitutive of the immaculate conception, observing how this dogmatic truth of our Lady reveals the intrinsic relation between the *eternal* and *temporal origins* of the human being simultaneously. Third, we will observe exactly how Mary's immaculate conception *illuminates* anthropological origins both eternally (predestined origin) and temporally (origin in time via the sacrament of baptism). Fourth and finally, we will explore how our Lady's immaculate conception *illustrates* human origination by arguing how, considering what philosophy discovers about anthropological *identity* and *vocation* in view of revelation, Catholic rationality recognizes the decisive incompleteness of the human being *until* a graced beginning is initiated.

## "I AM THE IMMACULATE CONCEPTION"

On March 25, 1858, four years after Pope Pius IX promulgated the document *Ineffabilis Deus* (December 8, 1854) declaring the immaculate conception of Mary as a dogma of the faith, our Lady said to Bernadette in reply to her query regarding who she was, "I am the immaculate conception." Considering these words in the private revelation received by Bernadette, one can muse on the depth of the intrinsic connection between who our Lady *is* as Virgin Mother and her *origin* as the decisively important foundation in which her total identity is rooted. So deep is this relation that the truth of her immaculate conception is not a mere fact concerning the manner of her origin that *was*, but *is* the very generative wellspring by which her total being and person usher forth and so is irrevocably ingredient to *who* she is as Virgin Mother. For Maximilian Kolbe, the truth of Mary's immaculate conception not only identifies this but also informs how one is invited to participate fully in this truth. In a circular letter he wrote in 1933 to the friar students of the order he belonged to, Maximilian shared the following:

> In her apparition in Lourdes the Immaculata did not say: "I have been immaculately conceived," but "I am the Immaculate Conception." With that, she determines not only the fact of the Immaculate Conception, but also the way in which that privilege belongs to her. Therefore, it is not some kind of casual feature, but a part of her very nature. She herself is the Immaculate Conception. As a result, she is such in us as well and transforms us into herself as immaculate beings. . . . She is the Mother of God, and also the Mother of God within us . . . and makes us gods and mothers of God, who generate Jesus Christ in the souls of men. . . . How sublime![1]

For Maximilian Kolbe, our Lady as the Immaculata continues to birth Christ in those who are open to this transformative embrace, allowing others to become, as it were, "immaculate beings." As we will see throughout this chapter, in addition to Mary's continued role in the life of the church, the immaculate conception of Mary uniquely enacts and recapitulates anthropological *origin* within pneumatic time, thus *illumined illustratively* theo-philosophically.

The doctrine of the immaculate conception, though formally defined only in 1854, found its doctrinal genesis in the medieval debates, particularly in the confrontation between Thomism and the subtle genius of John Duns Scotus. While Aquinas, committed to the universal necessity of Christ's atonement, found himself constrained by the inherited Augustinian paradigm, Scotus articulated a vision of grace so primordially prevenient that it preserved Mary from original sin *ab initio*—anticipating, rather than following, the redeeming act of Christ. This theological impasse, one seemingly locked in a dialectical tension between the necessity of redemption and the radical gratuity of prevenient grace, was resolved in a strikingly paradoxical manner by Pope Pius IX's *Ineffabilis Deus*. In defining the dogma, the pontiff simultaneously upheld the absolute mediation of Christ's redemptive work while affirming Mary's singular preservation from sin—thus dissolving the Scotist-Thomist debate not by favoring one over the other, but by elevating their common

1. As quoted in Fehlner, *Theologian of Auschwitz*, 136–37.

concern: the centrality of the cross. Mary's conception in grace was not apart from Christ's redeeming act but was its first and most perfect fruit, realized in her person before the event of Calvary but *eternally* dependent on its merits. In this way, the dogma affirmed what Scotus had already intuited and what Aquinas had not resolved: that redemption is not merely remedial but also preservative—a work of grace so complete that, in the singular case of Mary, it prevented the very occurence of sin.

The dogma teaches, "The Most Blessed Virgin Mary, at the first instant of her conception, by the singular grace and privilege of Almighty God and in view of the merits of Jesus Christ, the Savior of the human race, was preserved immune from all stain of original sin."[2] In articulating the inherent meaning of "conception," Ludwig Ott writes that this is to be understood as "*passive* conception," such that "the first moment of the conception is that moment of time in which the soul was created by God and infused into the bodily matter prepared by her parents." In addition, since the "essence of original sin consists formally . . . in the lack of sanctifying grace," our Lady, preserved from such a defect, "entered existence in the state of sanctifying grace," by which the "efficient cause" of such a conception is none other than "Almighty God."[3] The "meritorious cause," as is indicated in the dogma, is the proleptic application of the redemption procured by Christ—thus prevenient grace given—*redemptio praeservativa*. And since this is given in view of the great dignity she is to possess by becoming the Theotokos, the "final cause" of such a conception is made clear.[4] Notice, then, the temporal/eternal dynamic constitutive of this particular mystery: our Lady receives *proleptically*—in time from that *eternal moment* which *will* occur in *her future*—what her Son will merit through his sacrificial offering to the Father in the power and unity of the Spirit. Thus, *Lumen Gentium* states that Mary is "redeemed by reason of the merits of her Son and united to Him by a close and indissoluble tie, she is endowed with the high office and dignity of being the Mother of the Son of God, by which account she is also the beloved daughter of the Father and the temple of the Holy Spirit."[5] This is why the council fathers also declared, "It is no wonder therefore that the usage prevailed among the Fathers [of the church] whereby they called

2. Denzinger, *Sources of Catholic Dogma*, no. 1641.
3. Ott, *Fundamentals of Catholic Dogma*, 215; emphasis in original.
4. Ott, *Fundamentals of Catholic Dogma*, 216.
5. *LG* 53.

the mother of God *entirely holy and free from all stain of sin*, as though fashioned by the Holy Spirit and formed as a new creature."[6]

It is also part of the common teaching of the church (*sententia communis*) that, given her immaculate conception, our Lady was free from concupiscence. "Concupiscence cannot be reckoned among [Jesus and Mary] since it excites a person to commit acts which are materially contrary to God's Law, even where, through lack of assent, they are not formal sins. It would be incompatible with Mary's fullness of grace and her perfect purity and immaculate state to be subject to motions of inordinate desire."[7] In addition, a teaching proximate to faith (*sententia fidei proxima*) is that "in consequence of a Special Privilege of Grace from God, Mary was free from every personal sin during her whole life."[8] Thus, our Lady is free from the obscurity due to sin, both original and actual, and even free from the "motions of inordinate desire," which is the result of concupiscence (as Thomas Aquinas noted, though for different reasons since he did not hold to the immaculate conception, our Lady was free from the "seed of sin" [*fomes peccati*]).[9] This grants to our Lady a clarity and luminosity unlike any other creature, which is a dignity befitting both her *identity* as the Mother of God and her virginal *vocation*, and so she is rightly called in the Litany of Loreto "Mother most pure," "Mirror of justice," "Singular vessel of devotion," and "Queen conceived without original sin."[10]

This clarity and luminosity also mean that, unlike the rest of humanity (except for the sacred humanity of her Son), Mary's humanity is completely integrated and whole. Thus, if Christ is the perfect image of the Father (Col 1:15; Heb 1:3), then our Lady, fulfilling her complementary

6. *LG* 56; emphasis added.

7. Ott, *Fundamentals of Catholic Dogma*, 219.

8. Ott, *Fundamentals of Catholic Dogma*, 219.

9. Scheeben articulates the full significance of the privileges given to our Lady: "In the sense of the principles and considerations here formulated, the Church ascribes to the Mother of God, in contrast to the rest of mankind, three definite privileges: 1. Complete perpetual freedom from original sin, because of the sanctifying grace granted to Mary in her very conception; 2. Freedom from all the effects of original sin which, in one way or another, belong to the moral domain, i.e., from all inclination to sin, and in general, from all irregularity connected in the soul with the positive safeguarding against each, even the smallest, person sin; 3. Freedom from the reign of death, in so far as the latter is a consequence of original sin and the cause of the decomposition of the body; this freedom ensures the anticipated resurrection and glorification of the body" (*Mariology*, 28–29).

10. Vatican, "Litany of Loreto."

role as the second Eve, is the *perfect image of the Son* and so thoroughly models anthropological identity, vocation, origin, and end as one *in Christ*. Without competition, Mary, like her Son, is a perfect *icon* of the human being. This is why the French Dominican Édouard Hugon, OP, upon reflecting on the mutual eternal plan that they shared, compared our Lady and her Son in the following manner:

> But, as Jesus and Mary are united in the same eternal plan, and since God contemplated them in advance as part of the same design, *they are as the mold or mirror of one another*. There has never been a creature that so closely imitates and reproduces the beauty of Jesus as does the soul of Mary. *She is indeed the faithful mirror in which the soul of Jesus contemplates and recognizes itself*. She is therefore incomparably beautiful, and it was necessary indeed that the soul destined to bear all the marvels of grace herself already by the marvel of nature.[11]

The dogmatic truth of our Lady's conception indeed secures her as the perfect *icon* of the God-man, ever only as a mere creature, and so she is the center and channel of the highest aesthetic reality as a creature of God, who is the apex of creation. Thus, apart from Christ her Son, her beauty and glory are beyond comparison. Therefore, we can behold her (and, in a certain sense, we have no other choice but to do so!) as a true *icon* of God and humanity—a reality that is approximated only by the saints in varying lesser degrees. This stands over and against any temptation to render her an *idol* since the entirety of her reality, emanating from her origin, ever only points to God (since her immaculate conception is but a pure gift of grace preveniently given without synergistic participation on the side of creatureliness, which in turn renders all her subsequent acts truly free and thus hers, allowing for true synergistic participation vis-à-vis her lived existence). There, then, is no room for a Protestant critique against beholding Mary as *the* icon, either for fear of falling into idolatry or for somehow "limiting" or "taking away" God's action and glory, such a critique being the outcome of a theopanism[12]—which ironically loses sight of both the biblical God who upholds creaturely integrity in its

11. Hugon, *Mary, Full of Grace*, 8; emphasis added.

12. In the translator's introduction to *Analogia Entis*, John R. Betz offers an incisive response of the typical Protestant critique against an analogical metaphysics and so shows how real creaturely participation in God—a participation secured most perfectly in Our Lady through her immaculate conception, which allows her to be truly free in her integrity throughout her life— does not take away from God (John R. Betz, in Przywara, *Analogia Entis*, 1–15).

freedom (a freedom most secured for our Lady in the gift of her immaculate conception), and the human being as such, since God is viewed dialectically over and against human nature and human cooperation. Thus, the immaculate conception of our Lady allows us to reaffirm our thesis: we can *look* to Mary for a theo-philosophical anthropology.

That our Lady is a perfect icon of the God-man—and, so, an icon by way of *analogia entis* as described in our first chapter, since her life is the symphonic rhythm of the unspeakable union of God and humanity, and so an image of the unity in difference that is already the Trinity—all of creation is invited to behold her, to *gaze* upon her without fear of falling headlong into idolatry. She is the end upon which a longing gaze searches for the way *to* the Unconditioned. She is the gate *through* which glory is revealed. In her there is no room for an idolatrous quicksand but instead a bridge to the invisible *through* the visible. She is indeed, then, a true icon and not an idol.

Upon his phenomenological analysis of idols and icons, the philosopher Jean-Luc Marion identifies that the difference between gazing upon an *icon* and an *idol* is partly situated within the object itself. For while "the icon summons the gaze to surpass itself by never freezing on a visible, since the visible only presents itself here in view of the invisible," the idol "consigns the divine to the measure of human gaze," since "when the idol appears, the gaze has just stopped: the idol concretizes that stop."[13] For our Lady, her entire existence points ineluctably to the invisible Other and thus one's gaze is ever drawn onward—in and through her—into the infinite depth of God's loving economy so decisively revealed in her, established in her conception. The grace of her immaculate conception is the generative root that grounds and nourishes her entire being as one *solely for* and *from* God. This is why Mary could never be rendered an idol in and of herself since such a being—an idol—seeks to draw the gaze in upon itself as its end and culmination, rather than pointing only onward through it. Consider the following description of the idol's effect on the gaze by Marion:

> To stop the gaze: we could not do better than to say, to stop a gaze, allow it to rest (itself) in/on an idol, when it can no longer pass beyond. In this stop, the gaze ceases to overshoot and transpierce itself, hence it ceases to transpierce visible things, in order to pause in the splendor of one of them. No longer transpiercing itself, the gaze no longer pierces things, no longer

13. Marion, *God Without Being*, 18, 14, 11.

> sees them in transparency; at a certain point, it no longer experiences things as transparent—insufficiently weighted down by light and glory—and a last one finally presents itself as visible, splendid, and luminous enough to be the first to attract, capture, and fill it. This first visible will offer, for each gaze and in the measure of its scope, its idol. Idol—or the gaze's landing place.[14]

Our Lady's unmatched glorious luminosity and beauty as mere creature paradoxically leave no "landing place" for gaze to "stop" since her entire being is ordered toward God as one made ready to receive the gaze as a "transparent" being, like a stained glass window illumined by a higher light; God is glorious *in* his saints.

However, as Marion notes, "The gaze makes the idol, not the idol the gaze—which means that the idol with its visibility fills the intention of the gaze, which wants nothing other than to see."[15] He goes on to write,

> The gaze precedes the idol because an aim precedes and gives rise to that at which it aims. The first intention aims at the divine and the gaze strains itself to see the divine, to see it by taking it up into the field of the gazeable. The more powerfully the aim is deployed, the longer it sustains itself, the richer, more extensive, and more sumptuous will appear the idol on which it will stop its gaze.[16]

However, even though the intention "aims at the divine and the gaze strains itself to see the divine," such an intention—if eyes are given to see—will indeed be met with the *divine made visible*, the incarnate One, in the arms of our Lady. And while it is true that such a revealing of the divine as vulnerable babe, or as one crucified, with his Mother standing at the foot of the cross, is the height of paradox—and so such gazing never "arrives" at a beholding of the Unconditioned *without* flesh—the gaze will nevertheless find its proper resting place when seeking to behold its true end. This will occur if and only if the gaze is one of *faith* and thus reckons with the utter mystery and transcendence given in this enfleshed one, who is ever *with*, *in*, and *along* his Mother. This is why Marion states that "even presented by the icon, the invisible always remains invisible; it is not invisible because it is omitted by the aim (*invisable*), but because it is a matter of rendering visible this invisible as such—the unenvisageable."

14. Marion, *God Without Being*, 11.
15. Marion, *God Without Being*, 10–11.
16. Marion, *God Without Being*, 11.

Christ is the proper end of such a gaze that seeks God; our Lady—his Mother—is the *way* to that end; thus, a true *icon*, like her Son but in a different metaphysical register. "Whereas the idol results from the gaze that aims at it, the icon summons sight in letting the visible . . . be saturated little by little with the invisible."[17]

Mary's immaculate conception—which, as we will observe further below, is the condition of possibility for her maternal identity, virginal vocation, and glorious end—is the *root cause* of her unique status as an icon; she, ever only as a mere creature, is the highest possibility of beholding God *through* creatureliness (save the flesh of Christ, of which our Lady is the principle). This is why the following description of an icon by Marion applies fittingly to our Lady in a wonderfully unique manner:

> The icon regards us—it *concerns* us, in that it allows the intention of the invisible to occur visibly. Moreover, if man's gaze envisages the blind side of the first visible, or of its material consignment in the icon, he who sees it sees in it a face whose invisible intention envisages him. The icon opens in a face, where man's sight envisages nothing, but goes back infinitely from the visible to the invisible by the grace of the visible itself: instead of the invisible mirror [as in an idol], which sent the human gaze back to itself alone and censured the *invisable*, the icon opens in a face that gazes at our gazes in order to summon them to its depth. . . . The icon alone offers an open face, because it opens in itself the visible onto the invisible, by offering its spectacle to be transgressed—not to be seen, but to be venerated.[18]

The face of the Immaculata draws the gaze into the infinite depth of the invisible, as the invisible gazes back upon the gazes through the grace of visibility—substantiated by her conception—and so Mary as icon "can be measured only on the basis of the infinite depth of [her] face" since "the more [her] face becomes visible, the more the invisible intention whose gaze envisages us becomes visible." Thus, the Immaculata's countenance whose depth "opens to envisage, permits the icon to join the visible with the invisible, and this depth is joined itself with the intention." However, "the intention here issues from the infinity; hence it implies that the icon allows itself to be traversed by an infinite depth."[19] This is so for Mary in two ways: as *the* icon of the *imago Dei* as God incarnate, her Son; and as

17. Marion, *God Without Being*, 17.

18. Marion, *God Without Being*, 19; emphasis in original.

19. Marion, *God Without Being*, 20.

the gate by which the *imago Dei* appears concretely through the incarnation. Thus, beholding our Lady as a unique icon via her graced conception, the following additional lengthy quote undoubtably articulates her iconic nature:

> The icon recognizes no other measure than its own and infinite excessiveness [*démesure*]; whereas the idol measures the divine to the scope of the gaze of he who then sculpts it, the icon accords in the visible only a face whose invisibility is given all the more to be envisaged that its revelation offers an abyss that the eyes of men never finish probing. It is, moreover, in this sense that the icon comes to us from elsewhere: certainly not that it should be a question of recognizing the empirical validity of an icon "not made by the hands of men" but indeed of seeing that *ackeiropoiesis* in some way results necessarily from the infinite depth that refers the icon back to its origin, or that characterizes the icon as this infinite reference to the origin.[20]

Is it not the case that our Lady "comes to us from elsewhere" since her conception "results necessarily from the infinite depth that refers [her] back to [her] origin"? Indeed, this "infinite reference to the origin" is revealed precisely in her immaculate conception; she is a true icon. This being the case, not only does she reveal God uniquely, but also uniquely unfolds for us the anthropos as *imago Dei* as revealer of God—icon. So, while each person is a living icon albeit obscurely seen due to sin, only Mary perfectly unveils both God (as end) and humanity (as the dignified means to that transcendent end) as Immaculata, the one conceived without original sin, the Panagia—the all-holy one.

Since our Lady is the Immaculata, she uniquely reveals God and humanity in a coextensive manner as a mere creature. This is possible only because she is the one who is "full of grace"—a grace she received at the moment of her conception, and a grace that grows superabundantly throughout her life in response to her lasting fiat.[21] In reflecting on this grace, the Dominican Dom Xavier Perrin, OSB, states,

> This fullness is not simply an ornament, a covering or rich robe that one might place upon a very modest stand. *It is what she*

20. Marion, *God Without Being*, 21.

21. As Hugon states, "Mary, at her conception, attains God less than she does later when she conceives the Word of life. Thus, her initial grace is not a consummate grace. However, it is ever the preparation and foundation of the divine maternity" (*Mary, Full of Grace*, 8).

> *is in her deepest self. In perfect simplicity, her very being exists caught up by grace in a way innate to her, sanctified, divinized.* She is infinitely magnified in the original nuptials of a created participation in the divine nature.[22]

She *is* the immaculate conception; this grace is not a mere fact of her manner of coming into being but is, as stated above, constitutive of her personhood since it is the continual source of her foundational grace, the precondition for her maternal being, virginal vocation, and glorious end. Thus, "never has a creature corresponded so perfectly to the Creator's vision of beauty."[23] Therefore, she is uniquely an *icon* through her grace-filled conception; and this conception is no doubt the presupposition necessary for her immense dignity as Virgin Mother.

Clearly, then, we can note how our Lady's immaculate conception fashions her to be a unique icon, which, in turn, strengthens our thesis since we are called to look upon her *as an icon* to discover how she reveals a theo-philosophical anthropology. Since an icon, she uniquely showcases the intrinsic relation between God and humanity, substantiated by the metaphysics described in our first chapter, and so she indeed is an icon of a *theoanthropocosmic* synthesis. In addition, as icon Mary reveals how the gift of her grace-filled conception, her *origin*, is the essential cornerstone by which the entire edifice of her personhood is built. Thus, her *identity*, *vocation*, and *end* are radically situated in the truth of her immaculate conception as the necessary presupposition for the flowering of her being and person. As Édouard states, "From the first instant, Mary was marked as the Mother of God, and it was necessary that grace already dispose her in view of this destiny, that she receive the perfection of a future Mother of God." He goes on to state that "she did not yet have her supreme dignity [which she would receive in the incarnation], but she required a fitting preparation. In a word, her first sanctification had to be the foundation of the divine maternity."[24] This was necessary because without this initial grace, our Lady would have lacked the dignity befitting of the Theotokos.

> Was it possible that the temple where the Word would dwell be profaned for a single instant? Should not the Virgin receive, from the first moment, a preparation worthy of the future Mother of a God? The original disgrace would forever be reflected upon the

22. Perrin, *Radiance*, 9; emphasis added.
23. Perrin, *Radiance*, 9.
24. Hugon, *Mary, Full of Grace*, 21–22.

> Son. With what insolence could the Demon then say to Christ Jesus: "I defeated you once, for she from whom you received flesh was for an instant under my power."[25]

Thus,

> the initial grace, being the basis and the preparation for the divine maternity, must be proportioned to that dignity, since it is an axiom that every disposition is measured to the ultimate character for which it initiates and prepares. Here, the ultimate character, namely the divine maternity, is an incommensurable dignity that exceeds as does the infinite all the perfections and every dignity of creatures taken together. Therefore, the first sanctification, so as to have some bearing upon this dignity, even from afar, must surpass the gifts and graces of all creatures at once.[26]

Here we observe that in view of our Lady's *identity* and *vocation* as Virgin Mother of God, she was to receive a fitting conception as the necessary precondition for such an immense dignity. One might ask, given this unique origin of Mary, how then could her immaculate conception *illumine illustratively* anthropological origin as such? In what way, in other words, does her unmatched origin enact and recapitulate the "normal" origin of the *imago Dei*? To address this, we first need to unpack the intrinsic relation between the eternal and the temporal aspects of the origin of our Lady. In doing so, we will then be better positioned to see how Mary enacts and recapitulates the origin of anthropos.

## THE TEMPORAL/ETERNAL DYNAMIC OF THE IMMACULATE CONCEPTION

The immaculate conception of Mary possesses a twofold origination: it occurs *in time* ("at the first instant of conception") but is rooted *in an eternal decree*. As the council fathers of Vatican II state,

> The Father of mercies willed that the incarnation should be preceded by the acceptance of her *who was predestined to be the mother of His Son*, so that just as a woman contributed to death, so also a woman should contribute to life. That is true in outstanding fashion of the mother of Jesus, who gave to the

25. Hugon, *Mary, Full of Grace*, 18.
26. Hugon, *Mary, Full of Grace*, 25–26.

> world Him who is Life itself and who renews all things, and who was enriched by God with the gifts which befit such a role. *It is no wonder therefore that the usage prevailed among the Fathers whereby they called the mother of God entirely holy and free from all stain of sin, as though fashioned by the Holy Spirit and formed as a new creature.*[27]

As John Henry Newman notes concerning the state of our Lady, "Mary *never* was in this state [of original sin]; she was by the eternal decree of God exempted from it. . . . It was decreed, not that she should be *cleansed* from sin, but that she should, from the first moment of her being, be *preserved* from sin."[28] Moreover, Louis Bouyer notes that "Mary was not called, first to exist, then, subsequently, to be redeemed, but was created and redeemed at one and the same time."[29] It is in this way we can speak of our Lady's *origin* as having a twofold manner: occurring in time as the manifestation of an eternal decree—revealing the pneumatic time inherent in this mystery. That she was persevered from the stain at the *first instant* of her existence (and thus born "full of grace") signifies sharply the *eternal* cause of her unique conception, since this genesis could not be "natural." Thus, as Germanos of Constantinople articulates in a homily on the presentation of our Lady in the temple, "Accept her whom you have chosen, *predestined and sanctified* . . . , she whom you have chosen as a lily among the thorns of our unworthiness."[30] As Scheeben notes, "Hence it follows, how highly befitting to Mary is the privilege of the immaculate conception because of her original and hallowed destiny as Mother of God."[31]

By considering the twofold manner of our Lady's conception in the light of our thesis, we can begin to discern how Mary's utterly unique origin reveals the intrinsic relation between the eternal and temporal regarding human origination. For while God has *eternally* elected the anthropos to be "holy and blameless" in Christ (Eph 1:4–5), this is made manifest *in time* via the sacrament of holy baptism, bringing to pass the removal of the stain of original sin (as well as actual sin for those who receive the sacrament later in life) and the reception of new life in the Spirit. So, baptism is analogous to our Lady's immaculate conception—no

27. *LG* 56; emphasis added.

28. Newman, *Meditations on Mary*, 73–74; emphasis in original.

29. Bouyer, *Seat of Wisdom*, 104.

30. As quoted in Nichols, *There Is No Rose*, 49; emphasis added.

31. Scheeben, *Mariology*, 1:51.

doubt different in *mode*, *effect*, and *manner*, but nevertheless similar in that new life begins in grace *within* time—while also Mary's predestination is analogous to the predestined call of those elected in Christ. This is one of the reasons our Lady is the preeminent member of the church, while also being her Mother.[32] Therefore, the immaculate conception enacts and recapitulates anthropological origin, an origin rooted in eternity and actualized in time through grace.

## MARY'S IMMACULATE CONCEPTION ILLUMINATES ANTHROPOLOGICAL ORIGIN

Already we observe how our Lady *illumines* (grace/faith/theology) human origin. By reading her immaculate conception as an analogous correlate to the sacrament of baptism, we can see how she illuminates anthropological origin by revealing the initial sanctifying grace necessary for the actualization of anthropological vocation and identity—virginal and maternal—as well as the essential precondition needed for a glorious end. Her grace-filled conception reveals the necessity for the human being to be born of "water and the Spirit," to be "born again" in order to "see" and thus live (John 3).[33] That this is so also shows that the temporal

32. Reflecting on the deeply abiding connection between our Lady and the church, the council fathers write the following: "But while in the most holy Virgin the Church has already reached that perfection whereby she is without spot or wrinkle, the followers of Christ still strive to increase in holiness by conquering sin. And so they turn their eyes to Mary who shines forth to the whole community of the elect as the model of virtues. Piously meditating on her and contemplating her in the light of the Word made man, the Church with reverence enters more intimately into the great mystery of the Incarnation and becomes more and more like her Spouse. For Mary, who since her entry into salvation history unites in herself and re-echoes the greatest teachings of the faith as she is proclaimed and venerated, calls the faithful to her Son and His sacrifice and to the love of the Father. Seeking after the glory of Christ, the Church becomes more like her exalted Type, and continually progresses in faith, hope and charity, seeking and doing the will of God in all things. Hence the Church, in her apostolic work also, justly looks to her, who, conceived of the Holy Spirit, brought forth Christ, who was born of the Virgin that through the Church He may be born and may increase in the hearts of the faithful also. The Virgin in her own life lived an example of that maternal love, by which it behooves that all should be animated who cooperate in the apostolic mission of the Church for the regeneration of men" (*LG* 65).

33. Since our Lady's conception is the necessary condition for her virginal maternity and glorious assumption, and since, according to our thesis, she is the revealed cipher for anthropology, then baptism, as the analogous correlate to her conception, is the essential means by which the maternal being, virginal vocation, and glorious, ineffable end of the human being as such is realized. As the catechism states, "The whole

origins of anthropos—the waters of baptism—are decisively rooted in an eternal election since such a birth is "not of blood or of the will of the flesh or of the will of man, but of God" (John 1:13). Thus, Mary's immaculate conception illuminates human origin—human birth as "from above" (eternal) via the waters of baptism (in time).

Anthropological origin, illumined by our Lady's immaculate conception, is manifestly tied to the predestined origin and eschatological completion of the church as such. Enacted in time in each person (through the sacrament of baptism), the church finds her culminating holiness in the eschatological age. Nevertheless, she already finds this locus in her type in Mary, who is given the gift of her immaculate state at the beginning of her life rather than the end. As Ratzinger notes, "God does not act with abstractions or concepts; the *type*, of which the ecclesiology of the New Testament and the Fathers speak, exists as a *person*."[34] The originating source of holiness is Christ, which is applied preveniently to our Lady, preserving her, and applied to the church after the objective redemption procured on the cross. However, both the members of the church and our Lady receive this grace *in time* as the actualization of what is *predestined*. As Louis Bouyer states,

> The Virgin "without spot or wrinkle" (Eph. 5:27), to be presented to Christ at the end of time, is the Church; but Mary, at the beginning of the new epoch, is already this Virgin without stain. She is, thus, the promise already fulfilled, the pledge already actualized, of what all of us together are to become. She is, as it were, the living Image, present within time, of what will be brought about in us all only at the end of time. Though unique and pre-eminent she is yet the image of what we have to become, and so her sublime sanctity, from this point of view also, is seen to be part of the preparation and promise. . . . The Church, then, will extend, in a way, to the whole world what is now the exclusive privilege of Mary. By contrast, what Mary and the Church, in its final state, will possess in common has, with her, a pre-eminent dignity. The glory of each derives wholly from their union with Christ, their intimate association with the found and fulness of holiness.[35]

---

organism of the Christian's supernatural life has its roots in Baptism" (Catholic Church, *Catechism*, §1266).

34. Ratzinger, *Daughter Zion*, 68; emphasis in original.

35. Bouyer, *Seat of Wisdom*, 128–29.

In Bouyer's reckoning the church collectively arrives, so to speak, at the level of holiness akin to our Lady only eschatologically. As Manfred Hauke states, "The perfect holiness of Mary helps us to understand in its depth the holiness of the *church*, which is 'holy and immaculate' (Eph 5:27). This purity does not find full expression in the other members of the church, who continually need to confess that they are sinners. Mary, free of any sin, is the type of the church and assurance of its unshakable holiness."[36] Nevertheless, in a real and certain sense, such a holiness—and thus, a real *origin in holiness*—already begins *in time* for each member of the church, which is why the New Testament ascribes to Christians the title "saints," a title only ever possible through baptismal regeneration as the means by which the anthropos comes to pass. Again, we behold the intrinsic association between the origin that occurs in the temporal stream and that "origin," so to speak, established in the eternal election—predestined/eschatological. Therefore, the link between our Lady and the church within the context of a shared holiness in both origin and end, the source and summit of which is always in Christ, reveals the basis by which the human being as such truly comes to be: in holiness, in time, and as the temporal manifestation of that eternal election.[37]

Despite the frailty of human flesh, the true anthropos is born through the waters of baptism. This frailty no doubt continues post baptism, and the need for the sacrament of reconciliation and the continued strength afforded by the Eucharist are essential for the human being to perdure without destruction. Nevertheless, one could read analogously the elevation of nature by grace that occurs in baptism with that of our Lady's nature being supernaturally elevated by means of her grace-filled conception. Just as our Lady's conception presupposes the "ordinary"

36. Hauke, *Introduction to Mariology*, 234; emphasis in original.

37. In a document by the Pontifical International Marian Academy, the following articulates the decisive relationship drawn out between Mary and the church, and of each member through the sacrament of baptism: "The Church sees Mary in Ephesians 5:25–27, the marvelous account of Christ's love for his spouse, the Church. 'Christ loved the church. He gave himself up for her to make her holy, to present to himself a glorious church, holy and immaculate, without stain or wrinkle or anything of that sort.' The spousal and filial character of God's people, of which Mary is the personification and the perfect image, includes not only the ecclesial community as such, but also each of its members; the reading (Eph 1:3–6, 11–12) for the Mass for 8 December, recalls that the Father 'has blessed us in Christ with every spiritual blessing in the heavens, as he chose us in him, before the foundation of the world, to be holy and without blemish before him' (cf. Eph 1:3–5). Viewed in this way, *baptism, the immersion into the Paschal Mystery of Christ (cf. Rm 6:3–5), corresponds sacramentally to Mary's Immaculate Conception*" (*Mother of the Lord*, 52; emphasis added).

nature received through the conjugal act of her parents, so too baptismal regeneration presupposes the "ordinary" nature that is to be elevated by means of the grace of this sacrament, a nature (together with *personhood*) that is completed and thus "born again" through grace.[38] As John of Damascus beautifully articulates in his oration on the nativity of Mary,

> Nature has been defeated by grace and stands trembling, no longer ready to take the lead. Therefore when the God-bearing Virgin was about to be born from Anna, nature did not dare to anticipate the offshoot of grace; instead it remained without fruit until grace sprouted its fruit. . . . O blessed couple, Joachim and Anna, all nature is indebted to you! . . . O most all-blessed loins of Joachim, from which a *wholly unblemished seed was sent forth*! O renowned womb of Anna, in which slowly, with additions from her, *an all-holy infant grew, and once it had taken shape, was born*![39]

Here, John expresses poetically how Mary's nature is not destroyed but elevated by grace such that a "wholly unblemished seed" was given and "an all-holy infant grew" by way of the conjugal union of Joachim and Anna. So while it is true that Mary "was never subject to original sin" and thereby was "redeemed in a manner more sublime," as Pope Pius IX states,[40] the gift of her conception illuminates the decisive importance—the necessity, really—of a graced origin that allows for the anthropos to truly spring into being; an origin that doesn't disregard or negate nature as such but elevates and transforms it by heightening and fulfilling its integrity. That Mary's nature is brought about "naturally" through the marital act of her parents means she is very close to the rest of humanity, who are born through baptism despite the frailty and weakness found within human nature.

38. As Cabasilas states, "'New birth' and 'new creation' mean nothing else than that those who are born and created have been born previously and have lost their original form, but now return to it by a second birth. It is as when the material of a statue has lost its shape and a sculptor restores and refashions the image, since it is a form and shape effected in us by Baptism. It engraves an image and imparts a form to our souls by conforming them to the death and resurrection of the Savior" (*Life in Christ*, 67). This coincides with the description offered in the catechism of the Catholic Church: "Baptism not only purifies from all sins, but also makes the neophyte 'a new creature,' an adopted son of God, who has become a 'partaker of the divine nature,' member of Christ and co-heir with him, and a temple of the Holy Spirit" (Catholic Church, *Catechism*, §1265).

39. John of Damascus, "Nativity of Holy Theotokos," 54–55; emphasis added.

40 Pius IX, *Ineffabilis Deus*, s.vv. "Testimonies of the Catholic World."

This is why any thought of Mary's immaculate conception as possibly alienating her from the rest of humanity is simply unwarranted. In fact, it is by virtue of her unique conception that she is *fully* human (for human nature devoid of grace always tends toward dehumanization) and so she, along with her Son but in a different mode, really and truly reveals what it means to be human[41] and, specifically in this context, really and truly *illumines* the immaculate origin of the anthropos. In addition, our Lady's conception *actualizes* the level of holiness that the human being as such is oriented toward eschatologically but already begins *now* through the sacramental grace of baptism. Thus, Mary is both model and goal by which the anthropos discovers her origin and end *in* holiness. She is the fundamental paradigm by which the graced origin and end of the human being is unveiled. "Mary's Immaculate Conception is a forceful sign of God's grace operative within a creature: Gift of the Trinity's love, this grace allowed Mary, with her liberty rooted in grace, to live her life of freely welcoming love without limit."[42] Manfred Hauke explains:

> In the *anthropological* context, Mary Immaculate strengthens man, who finds himself on a journey and in struggle. She shows that the new existence is not a dream, but finds its perfect realization in a human person, in Mary. Freedom from sin does not distance the Immaculate from spiritual struggles because the disastrous character of evil is felt more profoundly by the saints. Help to overcome sin does not come from us, but from a greater holiness. The sign raised up with the Immaculate Conception shows "that man as willed by God, the 'ideal' man, so to speak, is man without guilt. So sin is not part . . . of man's nature. The human journey in the world and in history does not necessarily pass through sin."[43]

Thus, despite the facticity of sin that is found between the times (since the reign of holiness is *here* but *not yet*), Mary reveals that the human being has an immaculate origin, by way of both the eternal election and the temporal origin in and through the cleansing waters of regeneration

41. "The doctrine means that the Virgin of Nazareth fulfilled in herself the human condition which God wished: She was a woman oriented toward that which was on high, not bent over by the weight of sin; she was not enclosed in herself but open to the love of God, to the love of humanity, to the love of creation" (Pontifical International Marian Academy, *Mother of the Lord*, 53).

42. Pontifical International Marian Academy, *Mother of the Lord*, 53.

43. Hauke, *Introduction to Mariology*, 234; quoting Leo Scheffczyk, *Maria, crocevia della fede cattolica*; emphasis in original.

and rebirth. Mary's immaculate conception not only illumines the origin of anthropos in holiness by grace but also uncovers the necessity of a sustained holiness for the dynamic unfolding of authentic humanization. Reading this as the analogous correlate to baptism we are able to view the necessity, then, of this sacrament for both the *birth* and *flourishing* of the anthropos (no doubt a flourishing only ever possible through the frequent use of the sacrament of confession, which strengthens and recovers our baptismal grace, along with a frequent participation in the Eucharist coupled with a life of ascesis); as the Byzantine theologian Nicholas Cabasilas states, "The Mystery [of Baptism] is the beginning of the life in Christ, and causes men to *exist, live, and excel in true life and being*."[44] This is why in considering the complete humanity of our Lady in view of her grace-filled conception, the Pontifical International Marian Academy identifies a twofold way in which Mary truly illumines the human being:

> The doctrine means that the Mother of Jesus is the mirror of the two dimensions of existence. The Virgin, although full of grace (cf. Lk 1:28), was not exempted from the human condition of suffering, darkness, inner struggle, and sorrow. As disciple, Mary had to grow in faith, to overcome in hope difficult trials, to direct her virginal love to God, to Joseph of Nazareth, to her Son Jesus, to the ecclesial community, to all men and women, her brothers and sisters. But it also means that Mary presents the truest and most beautiful form of human existence, free from deception and turmoil; bright with the splendor of truth and goodness; radiant with the beauty of harmony and perfection, simplicity and transparency.[45]

So, while it is indeed true that the gift of her conception renders her the "truest and most beautiful form of human existence," this gift is also the precondition needed for her dignity as virginal Mother, which she would eventually fulfill and complete through her continued yes to God throughout her life. What the immaculate conception does not do is shield our Lady from the existential particularities of the postlapsarian state (except from concupiscence and other such privileges). Indeed, she "was not exempted from the human condition of suffering, darkness, inner struggle, and sorrow," and she "had to grow in faith."

Now we can see with greater clarity how our Lady illumines human origin through the grace of her immaculate conception. Through

44. Cabasilas, *Life in Christ*, 101; emphasis added.

45. Pontifical International Marian Academy, *Mother of the Lord*, 53–54.

an analogical reading of (1) our Lady's predestined call with the general predestined election of anthropos in Christ, (2) immaculate conception in time with the sacramental grace of baptism enacted in time, and (3) the nature that is presupposed and elevated by grace in Mary as it is in the anthropos who undergoes baptism, we observe the fitting way in which our Lady's unique origin *illuminates* the necessity of a graced origin in holiness for the human being as such, predestined but temporally realized. We can now proceed to examine how Mary also *illustrates* (nature/reason/philosophy) the immaculate origin of anthropos. As we have seen thus far in our previous chapters, a philosophical consideration of our Lady in view of the anthropos should yield further insights from the side of creatureliness as does a theological exploration from the side of grace.

## MARY'S IMMACULATE CONCEPTION ILLUSTRATES ANTHROPOLOGICAL ORIGIN

As stated in our previous chapters, since our Lady, like her Son though in a distinct way, is the non-reductive expression of the human being—and so, as mere creature, is the archetypal expression of the suspended middle, complementing Christ, who is that expression as God—there is ample room to explore philosophically her immaculate conception in view of the question concerning the origin of anthropos, as it remains open to what has been pondered by theology. This will allow us to consider how our Lady's origin *illustrates* (nature/reason/philosophy) in an explicative mode what is decisively revealed—*illumined*—by grace.

This grace elevates and perfects nature, presupposing it as a definitive given that is ever open to the transformative embrace of grace given superaddedly,[46] as our Lady shows in an iconic fashion via her grace-filled conception. Her nature is not destroyed but is truly perfected by the grace of her conception. *Gratia non destruit, sed supponit et perficit naturam.*[47] Curiously, then, this is why it could be said in a comparable manner that theology in some sense presupposes philosophy (and faith, reason) not only as a response to the questions explicitly asked by philosophy (reason), but also as an address to the question implied by its

46. As stated in our first chapter and understood in view of *analogia entis*, nature is *gift* given and sustained freely by God (as a finite, contingent creaturely reality) and thus is already grace in a nonidentical, non-repetitive way; yet nature is truly its own and so *is* nature.

47. Grace does not destroy but supposes and perfects nature.

very being. Yet, with Maurice Blondel, we can also say that philosophy "presupposes" or, better put, is prepared for and oriented toward theology, by way of a humble unearthing—as philosophy excavates and thus discovers the need for theology to bring about what philosophy cannot on its own accomplish—as nature/reason is prepped and oriented toward grace/faith as its perfection without destroying its creaturely integrity. In a manner of speaking, then, we can say that both theology and philosophy (revealing the necessity of their union without mixture, confusion, or separation) presuppose each other, albeit not symmetrically, in a way analogous to our Lady's grace-filled conception, which (1) reveals the perfection of her nature by grace—thus the need for grace *for* nature, yet paradoxically surprised by grace's gratuitous *vertical* descent—while at the same time (2) her nature at the first instance of her conception is really presupposed by grace, thus the presumption of nature *by* grace despite the distinction between the *horizontal* reality of nature and the *verticality* of grace. In this one could discern Mary's immaculate conception as an *icon* of the coextensive relationality of theology and philosophy, faith and reason, and nature and grace. If this, we can then also begin to sketch out a path by which we can readily observe how her conception specifically *illustrates* human origin *from the side of creatureliness* that is ever open to the verticality of grace. But first, let us consider more broadly the relationship between theology and philosophy in view of our Lady's conception. By reading Mary's nature as the creaturely correlate to philosophy, and her salvation by preservation as the gracious correlate to theology, our thesis will be strengthened, showing that Mary does indeed *illumine illustratively* (*theo-philosophically*) anthropology.

The philosopher Emmanuel Falque muses on the interpenetrative (without confusion or separation) relationship between theology and philosophy, arguing their mutually edifying presence with respect to each. In light of the above, this can be read loosely as analogous to the graced conception of Mary who, through grace, has her nature perfected, while the grace received is already presupposed in view of the great dignity she is to possess as Virgin Mother, also while this grace as illumination is such vis-à-vis nature and so revealing the *Giver* of grace uniquely. Thus, as Falque states, "theology renews itself by means of philosophy, although theology is never content to use philosophy, but to transform it through and through."[48] In our Lady, grace, in a manner of speaking, "renews it-

48. Falque, *Crossing the Rubicon*, 125.

self" by means of her nature insofar as it is brought to light by means of its *illuminating* power upon nature—while nature, then, *illustrates* grace vis-à-vis its "embodiment" of grace—all the while transforming nature "through and through." Nevertheless, "between philosophy and theology a *difference* must be maintained between (a) their ways, (b) their modes of proceeding, and (c) the status of the objects to be analyzed, while at the same time recognizing (d) the possible and paradoxical *community* of objects given to thought."[49] This recognized difference in unity between the two disciplines has been the presumption throughout this project as we behold our Lady theo-philosophically in view of anthropology, and it is a supposition that is reinforced by means of the very gift of our Lady's immaculate conception. Therefore, by taking contingency seriously *from the side of creatureliness*, the philosopher qua philosopher considers, by means of a certain heuristic approach, only what is *possible*—recognizing, among other things, the proper delineated "boundaries" given within the facticity of finitude—while the theologian qua theology receives what is *actual*, revealed and thus received by faith. As Falque notes,

> The philosopher [qua philosopher] does not actually believe in the Incarnation, the Eucharist, or the Resurrection—as they are revealed—apart from within the framework of theology itself. Theology opens itself, and paradoxically so, all the more to philosophy as it fears no damage to the actuality of the phenomenon due to the philosophical investigation: it allows its possibility [a "possibility" to the philosopher qua philosopher, but an "actuality" to the theologian qua theologian] to be analyzed by others.[50]

This is why the "force of theology as a discourse beginning with God does not hinder philosophy as a discourse on the God-phenomenon appearing to the human."[51] In fact, by providing philosophy with content "from above," philosophy, although receiving it only as a *possibility*, is nevertheless transfigured, paradoxically fulfilling without destroying its integrity as a discipline. Thus, just as Mary is the supreme and highest creature of God in and through the grace she received in view of her unique dignity, so too is philosophy elevated as theology is in and beyond philosophy analogically.[52] Thus, "we must theologize if we want to truly philoso-

49. Falque, *Crossing the Rubicon*, 125; emphasis in original.

50. Falque, *Crossing the Rubicon*, 126.

51. Falque, *Crossing the Rubicon*, 127.

52. See ch. 1 for the details concerning the analogical metaphysics underpinning this.

phize, at least when philosophy claims to reach theology's threshold."[53] Analogously, the anthropos is paradoxically completed and made whole by means of grace; Mary's nature, especially in view of her vocation—a vocation we all share analogously (ch. 3)—is indeed substantiated by the grace of her conception. Therefore, the "starting points are all the more *philosophical* when the endpoints are *theological*,"[54] akin to how our Lady's nature received "naturally" from the beginning is simultaneously perfected in integrity by grace coincident with her beginning; her nature is thus even more truly *nature* because of the *grace* she received. In short, Mary's grace-filled conception mysteriously points to the joint expression and collaboration between theology and philosophy in their respective mutually informing modes.

All of this, then, strengthens our resolve to continue to approach our Lady in view of those questions in anthropology both theologically and philosophically, doing so with the recognition that philosophy is elevated (and so truly made *philo-sophia*) by means of the datum of revelation given in our Lady. This in turn strengthens our theological exploration of those questions inherent in anthropology, in view of Mary, as theology is increasingly served by philosophy without its collapse or disintegration. Let us, then, now turn to our Lady's immaculate conception to observe how her conception specifically *illustrates* human origin from the side of creatureliness that is ever open to the verticality of grace.

Reckoning with the weight of finitude, philosophy observes that our Lady's origin in grace does not in any way negate her conditioned state as a contingent being. She is indeed human, all too human (ever more so precisely through *grace*). Receiving from the datum contemplated by theology in *faith*, Catholic philosophy opened to the presuppositions of that same faith receives in awareness the truth that the immaculate conception does not immunize our Lady from the existential particularities of the postlapsarian state (except, as stated earlier, from concupiscence and other such privileges in view of her great dignity); neither does it somehow remove the facticity of her contingency and finitude. Quite the opposite. It is precisely through her grace-filled conception that we can behold with proper clarity the creaturely being as such without the sort of obscurity or blinding spectacle that emanates from a creature that seeks to usurp its own contingency. Mary, as mere creature, perfectly embraces

53. Falque, *Crossing the Rubicon*, 149.

54. Falque, *Crossing the Rubicon*, 149; emphasis in original.

her limits, her finitude, unlike the first Eve, who transgressed those limits. Heidegger suggests, "In order to designate the finite in human beings it might suffice to cite any of our imperfections. In this way," he says, "we gain, at best, evidence for the fact that the human being is a finite creature."[55] While our Lady is "imperfect" to the degree that she is not God, she nevertheless—and by virtue of the grace received from God—is altogether *the* perfect creature *of* God by virtue of her total embrace of her identity and vocation accomplished in God, which is a *total embracing of her limits under* and *for* God, making her the freest and most perfect of God's creatures (save the flesh of Christ himself). Thus, by the grace of her conception, her finitude is ever secured.

With her creaturely finitude secured by means of grace, philosophy can advance by exploring how our Lady's immaculate conception *illustrates* (nature/reason/philosophy) human origin from the side of creatureliness that is ever open to the verticality of grace. It can do so by asking the following: In what way might the human being as such imply the need for a transcendent origin (that is, in and through grace), an origin that simultaneously confirms and presupposes an "immanent" origin (that is, nature)? Can reason perceive an implicit, inherent need for a *vertical* origin coincident with the *horizontal* origin of nature, and thus the perfecting of anthropological nature? The question of "need" is asked in the Blondelian spirit: "We see thereby how we have to excavate within ourselves the place where the supernatural solution will come to fill the abyss."[56]

Taking what we have discovered so far in this project, philosophy can begin to realize a profound *incompleteness*—an "abyss"—native to the human being *if* a vertical beginning, a graced origin, does *not* occur. Since, as we observed in our second chapter, anthropological *identity* is *maternal*, and since it is coextensive with anthropological *vocation* being *virginal*, as discerned in our third chapter—both the intimations of which are gestured toward according to our philosophical reading of our Lady in chapters 2–3—then a *vertical* origination is needed for the possibility of both human identity and human vocation to be actualized. (The human must be *born* to possess an *identity* and *vocation*!) This is so because a graced, transcendent origin in addition to its *horizontal* (nature) beginning is *implied* for the human *if* human identity as maternal is the *locus of*

55. Heidegger, "Possible Determination of Finitude," §39.

56. Blondel, *Philosophical Exigencies*, 21.

*union between the infinite and finite* as *finitude containing the infinite* (ch. 2); and *if* human vocation (virginal) is an *eschatologically oriented exocentricity* (ch. 3). Given that the vocational structure is exocentric—the eternal, transcendent One is to be the "center" of a contingent being whose identity is maternal pertaining to this infinite, transcendent Other—then this one must have a *graced origin*, born from above, as it were, since both its identity and vocation transcend its contingency paradoxically. To put it differently, if anthropological identity and vocation are uniquely inscribed by means of a transcendent, eternal Reality who is both their center and end as the One who desires to be "all in all," this, then, signals, in the most significant way, the need for a *transcendent origin* since this creature "naturally" could never arrive at either fulfilling its identity or vocation. This creature—the anthropos—then must have a supernatural origin whose foundation supports its (maternal) being and (virginal) vocation transcendently; thus, as theology observes, "no one can enter the kingdom of God without being born of water and Spirit" (John 3:5).

Given that the maternal identity and virginal vocation of the anthropos is definitively shaped by a transcendent Source, philosophy discerns a necessarily "higher" and "deeper" origination that constitutes the foundational structure of the human being without destroying its nature but elevating it to obtain the capacities ingredient to its (transcendent) identity and vocation. Such a transcendent identity and vocation, then, presuppose in a fitting manner a transcendent origin; the weight of glory revealed in anthropological identity/vocation (vis-à-vis theology, but only by way of intimations and gestures discoverable via philosophy), as it is observed in our Lady, would be too much to bear if anthropos were somehow *not* from above. Recognizing a proportionality, the degree to which human *being* and *vocation* are decisively rooted in and oriented toward this Other is the degree to which human *origin* must find its locus in this same Other, who is God. Its being and call point to this creature's higher origination.

In addition, such a philosophic reckoning of anthropos would conclude that this transcendent ground/origin must somehow be enacted *in time* given its finitude, which could ever only point to a *predestined* "origin" in the transcendent One. Thus, taking this into account philosophy could in fact begin to perceive, as a *possibility* (qua philosophy), the temporal/eternal dynamic inherent in human origin, thus recognizing hints of pneumatic time. In other words, if the human being is to be somehow "born from above" in concert with its *horizontal* ("natural") facticity, then the eternal must somehow be coincident with true temporal becoming for the anthropos to truly fulfill its vocation and identity. This is how our Lady *illustrates* (nature/reason/philosophy) the kind of beginning needed for the human being for such a creature to truly enact its authentic *identity* by means of this yes to its high *call*.

So, what we have here, in view of our Lady, is the (philosophic) "discovery"—a discovery of *intimations* and *gestures* from the side of philosophy alone, but more so a deeper discovery when philosophy is truly open to the datum of revelation—of a certain origin needed that corresponds proportionately to the specific *call* and *identity* uniquely inscribed in anthropos. A certain type of "equipping" or "augmentation," if you will, is clearly necessary for such a creature whose contingency is to become the home of the transcendent One. Clearly, though, a *naked* contingency, a *naked* finitude—that is to say a creatureliness devoid of transcendent (vertical and so, utterly surprisingly, paradoxically) *grace*—cannot on its own become the abode of the transcendent in a substantially existential way (that is, in addition to the fact that creatureliness as such is already sustained in and upheld by the eternal, transcendent One). The true identity and vocation of the human being, then, constitutes a sign of profound limitation ever while pointing to something greater than its inherent limits; thus, the *naked* human, then, is doomed to an existential frustration because of its inability to transcend this limit, unless this creature is somehow reconstituted to a "higher" order, which, in this sense, would be utterly gratuitous (since it arrives, as it were, from the "outside"). Like Adam's discovery of his own nakedness, the human, in the face of this profoundly glorious *call* and *identity* will seek to both clothe itself (a symbol, here, as the futile attempt to do what on his own he cannot) and hide (here symbolized as the inability to answer the *call* according to his true *identity*—Adam, "Where are you?" [Gen 3]). But, as Genesis reveals, only God can truly clothe and thus reinstate the human as such, creating the conditions necessary to fill its task as anthropos. Since this existential frustration is inevitable without recourse to a transcendent "birth," philosophy, then, would on its own terms recognize this as a sort of metaphorical "new birth" from "above" since this needed reconstitution utterly transfigures the contingent, finite creature to fulfill *without destroying* its very end. A philosophy closed off to the possibility of the transcendent, however, will forever be haunted by the inklings and rumblings that emanate from the subtle intimations discernible to a probing mind and aching heart, and will thus attempt to construct its own systems, thoughts, movements (the "figs") that could potentially respond to such quivers, but which will result in utter futility.

In thinking about other potential ways in which a transcendent birth is hinted in anthropos, one might perhaps even consider the human desire *for* transcendence and permanence, a desire that seeks to overcome the existential facticity of its *horizontal* constitution, which is given over to flux, impermanence, and thus remains as an ever-present reminder that any such grasping *on the side of creatureliness alone* is vain and fruitless. In view of this, philosophy could ask, "Whence does this desire come?" Is it wishful thinking, a desire to escape what anthropos cannot? Or does it indicate a corresponding truth: Does the desire indeed find its fulfillment *in* the transcendent/eternal? A Nietzschean resignation is optional; a stoic resolve is too. Or, perhaps, the very desire indicates something paradoxical about the human: anthropos yearns for, longs for its true *home*—a home that is indeed transcendent, eternal, even though the human is *horizontally* constituted as a conditioned, finite being. Perhaps, the philosopher may muse, there is a mystery here, at the very heart of this perennial desire, that reason itself cannot penetrate. Perhaps it points to something *more*—a more that, in principle, cannot be achieved on *this side of creatureliness*. In the face of this mystery, one can either accept, on the grounds of nihilism, that there is nothing that can be done, or one can "hope against hope" by looking up, humbly opening oneself to the possibility that this desire does not signify an inescapable contradiction within the heart of anthropos but instead signifies the paradoxical presence of the truth that the human being is made for this *more* precisely because it somehow mysteriously ushers forth from this *home*, which, perhaps, can be enacted in time. *Exitus et reditus*.

This "abyss" that philosophy encounters reveal the ways in which anthropos inherently implies and so gestures toward a *vertical* origin somehow coincident with its *horizontal* being. This discovery made by philosophy is in the mode of excavation, a digging around to discover what nature *on its own* paradoxically needs for its fulfillment. This is why Maurice Blondel states,

> Let no one say then that it is ridiculous and useless to put so much effort into indicating such an emptiness, into proving such an abyss: the acknowledgment of this impossibility the philosopher finds himself in of completing himself, of tying thought and life into one another, is on the contrary the highest service reason can render; and the Christian spirit, which has no greater

> enemy than the false sufficiency of egoistic autonomy, has no better auxiliary than this sense of mystery and of humility. God, says Scripture, loves empty vases in which to pour Himself. And it is already a beautiful role to have to shape and to purify these vases of nature and of man that to contain the divine presence.[57]

It is here, then, that the philosopher qua philosopher, echoing Blondel, can affirm only the *hypothetical* necessity of the *vertical* for the *horizontal* to be completed. As Fr. Cathal Doherty, SJ, states, "This supernatural complement is 'hypothetical' because philosophical reasoning reaches its limits here. Human reason can demonstrate only that a supernatural complement is necessary and that human action would be its receptacle."[58] This is to be carefully maintained if (orthodox) Catholic theology is to remain intact and philosophy qua philosophy is to maintain its integrity. As Blondel notes,

> For if one tries to begin with the supernatural, treating it as a factual datum, one would be abandoning philosophy. If one tried to produce the supernatural from natural premises as an apodeictic conclusion, an undertaking which has been condemned under the name of semi-rationalism, one would be abandoning orthodoxy.[59]

Again, however, this does not in any way mean a divorce between theology and philosophy, but rather a mutual synergistic participation and co-operation.

> Both the one and the other demand a separation of competences; they remain distinct from one another, but distinct in view of an effective cooperation: *non adjutrix nisi libera: non libera nisi adjutrix philosophia* (philosophy is not a helper unless it is free and not free unless it is a helper). The fullness of philosophy consists, not in a presumptuous self-sufficiency, but in the study of its own powerlessness and of the means which are offered from elsewhere to supply for its powerlessness.[60]

Thus, while our Lady no doubt reveals—*illumines*—the *verticality* of human origination, she also, by means of this same truth though perceived *on the side of creatureliness* via philosophy, *illustrates* this by inviting the

57. Blondel, *Philosophical Exigencies*, 21.
58. Doherty, *Maurice Blondel*, 119.
59. Blondel, *Letter on Apologetics*, 138–39.
60. Blondel, *Action*, 361–62.

philosopher to "look again" at the anthropos to carefully discern its implicit *identity* and *vocation*, along with its perennial desire for the *more*. Taken as a whole, philosophy then humbly receives what according to its own resources cannot produce. As Fr. Doherty notes, in view of Blondel,

> What revelation brings to philosophy, then, is not some kind of arbitrary "excess baggage" or even worse a repression of reason. On the contrary, Blondel claims that religious dogma brings real solutions to philosophical enigmas. That is, the Christian mysteries provide their own lights for the philosopher and assure that philosophy remains "open," not only through internal intellectual coherence but also by a co-operation comparable to a sort of conjugal union, or "symbiosis." What may seem like an impasse for reason can, in fact, turn out to be a passage opened by Revelation.[61]

This is why philosophy ought not to fear such an opening to *verticality*. Philosophy does not surrender its claim as *philo-sophia* but instead finds its fulfillment therein. It is through the limit, the "abyss," that *verticality* both confirms and addresses transcendently what is in fact discoverable to reason *horizontally*. As Blondel notes,

> If as soon as philosophy touches on the simple *notion* of the supernatural [*verticality*] one dreads an abuse of power or a confusion of competences, it is because one knows nothing of the *essence* of this supernatural itself. Being above everything we can suspect or hope for [qua philosophy], this mystery, far from dreading the encroachment of thought, opens up for it an infinite quarry, without thought ever being able to attain it. To be sure, in what faith proposes, all is not inaccessible to our efforts; and in what reason can discover, there is a part covered and confirmed by revelation. But beyond all advances of human science and virtue, there is a truth impenetrable to any philosophical view, a good higher than any aspiration of the will.[62]

Thus, the *noncompetitive* and so synergistic partnership of theology and philosophy, grace and nature, faith and reason. All this is *illustrated* (nature/reason/philosophy) via our Lady as it is *illuminated* by her too. The *horizontal* is fulfilled paradoxically by *verticality*, in imitation of Mary's immaculate conception. And it is this, the *necessary* precondition for the enactment and fulfillment of anthropological *identity* and *vocation*—ever

61. Doherty, *Maurice Blondel*, 122.

62. Blondel, *Action*, 374–75; emphasis in original.

only observed as a *hypothetical* option qua philosophy considering the mysterious intimations and gestures implicit in human identity, vocation, and its corresponding desire—that Mary's grace-filled conception *illumines illustratively* the *vertical* origination of anthropos.

## CONCLUSION: ANTHROPOLOGICAL ORIGIN

In this chapter we examined how Mary distinctively reveals (*illumines*) and presents (*illustrates*) the decisive response to the question concerning anthropological origin *theo-philosophically*. Initially, we explored the dogmatic claims regarding our Lady's immaculate conception to trace the theological meaning of this unique origination. Her grace-filled origin is not ancillary to her being (as if it were just *merely* a historical fact about our Lady's manner of conception) but is profoundly ingredient to her identity and vocation as the generative source of her being and person: "I am the immaculate conception." By considering the gravity of the dogmatic truth articulated about our Lady coupled with the private revelation given to Bernadette from our Lady of Lourdes, we discovered that, by means of this unique grace received "at the first instance of her conception," she is, as mere creature, the decisive *icon* of the human being as such (in concert with her Son but in a distinct manner). This provided space for further analysis à la Marion into the nature of our Lady's *iconic* reality, recognizing that this in fact strengthens the thesis of our project: we can and should behold our Lady theo-philosophically in view of anthropology.

This then gave way for us to explore exactly how our Lady's *unique* conception *illumines illustratively* anthropological origination. By first examining the temporal/eternal dynamic inherent in our Lady's conception, we discovered a twofold origin: it occurs *in time* ("at the first instant of conception") but is rooted *in an eternal decree*. Therefore, reading our Lady's conception as analogous to human origination, we discerned that while God has *eternally* elected the anthropos to be "holy and blameless" in Christ (Eph 1:4–5), this is made manifest *in time* via the sacrament of holy baptism. Thus, baptism is analogous to our Lady's immaculate conception—no doubt different in *mode*, *effect*, and *manner*, but nevertheless similar in that new life begins in grace *within* time—while also Mary's predestination is analogous to the predestined call of those elected in Christ.

This positioned us to explore specifically how Mary *illumines* human origination, examining the ways in which grace elevates without destroying nature *within* the temporal unfolding of sanctification eschatologically completed for the church but truly begun *in time* via baptism, which is already given through our Lady's conception, thus she is "full of grace." Through, then, an analogical reading of (1) our Lady's predestined call with the general predestined election of anthropos in Christ, (2) immaculate conception in time with the sacramental grace of baptism enacted in time, and (3) the nature that is presupposed and elevated by grace in Mary as it is in the anthropos who undergoes baptism, we detected the fitting way in which our Lady's unique origin *illuminates* the necessity of a graced origin in holiness for the human being, predestined but temporally realized.

Finally, we proceeded to examine how our Lady's immaculate conception *illustrates* the origin of anthropos by initially considering the non-reductive relationship between theology and philosophy, reading Mary's nature as the creaturely correlate to philosophy, and her salvation by preservation as the gracious correlate to theology. Mary's grace-filled conception mysteriously points to the joint expression and collaboration between theology and philosophy in their respective mutually informing modes, which, in turn, strengthened our resolve to continue to approach our Lady in view of those questions in anthropology *both* theologically and philosophically, doing so with the recognition that philosophy is elevated (and so truly made *philo-sophia*) by means of the datum of revelation given in our Lady. By considering Mary *from the side of creatureliness*, distinguishing her finitude, we were able to then identify a profound *incompleteness*, a Blondelian "abyss," in the intimations and gestures discoverable by philosophy within anthropos in its identity, vocation, and perennial desire for *more*. It is in this way that our Lady *illustrates* what is fulfilled and completed *illuminatively* by grace.

We now are prepared to consider Mary in the light of the final dogma that reveals her *end*, her definitive telos, in view of anthropology: her assumption. Such an *end* illumines illustratively the ultimate mystery of anthropos, a creature destined for glory and so one who cannot, even in principle, be collapsed into and merely identified with the *horizontal* but is truly "hidden with Christ in God" (Col 3:3). As *verticality* is the necessary constitutive foundation for the origin, identity, and vocation of the human being, so it is for the very *end* of anthropos. As we will now see, such an eschatological end proleptically reveals the utter mystery—verticality—of the entire human being: *the* theoanthropocosmic synthesis. Therefore, anthropos is completed apophatically, and so rejects any attempts at seeking a "fallen" eschatology according to the dictates of a horizontal logic.

*The touch of an infinite mystery passes over the trivial and the familiar, making it break out into ineffable music. . . . The trees, the stars, and the blue hills ache with a meaning which can never be uttered in words.*

~ Rabindranath Tagore

*The immortal is that which is now growing and developing in our present life.*

~ Joseph Ratzinger/Benedict XVI

# 5

# Assumption

## *The Human as Eschatologically Deferred*

We have hitherto reflected on how Mary's virginal maternity and grace-filled beginning *illumine illustratively* anthropological origin, identity, and vocation. By doing so we have had an opportunity to not only observe the significance of cultivating an anthropology predicated on our Lady (which, among other things, allows for the preservation of the *archetypal pair*—new Adam and new Eve), but also have recourse to one who perfectly reflects the divine hypostasis that is her Son but ever only as *mere* creature, as a human hypostasis. Thus, without minimizing but complementing our Lord, our Lady answers the enduring questions implied in human existence itself. While also recognizing the distinction without divorce between grace and nature, faith and reason, theology, and philosophy, we have also been able to explore how both a theological *and* philosophical assessment of our Lady's anthropological significance offers us a deeper assessment of the anthropos as such, thus allowing us to fly with both "wings," faith *and* reason.

By coordinating the four Marian dogmas with the four perennial questions concerning the origin, end, identity, and vocation of anthropos in our previous chapters, we have also discovered how *pneumatic time*—the temporal/eternal dynamic eschatologically construed—profoundly constitutes the temporal mechanics of the human being. Thus, we have discovered the importance of engaging such an analysis to acquire the full scope of how pneumatic time determines the "shape" of anthropos with respect to its origin, end, identity, and vocation. The significance of this is revealed insofar as pneumatic time holds together, without confusing, both (the creatureliness of) time and the eternal; or to put it another way, it identifies how time as such (vis-à-vis the human being) is eschatologically determined.

Our current chapter will explore how the fourth Marian dogma, the assumption, enacts and recapitulates human *completion* such that anthropos is an *eschatologically deferred being*, observed both *illuminatively* (grace/faith/theology) and *illustratively* (nature/reason/philosophy). The argument will proceed as follows: First, we will in brief examine the meaning of Mary's assumption to explicate its significance in revealing the human as the *theoanthropocosmic synthesis*. Second, we will assess how *pneumatic time* is ingredient to understanding how her assumption is, like her conception but in an inverted manner, a twofold *end*: it is enacted (in time) at the completion of her earthly life while it is ever only finally realized as an eschatological (eternal) reality in the hereafter. Here we will investigate how Mary's assumption is the eschatological completion of her maternal being, virginal vocation, and so is the "omega" to the corresponding "alpha" of our Lady's immaculate conception. Third, we will study how Mary's assumption *illumines* the ineffable reality of anthropos as the proleptic appearance of the *yet unknown*—theosis *in time*—such that the human being is definitively the *apophatically concealed, eschatologically deferred being*. Fourth, we will explore how Mary's assumption *illustrates* human telos by arguing how, in light of what philosophy discovers about anthropological *origin*, *identity*, and *vocation* in view of revelation, Catholic rationality recognizes the *fitting end* of such a creature, thus also discerning an ineffability to the human being.

## MARY: THE HUMAN IN GLORY

That Mary was assumed body and soul into heaven signals, anthropologically, a certain telos that at once reveals the glorious end (and thus, a new and final *beginning*) of the human being while also indicating a profound, even ineffable mystery that *is* the anthropos since this eschatological inbreaking, this ultimately futurity, like that of the resurrection, proleptically invades the present, thus unveiling the true being of anthropos. The question, however, of whether or not Mary's assumption occurred after an actual temporal death is one the church is dogmatically silent about, although "the fact of her death is almost generally accepted by the Fathers and Theologians, and is expressly affirmed in the Liturgy of the Church," as it is expressed, for example, in *Sacramentarium Gregorianum*, transmitted by Pope Adrian I to Charlemagne in the eighth century.[1] Supposing an actual temporal death, such an end would in no way presuppose the presence of original or actual sin in our Lady but rather, given the mortal nature of her body, is simply the result of her conformity to her Son who died.[2] Leaving the question of her death open, the dogmatic declaration of our Lady's assumption by Pope Pius XII states the following: "We pronounce, declare, and define it to be a divinely revealed dogma: that the Immaculate Mother of God, the ever Virgin Mary, having completed the course of her earthly life, was assumed body and soul into heavenly glory."[3] The phrase "body and soul" here means the totality of our Lady, the fullness of her humanity, was taken up and entered into her glorious eschatological abode, realizing in her person what is the abiding destiny of the church militant and suffering.[4] Thus, the catechism states that "the Assumption of the Blessed Virgin is a singular participation in her Son's Resurrection and an anticipation of the resurrection of other Christians."[5] Therefore, she is the forerunner of

1. Ott, *Fundamentals of Catholic Dogma*, 224.

2. Ott, *Fundamentals of Catholic Dogma*, 225. Newman expresses his view of the death of our Lady and subsequent assumption: "As soon as we apprehend by faith the great fundamental truth that Mary is the Mother of God, other wonderful truths follow in its train; and one of these is that she was exempt from the ordinary lot of mortals, which is not only to die, but to become earth to earth, ashes to ashes, dust to dust. Die she must, and die she did, as her Divine Son died, for He was man; but various reasons have approved themselves to holy writers, why, although her body was for a while separated from her soul, and consigned to the tomb, yet it did not remain there, but was speedily united to her soul again, and raised by our Lord to a new and eternal life of heavenly glory. . . . And the most obvious reason for so concluding is this—that other servants of God have been raised from the grave by the power of God, and it is not to be supposed that our Lord would have granted any such privilege to anyone else without also granting it to His own Mother. . . . Therefore we confidently say that our Lord, having preserved her from sin and the consequences of sin by His Passion, lost no time in pouring out the full merits of that Passion upon her body as well as her soul" (*Meditations and Devotions*, 89–91).

3. Pius XII, *Munificentissimus Deus* 44.

4. As the catechism states, "In her we contemplate what the Church already is in her mystery on her own 'pilgrimage of faith,' and what she will be in the homeland at the end of her journey" (Catholic Church, *Catechism*, §972). Also: "In the interim just as the Mother of Jesus, glorified in body and soul in heaven, is the image and beginning of the Church as it is to be perfected is the world to come, so too does she shine forth on earth, until the day of the Lord shall come, (Cf. 2 Pt. 3:10) as a sign of sure hope and solace to the people of God during its sojourn on earth" (*LG* 68).

5. Catholic Church, *Catechism*, §966.

the church, the expressed realization of what is to come, complementing Christ as the new Eve, mirroring him as *mere* creature (thus, for example, she is *assumed*—passively receiving this gift/grace—and not *resurrected* by way of her own prerogative as was the case with her divine Son).

The Pontifical International Marian Academy highlights Mary's assumption in view of the church:

> In relation to the Church, the Virgin assumed into heaven is: The *beginning* of the Church both in a theological and in a chronological sense. . . . As eschatological *icon*, the image of the *assumpta* shines before the pilgrim Church on earth. Mary is that human creature who has arrived at the fullness of her divine vocation, the prototype of the eschatological Church; the icon of the *assumpta* is not static but has a drawing power.[6]

Note that our Lady's assumption brings to pass the full realization of her "divine vocation." Chapter 3 of our project examined how our Lady's perpetual virginity, intimately linked to her divine maternity, is the expressed *shape* of anthropological vocation: *eschatologically oriented exocentricity*. Here, then, we can see how the assumption fulfills and completes (eschatologically) the vocation of our Lady (and the anthropos, by extension) as it does her identity (maternal) insofar as she is filled transcendently with her glorified Son.[7]

Concerning the various reasons for the assumption, Ludwig Ott identifies four items of revelation that the church uses to argue for the incorruptibility and transfiguration of Mary at the end of her life: (1) her freedom from sin; (2) her divine maternity; (3) her perpetual virginity; and (4) her participation in the work of Christ.[8] This coincides well with what we have thus far discovered in our project: Mary's grace-filled origin, her immaculate conception, coupled with her divine maternity and perpetual virginity, points ineluctably to her glorious end. In a fitting way, the relations among the dogmatic truths of our Lady are intrinsically linked, mutually informing each within the totality of Mary, and thus,

6. Pontifical International Marian Academy, *Mother of the Lord*, 64–65; emphasis in original.

7. "Mary, in her glorification, is the sign of the completion of the human vocation, the only one who fulfills this vocation: to be enveloped in the glory of the living God, to resonate the hymn of pure praise, and to respond in pure love" (Pontifical International Marian Academy, *Mother of the Lord*, 61).

8. Ott, *Fundamentals of Catholic Dogma*, 226.

anthropologically, the human being as such, analogically understood.[9] Manfred Hauke explicitly identifies how the three Marian dogmas relate to the assumption: (1) "The Assumption appears as the ultimate consequence of the Immaculate Conception." (2) "The divine maternity creates a spiritual and corporeal bond between Mary and Christ, a bond destined to be fulfilled in her final glorification with soul and body." (3) "The cooperation of the Mother of God in the plan of salvation." (4) "The divine maternity is closely tied to Mary's virginity,"[10] thus, as John of Damascus states, "It was necessary that she who had preserved her virginity intact in birth, would see her body kept sheltered from any corruption, even after her death."[11] Scheeben also gives similar reasons for the assumption.[12] Seeing, then, the inherent logical connection among the dogmatic truths of our Lady via *analogia fidei*, we consequently discern how anthropos is oriented toward a supernatural end.

Given what we have thus far observed—that our Lady's identity, vocation, and grace-filled beginning are intimately linked to her telos—we can conclude that the assumption of Mary is the definitive seal and guarantee that she is, in complementarity to her Son and not in contradistinction, *the* theoanthropocosmic synthesis. Her eschatological "arrival" reveals the glorious end and thus fulfillment of her virginal maternity within a transcendent mode, which is also the fitting outcome of her grace-filled beginning. In her, God unites the world to himself, both in time (via the incarnation, and as the Mother of the crucified) and in eternity (realized eschatologically in Mary's assumption). And since her assumption, though "beginning" in time, transcends time (as we will see below) as an eschatological "event," our Lady as theoanthropocosmic synthesis can only, in the final analysis, be indirectly spoken of since her assumption is ineffably mysterious. In other words, while we explored how our Lady is such a synthesis in chapter 1 (metaphysically understood), and examined how her virginal maternity and immaculate

9. Aidan Nichols offers insight into the grounding of the dogma of the assumption in light of other dogmas via *analogia fidei*: "The assumption doctrine could be dogmatized—in other words, defined as a truth of faith which all the faithful are obliged to hold—simply because in a certain way it is an inference from other truths in the doctrinal corpus, some of them already dogmatically in place" (*There Is No Rose*, 89). See also Kilian Healey's treatment on the question of the intrinsic relations among the Marian dogmas: "Assumption Among Mary's Privileges." Thomist 14 (1951) 72–92.

10. Hauke, *Introduction to Mariology*, 283.

11. John of Damascus, *Dorm*. 2.14 (Galot, *Maria*, 319).

12. Scheeben, *Mariology*, 2:166–68.

conception bring about *in time* this synthesis (chs. 2–4), her assumption additionally reveals the utter mystery that surrounds this synthesis, showing its apophatic reality. As Aidan Nichols notes,

> That mystery concerns divine acts transforming definitively the status of the ontological elements (body and soul, or flesh and spirit) that entered into the making of Mary's personhood. *Those divine acts escape the bounds of natural human enquiry of any kind.* That is so, of course, because the kind of agency involved is eschatological and Trinitarian, and so can hardly be factored into any naturally derived formula, never mind a purely empiricist one. The action concerned is what God the Trinity is doing to consummate the existence of the Mother of Jesus.[13]

Therefore, "the Assumption of Mary is the emblematic symbol of God's way of acting: The Virgin of Nazareth, an insignificant creature in the eyes of the world, has become, through God's grace, the most important person in history and in eternity."[14]

Thus, as we will explore in greater depth below, the assumption unveils anthropologically the human being to be the *apophatically concealed, eschatologically deferred being.* Anthropos will be fully and finally revealed only eschatologically, as seen in our Lady's assumption (complementing the resurrection [1 John 3:2]). However, though mysteriously enveloped by virtue of its transcendent reality, the assumption does nevertheless show a glorious, supernatural end, destined for those in Christ. This much is known. Her end reveals the proper telos of anthropos.

> After the resurrected Christ, the Virgin's Assumption is a sign of dignity of persons—male and female—and of their future destiny to glory. Both events—the Resurrection of Jesus and the Assumption of Mary—teach us that the destiny of humanity, made to the "image and likeness" of God (cf. Gn 1: 26–27), is not an undoing of personhood and a dissolution into nothingness, but the full realization and total conformity to Christ, by having arrived to "the full stature of Christ" (cf. Eph 4:13), or, as the East prefers to say, to "divinization."[15]

Therefore, contrary to the "undoing of personhood," the anthropos ever only becomes fully itself, fully human *in* glory. Such an end signifies the

13. Nichols, *There Is No Rose*, 92; emphasis added.
14. Pontifical International Marian Academy, *Mother of the Lord*, 67.
15. Pontifical International Marian Academy, *Mother of the Lord*, 61.

human being as a *being in the making, being in time* who is finally "completed" eschatologically. As the then Joseph Cardinal Ratzinger stated concerning the church's proclamation of the assumption of Mary, "She [the church] herself was turning us to the future by interpreting man, on the basis of her faith, as *a being who is yet to come*, a being with an endless future, *a being who can attain full stature only by advancing*."[16]

Thus, we can conclude by summarily identifying why the dogma of Mary's assumption is anthropologically significant: (1) it unveils the glorious end anthropos is made for both collectively (the church) and individually; (2) it reveals the fitting fulfillment of anthropos in proportion to its given *origin* (immaculate), *being* (maternal), and *vocation* (virginal); (3) it affirms the theoanthropocosmic synthesis that is anthropos; and (4) it shows that anthropos is the *apophatically concealed, eschatologically deferred being*, the yet-unknown being who is an ineffably dignified mystery.[17] Part 3 of this chapter will unpack these anthropological implications as we examine how the assumption *illumines* (grace/faith/theology) the ineffable end (and thus, reality) of the human being as such. We will first turn our attention to the question of how pneumatic time shapes this doctrinal truth, and how this then informs the curious question concerning the glorious ending of such a lowly creature that is the human being.

## THE TEMPORAL/ETERNAL DYNAMIC OF THE ASSUMPTION

Like the way in which the immaculate conception possesses a twofold origin, the assumption of Mary reveals a twofold ending: it occurs *in time* ("having completed the course of her earthly life"),[18] though actualized as an eschatological (and thus, eternal) event in the hereafter *within* the stream of temporal events. This "within" simply means that the body and soul of our Lady are assumed on a particular day and hour, while simultaneously being a transcendent event. Like the resurrection of our Lord, who on *the third day* rose, so too our Lady is assumed at a specific time only known to God. Insofar as the assumption is a participation in the

16. Ratzinger/Benedict XVI, *Dogma and Preaching*, 358; emphasis added. As he also states on the same page, "The Church proclaims that the entire greatness possible to man is embodied and fulfilled in this woman, quite independently of descent or class."

17. See Rev 2:17. Perhaps this passage could be read as gesturing toward this truth.

18. Pius XII, *Munificentissimus Deus* 44.

resurrection, we can recognize this eternal/temporal event and therefore conclude that this mystery of faith is indeed informed by *pneumatic time*; that is, the temporal events surrounding the culmination of the life of the Virgin are undoubtedly marked by an eschatological reality. As the catechism states, "The mystery of Christ's resurrection is *a real event*, with manifestations that were historically verified."[19] Also, "although *the Resurrection was an historical event* that could be verified by the sign of the empty tomb and by the reality of the apostles' encounters with the risen Christ, still *it remains at the very heart of the mystery of faith as something that transcends and surpasses history*."[20] So too, on the side of Mary, the assumption itself presupposes a temporal ending—the end of this eon—so that the eternal, eschatological "event" may come to pass as the finalization of the temporal age.

By considering the twofold manner of our Lady's telos in the light of our thesis, discernment begins to open before us regarding how Mary's ending, her assumption, concurrently reveals the intrinsic relation between the eternal and temporal regarding anthropological culmination. Pneumatic time is the constitutive grammar of the culminating telos of anthropos insofar as the totality of the human being—"body and soul"—is inextricably bound up within an eternal frame that "resolves" all the tensions that naturally arise within a temporal being whose *beginning*, *vocation*, and *identity* are indissolubly united to an eternally transcendent Source. Death, the temporal end of the human being, is, in Christ, a "falling asleep" until that day when, in imitation of our Lady, anthropos is taken up, fully restored, and (bodily) glorified, completing what was begun both temporally (physical birth and baptism, and the subsequent life that enacts anthropological identity and vocation) and eternally (election).[21] Death and (eternal) life, then, are *intrinsically* related, which, of course, is in fact intimated and even articulated in the sacrament of baptism. Recognizing how the eternal (via Mary's assumption) begins and transcendently incorporates the temporal unfolding of *this* life, Ratzinger identifies the anthropological implication of the assumption in the following way:

19. Catholic Church, *Catechism*, §639; emphasis in original.

20. Catholic Church, *Catechism*, §647; emphasis added.

21. I am here setting aside the question concerning those who will be alive at the Lord's return, as Paul notes (1 Thess 4:17).

> The immortal is that which is now growing and developing in our present life. The immortal is that which is developing in this body of ours wherein we hope and rejoice, feel sadness, and move forward through time; that which is developing *now* in our present life with its present condition. In other words, what is imperishable is whatever we have become in our present bodily state; whatever has developed and grown in us, in our present life, among and by means of the things of this world. It is this "whole man," as he has existed and lived and suffered in this world, that will one day be transformed by God's eternity and be eternal in God himself.[22]

Given that the entirety of one's being is taken up transcendently, and noticing how this being *begins* (via baptism) under the sign of new life through death, we can observe, then, how the assumption is the "omega" to the corresponding "alpha" of our Lady's immaculate conception, and so for the originating (immaculate) and culminating (glorified) events of anthropos as such. Therefore, the assumption enacts and recapitulates anthropological ending, an ending actualized eschatologically though temporalized in a graced death.

## MARY'S ASSUMPTION ILLUMINATES THE INEFFABLE END (AND REALITY) OF ANTHROPOS

Clearly, we can begin to observe how our Lady *illumines* (grace/faith/theology) human telos. By understanding Mary's assumption as an analogous correlate to the *death and resurrection* event for the human being, we can see how she illuminates anthropological ending by revealing the transcendent culmination necessary for the actualization (eschatologically) of anthropological vocation and identity initiated in a grace-filled beginning. If we keep before us what we have thus far discovered in our previous chapters, how Mary enacts and recapitulates human identity (maternal), vocation (virginal), and origin (immaculate), we are then able to see how in an analogous mode her glorious end fittingly describes that supernatural end for those who enacted their authentic identity and vocation as the subsequent outcome of a baptismal—and thus, grace-filled—"conception" both temporally (sacramentally) and eternally (election). Laurentin's description of how the dogmatic truths of our Lady

22. Ratzinger/Benedict XVI, *Dogma and Preaching*, 360; emphasis in original.

presuppose her telos fittingly can also help us to think through how such an end is inscribed anthropologically.

> The body of the immaculate one, preserved from all sin, the body of the Theotokos who engendered the Word of God, this body whose virginity the Holy Spirit integrally preserved, even in conception and childbirth, did not remain prisoner of the bonds of death. In the totality of her being, the immaculate Mother of God, ever a Virgin, rejoined Christ in the communion of glory.[23]

Notice Laurentin's stress on the body in relation to her immaculate origin, maternal identity, and virginal vocation. Taking this into account, a Theotokion theo-philosophical anthropology must acknowledge the irreducible nature of the body in its integrative place within the maternal identity of anthropos—the locus of union between the infinite and finite as finitude containing the infinite—and within the shape of the virginal vocation—eschatologically oriented exocentricity—all together initiated and galvanized by an immaculate origin via baptism. Just as there is no baptism of "spirit" but of the full human (ch. 4), and just as the yes offered is manifested via the total being (ch. 2), coupled with a *chaste existence* of mind and body, which is the analogical correlate to Mary's virginal disposition, *virginitas mentis* (ch. 3), so too the bodily reality of anthropos, ingredient in the fullness of humanity, cannot end in dissolution but will be gloriously taken up at the "end of time." This anthropological culmination vis-à-vis the completion of one's life is the fitting capstone that fulfills and crowns the *total* human being. As Fr. Paul Haffner states, "The Assumption is a triumph for the nobility of maternity and also of virginity. The Assumption is also an indication of the glory which awaits the body of the Christian, who in this life has been the home of the Body of Christ in the Eucharist."[24] In imitation of Mary, then, anthropos—"body and soul"—is destined for an ineffable union with the One who is in fact the inexorable beginning (immaculate), middle (maternal and virginal), and end (glory) of the human being.

> Henceforward their union is *definitive*. It is *without shadow*. Mary knows her Son no longer by dint of earthly signs, in a way obscure and limited, but face-to-face with his divinity. Earlier

23. Laurentin, *Treatise on Virgin Mary*, 250.

24. Haffner, "Our Lady's Earthly Life," 84.

> she knew him as God through his humanity. Now she knows his humanity through his very divinity.[25]

Considering the totality of the human being eschatologically, albeit doing so apophatically because of the ineffable mystery that pertains to such a gloriously transcendent end, what more could be said about the body anthropologically? A Mariologically informed anthropology that takes seriously the assumption ought to offer some word about the nature of eschatological flesh/body. Using the resurrection as a template, Maximus can help to elucidate this. Knowing that the assumption is a (unique) participation in the Lord's resurrection, we ought to be able to glean from Maximus's reflections further insight into this query.

In chapter 1 of this project, we examined Maximus's theology to consider the unity of the body and soul. There we observed how Maximus's anthropology informs his thinking concerning anthropos as a theoanthropocosmic synthesis, as we also noted the profound relation, then, between Mary and Christ. For our purposes here, considering Ambiguum 42 is a helpful beginning in thinking about the body at the terminus of one's life since it is here that Maximus argues that the body cannot simply pass out of existence since "every essential existence created according to the divine purpose remains in being and cannot pass into nonbeing."[26] The body, then, which is part of the essential unity of the anthropos, must somehow persist beyond dissolution. Maximus goes on to state the following:

> But if whatever essentially exists cannot pass from being to nonbeing once it has been brought into existence, then its principles must be solid and unchanging, having the sole origin of their being in divine Wisdom, from which they come and thanks to which they remain in existence, and by which they have the power to remain firmly anchored in being. But if the principles of things exist permanently in God, then the purpose of God, who created all things, must be changeless concerning them—for God's purpose cannot be contained within the boundaries of time, nor does it admit change relative to the changes that take place among the things that are subject to it—and thus the existences of these principles are clearly incorruptible.[27]

25. Laurentin, *Treatise on Virgin Mary*, 251; emphasis in original.
26. Maximos the Confessor, *On Difficulties*, 1:151.
27. Maximos the Confessor, *On Difficulties*, 2:151.

Maximus's Logos/logoi distinction, which was discussed in our first chapter, is the metaphysical bedrock beneath his here description, instructing that the body and the soul coexist in time and thus their "principles"—that is, their logoi—"must be solid and unchanging, having the sole origin of their being in divine Wisdom"—that is, Logos. Nikolaos Loudovikos describes Maximus's ontology as eschatologically construed: "The doctrine of the *logoi* is an eschatological ontology, as they form not immovable archetypes but divine wills, destinations and existential vocations for the creatures, waiting for the human logos/response."[28] This lends credence to the idea that the total anthropos—"body and soul"—will only fully be actualized in the eschatological age, as Loudovikos himself states:

> Thus, the essence of beings for Maximus can be found, in a way, not in the "origins" but fundamentally in the "end" of beings: beings *shall be* as they really are, the kingdom to come is the kingdom of the ontological/eschatological consummation of things.[29]

It is in Ambiguum 42 that Maximus also argues that the formation of the body and soul, though metaphysically distinct and so differ in how they come about, are nevertheless coincident in time: "We, however, adhering to the middle course . . . speak neither of preexistence nor postexistence of either soul or body, but of coexistence."[30] In his polemic against those who assert that either God did not create bodies or did create bodies contrary to his purpose,[31] Maximus grounds the mystery of embodiment in Christ's incarnation and resurrection. In the following lengthy passage, we can begin to see, given Maximus's use of revelation along with his metaphysical perspective, the decisive importance of the body in glory as a continuous reality, albeit transcendently changed:

28. Loudovikos, *Eucharistic Ontology*, 4.

29. Loudovikos, *Eucharistic Ontology*, 4; emphasis in original.

30. Maximus, as quoted in Loudovikos, *Eucharistic Ontology*, 145. "The soul does not originate from underlying matter, as bodies do, but by the will of God, through the *vital inbreathing* in a manner which is ineffable and hidden, known only to the soul's Creator. Receiving its existence at the moment of conception simultaneously with the body, the soul contributes to the completion of a single human being, whereas the body is created from the underlying matter of another body at the moment of conception, and is synthesized together with the soul into a single form with it" (Maximos the Confessor, *On Difficulties*, 1:140–41; emphasis in original).

31. Loudovikos, *Eucharistic Ontology*, 153.

> For all the divine mysteries are surpassed by the mystery of Christ, and this mystery is definitive of every conceivable perfection in all things either present or to come, and it exists above and beyond every limit and boundary. Now this mystery teaches us that the body of God the Word—which was taken from us and which is consubstantial with us, and which was united to Him in a union according to hypostasis when He assumed flesh and perfectly became man—is the same body with which He ascended into the heavens, *far above all rule and authority and power and dominion, and above every name that is named, not only in this age but also in that which is to come*, so that now and for infinite ages He is seated together with God the Father, *having passed through* all *the heavens* and *surpassing all* things, and He shall come again to refashion and transform the universe, and for the salvation of our souls and bodies. . . . These things being so, who would be so obstinate and reckless . . . to entertain even the merest thought that bodies will pass into nonbeing after rational beings will have completed their progress to perfection . . . how, I wonder, could anyone think such a thing, believing at the same time that our Lord Himself, the God of all, is now and will be forever embodied, for it is He who grants to others the power enabling them to make progress, and it is He who leads and calls everyone to His own glory (as much as this is possible for them) by the power of His Incarnation.[32]

Following after her Son, Mary's assumption includes the totality of her being, reaffirming eternal embodiment. As Maximus imaginatively expresses the archangel Gabriel saying to our Lady at her dormition, "Your prayers and supplications have gone up before your son in heaven, and according to your request, he bids you to relinquish this world and ascend to the dwelling places of heaven and to be with him in the true and unending life."[33] And closely imitating the elements of the resurrection account, Maximus describes the following events surrounding the assumption:

> So then the tomb was found empty. They found only the burial wrappings and the shroud in which they had laid her to rest, and the body of the immaculate Virgin was not there, but it had been raised up to her son and God so that she will live and reign with him completely, and thus our nature was raised up to heaven

32. Maximos the Confessor, *On Difficulties*, 2:155–57; emphasis in original.
33. Maximus the Confessor, *Life of the Virgin*, 130.

> in the eternal kingdom not only by her son but also by the immaculate mother.[34]

Here we see how the assumption is a decisive participation in the resurrection, "For the body was united to the Word of God together with the soul, and so the body is saved together with the soul."[35] Mary as Theotokos no doubt "runs ahead" of us, as it were, in the assumption since she alone uniquely bore in her body that Word who is the unity of divinity and humanity; and so it will be for the church, for those who bear Christ by way of fiat, gestation, birth giving, and parenting (ch. 2).

Thus far, recourse to Maximus offers us a clear theologically informed metaphysics as to the continuation of the body into glory, transcendently transformed. What, then, does Maximus say directly about the dynamism of the body in glory in relation to the soul and God?

Fascinatingly, in Ambiguum 7 he presents a description of the eschatological body in view of the theoanthropocosmic synthesis that is the human being in glory. Anthropologically, such a telos described by Maximus is possible only for those who "did not, out of negligence, violate any of the divine logoi, who by their natural motion were inclined to the end established by the Creator, but kept themselves wholly chaste and faithful to their end."[36] This is a fitting description given what we have thus far articulated concerning the enactment of the maternal being and virginal vocation of anthropos (chs. 2–3). A Mariologically informed anthropology recognizes the intrinsic need for God for its origination and sustenance if the human being is to ever be fully realized and completed both in time and eschatologically. Thus, those who keep themselves "wholly chaste and faithful to their end" will do so "knowing that they are and will become instruments *of the divine nature*."[37] Maximus goes on to clearly explain how God will be "all in all" in this eschatological state in the following extensive passage:

> For God in His fullness entirely permeates them, as a soul permeates the body, since they are to serve as His own members, well suited and useful to the Master, who shall use them as He thinks best, filling them with His own glory and blessedness, graciously giving them eternal, inexpressible life, completely

34. Maximus the Confessor, *Life of the Virgin*, 141.
35. Maximos the Confessor, *On Difficulties*, 2:159.
36. Maximos the Confessor, *On Difficulties*, 1:111–13.
37. Maximos the Confessor, *On Difficulties*, 1:113; emphasis in original.

> free from the constituent properties of this present life, which is marred by corruption. The life God will give does not consist in the breathing of air, or in the flow of blood . . . but in fact that God will be wholly participated by the whole human beings, so that He will be to the soul, as it were, what the soul is to the body, and through the soul He will likewise be present in the body (in a manner that He knows), so that the soul will receive immutability and the body immortality. In this way, man as a whole will be divinized, being made God by the grace of God who became man. Man will remain wholly man in soul and body, owing to his nature, but will become wholly God in soul and body owing to the grace and the splendor of the blessed glory of God, which is wholly appropriate to him, and beyond which nothing more splendid or sublime can be imagined.[38]

This is the telos anthropos is naturally oriented to, realized first in the resurrection, then in the assumption, and will be so for the rest in Christ *and* Mary. What is in fact being articulated here, however, is a profound, unutterable mystery since we really cannot imagine what it means to be "completely free from the constituent properties of this present life," or that God will be "wholly participated by the whole human" and "man . . . will become wholly God in soul and body" since it will be done "in a manner that He knows." Paul reminds us that no one has recourse to what this actually looks like or to a proper conception of it (1 Cor 2:9). Only faith gains access to this mystery, and reason so enlightened can reflect thereupon. What we do see, nevertheless, in the light of Maximus's description is a fuller meaning of how the human being as such, illumined by the mystery of the assumption of our Lady, is the theoanthropocosmic synthesis, and how such a synthesis is only ever entirely realized eschatologically, while substantively real intimations of this synthesis do occur in

38. Maximos the Confessor, *On Difficulties*, 1:113. Maximos also describes the culminating state in the following way: "For just as the flesh was swallowed up by corruption as a result of sin, and likewise the soul by the flesh (since it is known only through the activities of the body), and the knowledge of God by the soul's complete ignorance (to the point of not even knowing whether or not God exists), so too, in the time of the resurrection—when the Holy Spirit will restore the correct order, for the sake of the God who became flesh—the flesh will be spiritually swallowed up by the soul, and the soul by God, who is true life, inasmuch as the soul will possess God exclusively, wholly manifested through all things to the whole soul, and, to put it simply, in contrast to the present state of affairs in which we now exist and live, all that is ours will be revealed under the aspect of the future by the divine grace of the resurrection, so that, just as death prevailed over this life and swallowed all through sin, death itself will be justly defeated by that life, and swallowed up by grace" (1:437–39).

time by the one who, in virtue of an immaculate origin (baptism), enacts one's own maternal identity and virginal vocation. Thus, the assumption beautifully enacts and recapitulates anthropological telos.

Considering how the assumption illumines the end of anthropos, both "body and soul," and bearing in mind how pneumatic time is the constitutive grammar of the culminating telos of anthropos insofar as the totality of the human being is inextricably bound up within an eternal frame, "resolving" all the tensions that naturally arise within a temporal being whose *beginning*, *vocation*, and *identity* are indissolubly united to an eternally transcendent Source, we are now better positioned to consider how this mysterious culmination of our Lady *proleptically* informs anthropological vocation and identity.

As we began to examine in our second chapter and further unpacked in our third, Mary's *maternal* identity and *virginal* vocation are the outworking *in time* of what is *predestined* (eternal) regarding her origin, her conception (beginning in eternity but executed in time at the first moment of her conception), and what is also *eschatologically realized* (eternal) in her assumption (beginning in time as a historical event but transcending it since it pertains to the eschaton as such). While her *origin* is made manifest in her maternal *identity* and virginal *vocation* along the arrow of time as the fitting presupposition, so too are both her *identity* and *vocation* the proleptic realization of her *eschatological end*.

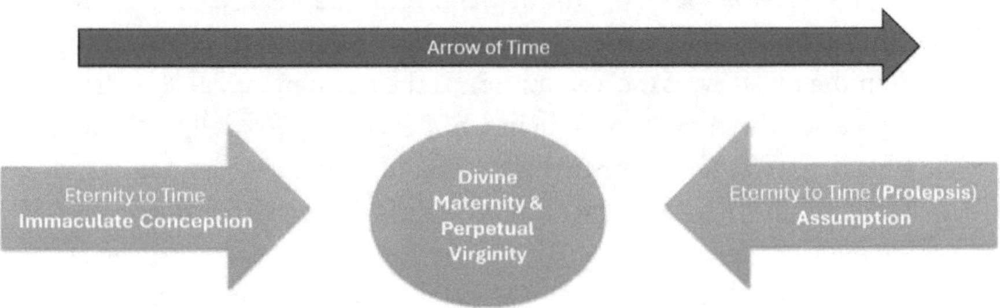


Contemplating the assumption, we observe in Mary the temporal/eternal dynamic that is an eschatological tension between the *here* of temporal events and the *not yet* of the eschaton. As stated in our third chapter, since it is God the Spirit who mediates this temporal and eternal dynamism as Lord of creation without collapsing either into the other, and since it is the Spirit himself who sanctified, empowered, and made fruitful the virginal womb of our Lady[39]—spouse of the Spirit—we call this temporal/eternal dynamic *pneumatic time*.[40] Our Lady's assumption, then, is manifested in time proleptically via Mary's virginal maternity. This is so given that, through her virginal maternity, she enacts in time what will eschatologically come into full bloom: God being "all in all"; "the Logos of God (who is God) wills always and in all things to accomplish the mystery of His embodiment."[41]

What this then tells us is that the human being enacts in time what will in fact only fully come in the end if and only if anthropos is true to the strictures of maternal identity and virginal vocation. Given that maternal identity is, in view of our Lady, the locus of union betwixt the infinite and finite as finitude containing, paradoxically, the infinite; and presuming, as we have in fact argued, that virginal vocation is, in consideration of Mary, eschatologically oriented exocentricity, then the death and resurrection of anthropos are the only finalities that will truly complete the human being. Therefore, enacting in time one's maternal identity and virginal vocation—an enactment described in chapters 2–3 of this project—is the dynamic unfolding of theosis, of sanctification. Theosis/sanctification is, then, the proleptic arrival of the *yet unknown*. As John describes in his letter, we simply do not know what we *will* be; nevertheless, at the parousia we will come to know that we are in fact like him (Christ) since we will "see him as he is" (1 John 3:2). Thus, the end is, in a manner of speaking, in the beginning (baptism/election) and so also throughout the fabric of existentiality from birth to death. If this is so, then the mystery of the assumption is the hermeneutical lens through which we see the *total* human being, but ever only partially—through a dark glass, as it were—since this end, this culmination is, as stated above, ineffably mysterious; thus, the human being is the *apophatically concealed, eschatologically deferred being*. This is the meta-anthropology given at the end, an anthropology that transcends any reductionistic account.

Noting how *pneumatic* time expresses the intersection and relation between time and eternity (without the collapsing or confusing of either)

39. Catholic Church, *Catechism*, §§721–26.

40. As stated earlier in our project, this term is coined to describe the unique temporal/eternal dynamic observable in Our Lady and, subsequently, in the anthropos as such. What I mean by pneumatic time is this: Our Lady (and the human being as such) is a historical being (with all the existential particularities that accompany this: risk, anticipation, change, etc.) that is nevertheless definitively shaped by an eschatological, eternal grammar.

41. Maximos the Confessor, *On Difficulties*, 1:107.

in Mary and thus the human being, we can also reflect on the presence of the Third Person of the Blessed Trinity in the formation and sustenance of the human being vis-à-vis Mary. This can be done within the framework of the mystery of the assumption since it is this mystery that principally brings about the proleptic reality that shapes and informs anthropos.

The Orthodox theologian Sergius Bulgakov offers a sustained reflection on the role of the Spirit in relation to the dormition, and in doing so offers us further insight into the way Mary (and thus the human being) is the theoanthropocosmic synthesis in complementarity to Christ. His work *The Burning Bush* is where this reflection is most thoroughly worked out.[42] Here, Bulgakov praises Mary insofar as the mystery of the dormition reveals the "glorification of human nature," making her "the ladder which Jacob saw" since "heaven and earth have been reunited and made one" in Mary. It is this mystery that reveals the *imago Dei* in the archetypal pair as the new Adam and new Eve: "The Divine image in humankind is disclosed and realized in the heavens as the image of two: of Christ and of His Mother."[43] All this is possible for Bulgakov only because Mary is the "Pneumatophoric Human"—since "such a being . . . is not a personal incarnation of the Holy Spirit, but she becomes His personal, animate receptacle, an absolutely spirit-born creature."[44] The asymptotically close link between the Spirit and Mary perhaps accounts for the pneumatic time that informs the virginal maternity and glorious telos of our Lady and thus, analogously, the human being as such. Therefore,

> it is incumbent on us to consider that the human essence of the Mother of God in heaven together with the Godman Jesus displays the full image of humankind. *The Icon of the Mother of God with Child*, the Logos and the creature receiving Him, filled with the Holy Spirit, in unity and its indivisibility, is *the full image* of humankind. The Godman and the Pneumatophore, the Son and the Mother, displaying the revelation of the Father through the Second and Third Hypostases, also display the fullness of the Divine image in humankind or, to put it another way, of the human image in God.[45]

42. Despite his brilliance, Bulgakov nevertheless descends into several false characterizations concerning the Catholic Church in this work. Robert F. Slesinski offers a fitting correction to Bulgakov's more polemical remarks while wonderfully expressing the richness of his theology: *Theology of Sergius Bulgakov*.

43. Bulgakov, *Burning Bush*, 80.

44. Bulgakov, *Burning Bush*, 81.

45. Bulgakov, *Burning Bush*, 82; emphasis in original.

Bulgakov's description helps us to see how the archetypal pair in glory, via the Spirit, bring about the full expression of anthropos, thus the theoanthropocosmic synthesis as a meta-anthropology. The Son "expresses the fullness *of the image* of human nature only together with the Mother of God, who thus has found her place in the heavens beside the glorified human nature of her Son, so that not only the male but also the female nature is glorified and divinized (though *in a different way*)." Therefore, this is "a revelation and realization of the fullness of the human image in the Godman and His Mother, which is given in any icon of the Mother of God."[46]

So, what we have here is this: the dormition—assumption—is the hermeneutical lens through which we behold the archetypal pair as the *full* and *complete* expression of anthropos, the theoanthropocosmic synthesis as *mere* creature through the Spirit, intrinsically united to the theoanthropocosmic synthesis as God the Logos, according to the providential will of the Father. Through this mystery of faith, we also see the *end* that fulfills the *beginning* and *entire course* of the life of anthropos, revealing the profoundly dignified human mystery apophatically—since it is an eschatological mystery—while nevertheless unveiling the ways in which the *origin*, *identity*, and *vocation* of the human being as such are substantively real intimations, patterns even, of what will come only in the *end* (possible only because *pneumatic* time constitutes the grammar of anthropos). Thus, the assumption, the fourth Marian dogma, enacts and recapitulates in an *illuminative* manner (grace/faith/theology) the glorious telos of the human being, while it also shines light on the mystery of the total human being as one who is in the process of becoming, the eschatologically deferred being.

> Glorified Mary, Heavenly Queen, is a creature and no longer a creature, for she made room in herself for the fullness of divine life. In her God is already "all in all," for her there no longer exists a further development or perfecting, as is still true for all creation, angelic and human. This is eternal life, if not of the Godhead itself, then eternal life in the Godhead, in the unfathomable deep of the ocean of the absolute. Creation became here perfectly transparent for the Creator.[47]

46. Bulgakov, *Burning Bush*, 83; emphasis in original.
47. Bulgakov, *Burning Bush*, 107.

We can now proceed to examine how Mary also *illustrates* (nature/reason/philosophy) the glorious end of anthropos. As we have observed thus far in our preceding chapters, a philosophical consideration of our Lady in view of the anthropos ought to yield further insights from the side of creatureliness as does a theological exploration from the side of grace.

## MARY'S ASSUMPTION ILLUSTRATES THE INEFFABLE END OF ANTHROPOS

Mary, as we have once again seen above, is the non-reductive expression of the human being as such—and so, as mere creature, she is the archetypal expression of the suspended middle, complementing Christ, who is that expression as God. Thus, there is ample room to explore philosophically her assumption in view of the question concerning the telos of anthropos, a question that no doubt remains open to what has already been pondered by theology. Doing so allows us to consider how our Lady's end *illustrates* (nature/reason/philosophy) in an explicative mode what is decisively revealed—*illumined*—by grace.

However, (Catholic) philosophy, although open to the datum of revelation and thus the *verticality* of grace, is nevertheless essentially operative within the *horizontality* of nature, concerned with the "rational" structure of being and reality, albeit not to the exclusion of what is beyond its reach. Just as grace presupposes nature without its destruction, so too philosophy is not undone but rather points to theology; thus, a real distinction between the two without schism or destruction.[48] How, then, ought we proceed in exploring philosophically the grace-filled reality of the assumption in view of its anthropological consequences? Perhaps we can begin with the existential, with the mode of human existence, with the circumscribed limits of the anthropos, and consider in what ways the givenness of such "boundary conditions" hints toward the requirement of a *vertical* reality, of transcendence, in order to fulfill and complete what is present *horizontally*, in the Blondelian spirit. Given the datum of theology, philosophy is justified in such a pursuit.

48. This interpenetration without confusion between grace/faith/theology and nature/reason/philosophy has been explored throughout our project and is maintained here. Consider again, for example, Falque, *Crossing the Rubicon*.

Emmanuel Falque articulates a vision of theology, like that of philosophy, that begins with finitude as the first given as it proceeds forward. While we may question whether such an approach for theology is strictly speaking warranted, he nevertheless offers a rationale for this beginning within the philosophical enterprise: "Finitude doesn't summarize a doctrine, but simply sums up the most ordinary existence of all human beings, including that of the Son of God, who was exactly 'made man' (*et homo factus est*)."[49] This, of course, applies also to Mary, and, without exception, to the human condition itself. This "ordinary existence of all human beings" can be our starting point in considering the telos of anthropos philosophically in view of the assumption. Doing so anchors our philosophic gaze to the facticity of lived existence and so takes seriously the conditions in which such queries about the end press.

Falque, using Heidegger's analysis in *Being and Time*, states that "Finitude (*Endlichkeit*), 'the impassable limit of our life,' means that life is completely dominated by care (*Sorge*), and it makes our Being-there (*Dasein*) a simple 'between,' caught between birth and death."[50] If this is the case, then (Catholic) philosophy must proceed with all seriousness *within* such limits without quickly escaping to "the other side" in order to do justice to the lived experience. It must root itself in the immanent without at the same time being dogmatically foreclosed to the transcended.[51] The glory of the resurrection shines all the more when the gravity of the carcass of Christ is truly felt. So too, the existential particularity of our Lady is the springboard from which we can philosophically explore the assumption. As was discussed earlier in our project, Maurice Blondel is a model for this way of immanence.[52] As Falque says, "Finitude as an access to the Christian path of human beings, though not as the last word

49. Falque, *Metamorphosis of Finitude*, 13.

50. Falque, *Metamorphosis of Finitude*, 13.

51. As Falque notes, "The return to, or rather the securing in place, of an *impassable immanence* does not then signify a refusal of transcendence, far from it; it only implies that we must think of both the one and the other differently, think of them better, in the way that phenomenology has today revised these concepts: Immanence must be understood as 'strictly confined with the bounds of internal *experience*' (Husserl), and transcendence as an 'openness [horizontal] of subjectivity' and no longer as a 'relation [vertical] of a subject to an object' which is exterior to it (Heidegger)" (*Metamorphosis of Finitude*, 18; emphasis in original). While we may quibble about the phenomenological approach Falque offers for "thinking better," he nevertheless identifies the *need* to properly parse the distinction between the two.

52. Falque even argues that we must "develop the method of immanence further" given to us by Blondel (Falque, *Metamorphosis of Finitude*, 19).

concerning that path, demands rather that we have the courage to loiter with all those who are our contemporaries, within the blocked horizon that comes from the simple fact of existing."[53]

In what way, then, is the givenness of our existential boundedness a hint toward a *vertical* reality, a transcendence? Does human time, for example, bound finitely, gesture toward the eternal? Is this even possible? "Man's first experience is initially that of his mortality; he sees that in and of himself he has no permanence."[54] Can knowledge of the eternal, then, somehow even arise from time? Without being dogmatically foreclosed to the datum of revelation, Thomas thought so: "As we attain to the knowledge of simple things by way of compound things, so must we reach to the knowledge of eternity by means of time [*per tempus*]."[55] These are serious philosophical queries as Ratzinger writes:

> The question of whether there is a future beyond death has always occupied men afresh and probably will never let go of them. . . . The man who has enjoyed the gift of being, of life, is terrified of the nothingness into which death seems to hurl him; he tries to flee from it. He yearns for life, for a future; indeed, man is so future-oriented that someone who no longer sees any future at all ahead can no longer endure the present, either—this is precisely why we are afraid, for example, to give an incurable patient unambiguous information about his condition.[56]

If the human being is to be completed, if anthropos is to not end in nothingness, a *nihil* that would run contrary to the very givenness of anthropological origin, identity, and vocation as discovered in our previous chapters, then, we can say, such a being would simply need *more* than the merely *horizontal*; it must somehow transcend its own death; it must be *more* than what death itself *appears* to be. For if death itself is the finality that results in nothing, then the human being, in the final analysis, is nothing.[57] And that would mean that what was hitherto discovered by way of a philosophical examination of our Lady's origin, identity, and vocation (chs. 2–4) is in fact wrong. It would mean that pneumatic time doesn't at all constitute the grammar of anthropos but rather nihilism

53. Falque, *Metamorphosis of Finitude*, 17.

54. Ratzinger/Benedict XVI, *Dogma and Preaching*, 257.

55. *ST* Ia, q. 10, a. 1 co.

56. Ratzinger/Benedict XVI, *Dogma and Preaching*, 255.

57. As F. H. Jacobi wrote, "Man has this choice, however, and this alone: Nothingness or God" ("Open Letter to Fichte," 534).

does. The proleptic appearance of death as nothing would reveal the human being as decisively *no-thing*.

The continued existence of *this* time, however—if it were at all possible—doesn't resolve this issue either given that finitude is the very condition of *this* existence; thus, everlasting life *here*, in this eon, is hell. As Ratzinger articulates, "No one can wish for himself that things will continue endlessly in this way; the endlessness of our everyday life is not a worthwhile goal, and therefore a medically induced immortality for man and mankind can only be a nightmare after all." This is so because "man is not psychologically equipped for the immortality of the body, and humanity would necessarily break into pieces from the internal tensions caused by the coexistence of generations that were speeding away from each other." Thus, the human being is bound to experience an irresolvable tension, "in that he wants infinity but necessarily fears endlessness; he needs a future, on the one hand, and, on the other hand, he cannot endure it."[58] How can this be resolved? Ratzinger explains:

> If the proper direction of the human yearning for the future compels us to distinguish between the tangible foreground of human routine and the authentic life that can be touched only occasionally and clandestinely, *then with an intrinsic necessity the question about what is to come must lead beyond what is tangible and onto the trail of mystery*. On the other hand, when it is a question of being or not being, man needs certainty more than anywhere else; if it is not given to him automatically, he tries to create it for himself.[59]

Thankfully, the human being doesn't need to have recourse to its own contriving. *If*, as Catholic philosophical thinking about our Lady in view of anthropos recognizes, it is the case that anthropological identity as maternal is the locus of union between the infinite and finite as finitude paradoxically containing the uncontainable infinite (ch. 2), and *if* anthropological vocation (virginal) is an eschatologically oriented exocentricity (ch. 3)—all of which presupposes a graced origin (immaculate) since both identity and vocation transcend its contingency paradoxically (ch. 4)—*then* it is supremely fitting that the proper end, the true telos, of this creature is the final and full realization of its eschatologically inscribed (pneumatic time) grace-filled virginal maternity. Rather than

58. Ratzinger/Benedict XVI, *Dogma and Preaching*, 256.

59. Ratzinger/Benedict XVI, *Dogma and Preaching*, 256; emphasis added.

considering the human being as a being toward death, death being death as nothing, Catholic philosophy can behold the human as a *being toward life via death* since death is *death then resurrection*. A philosophical appraisal of the telos of anthropos in view of the mystery of the assumption, then, is anchored in *hope* rather than despair. Since human identity, vocation, and origin are uniquely inscribed by means of a transcendent, eternal Reality who is its origin and center as the One who desires to be "all in all," then reason can discern an ineffable culmination and completion as the proper telos, ineffable only because the end to which the anthropos is oriented toward is an eternal, transcendent one: *God*! And as we have discussed in our first chapter, that we "live, move, and have our being" in this eternal Source means that the Trinitarian ontology discoverable does in fact already reveal the deep intimations of what will eventually and uniquely come to be in Mary in a decisively new mode, and, by extension, the anthropos. Metaphysically speaking, in other words, God is indeed already "all in all," and this is the very bedrock by which pneumatic time stands, revealing, as it were, the unfolding relation between time and eternity. The following extensive quote from Erich Przywara is helpful in elucidating this:

> The full mystery of time and eternity is apparent . . . only when *time and space* appear, in their correlation, in a relation of contrast to the divine. *Augustine* conceived this contrasting relation as a single "*transcending immanence*": God as the innermost "in" of space-time as well as its highest and deepest "beyond." The essentially supraspatial and supratemporal God pervades the intraspatial and intratemporal realm of the creature so thoroughly that, in relation to space, he is the one who is "both interior to all things, because all things are in him, and exterior to all things, because he is beyond all things"; and that, in relation to time, he is "both older than all things, because he is before all things, and newer than all things, because he is the same after all things."[60]

All this means that human time, determinatively finite because circumscribed by birth and death, cannot in fact be the only mode of being there is. There must be a different mode of existence capable for that creature who, in view of this telos, is in the process of becoming far more than what it appears to be now. This "far more" of course doesn't negate the givenness of its facticity but transfigures it from the inside out. The assumption, like the resurrection, is the taking up of "body and soul"

60. Przywara, *Analogia Entis*, 589; emphasis in original.

into glory—thus, the *inclusion* of its givenness into something *more*. As Falque notes, "If the closure of time remains necessarily a given from the point of view of human beings . . . only God possesses the capacity of transfiguring the structure of time and our relationship with him, because he did so 'once for all when he offered himself' (Heb 7:27)."[61] "Only the resurrection is capable of breaking through the chains of both finitude and of temporality,"[62] as the assumption itself reveals anthropologically. Again, this eternal—eschatological—"end" does not destroy time, negating it as some phantom, but rather *reveals the mysterious relation between the eternal and the temporal*. The eternal, in fact, is inaugurated by means of the temporal end of this life. The eternal comes by way of death and not despite it. This itself is sustained by the metaphysics we have hitherto explored in this project. As Przywara notes,

> Rather, the utterly incomprehensible mystery of time and eternity lies in this: that every particular "neutral" moment is both a divine "infinite moment of fullness" and a creaturely "finite moment of emptiness." Time and eternity are thus . . . the site where, in the "moment," God and creature so nearly coincide in a, so to speak, natural "divine-human moment" that precisely herein they are distinguished by an "infinite difference."[63]

Thus, time relates to God's eternality within the analogical difference between the "nearly" coincident and the "infinite difference." Thus time—like nature, reason, and philosophy—is sustained and not undone; and it is by its very modality that the eternal—correlating to grace, faith, and theology—comes into view. As Ratzinger puts it, "Death is redemption, a blessing, because in it this entire unrefined existence, which is prone to sin and so ill disposed, is renovated and reworked into a new one."[64] Given what has been discovered thus far concerning anthropological origin, identity, and vocation, death is indeed *death*—the cessation of *this life*—since the origin, like its identity and vocation, is eschatologically informed; as Aquinas articulates, we are naturally oriented to the supernatural, thus *death and resurrection* as the telos of anthropos.

> This means that death in itself remains for us a frightful negation of the whole man, but, in a marvelous reversal, this negation

61. Falque, *Metamorphosis of Finitude*, 112.
62. Falque, *Metamorphosis of Finitude*, 22.
63. Przywara, *Analogia Entis*, 589.
64. Ratzinger/Benedict XVI, *Dogma and Preaching*, 252.

> now becomes the prerequisite for a new, positive reality: out of the destruction is born the new thing. Thus Christianity, unlike idealism, does not simply deny the terror and frightfulness of death. Instead, that continues to exist, but it becomes, precisely as such, the instrument of grace and salvation, in a reversal that could never be imagined from an earthly perspective but can only be decreed by God.[65]

And so just as our *beginning* is one both in time and eternity (baptism/election), so our end, the "omega" to the "alpha" of our beginning, is its perfect culmination:

> Death as a whole, that is, that *processus mortis in vitam* which permeates our whole life, is as such our baptism, the gradual success of the new Adam. . . . It is a grace-filled event, inasmuch as God snatches away from us our natural, self-willed, rebellious life at the tribunal of death so as to recreate us for the life of holiness and love. Basically everything is said with the observation that death (taken in each case as a whole) is the realization of our baptism.[66]

Anthropological *culmination* recapitulates its (baptismal) *origination*, and so fulfills what begins (in time) in anthropological *identity* and *vocation*. This is the end that is *illustrated* (nature/reason/philosophy) by our Lady's assumption, the culminating reality of the human being as such, which is simultaneously *illumined* (grace/faith/theology) by such a glorious end. The mystery of the assumption *illumines illustratively* the human telos; thus, this mystery of faith both enacts and recapitulates such a telos theo-philosophically. Therefore, the telos of anthropos is *love*, for the culminating end that completely and entirely fulfills anthropological reality, the end that realizes the *beginning* and sustains the *middle* proleptically, is God, and God is love (1 John 4:8). The anthropos, then, is entirely made for love—God. Mary, forever Virgin and Mother, Immaculata, Panagia, Queen of Heaven, assumed into glory, reveals this theo-philosophically.

> Immortality, according to the Christian faith, fundamentally has to do with love. The only eternal thing is love; as *love*, God is eternity. And *his* love, in turn, is man's eternity; in being loved by eternal Love, he is lifted up imperishably. He is lifted up, because he himself can love. For him, too, love is the only thing that gives eternity; the measure and manner of his eternity depend on the

65. Ratzinger/Benedict XVI, *Dogma and Preaching*, 252.

66. Ratzinger/Benedict XVI, *Dogma and Preaching*, 253.

> measure and manner of his loving. But if his loving is his future, then the future for him is both doing and receiving—at the same time entirely his own and entirely what is given to him.[67]

## CONCLUSION: ANTHROPOLOGICAL TELOS

This chapter offered an examination of Mary's assumption in view of anthropological telos theo-philosophically, wherein we discerned how this mystery of faith concerning our Lady both *illumines* and *illustrates* the end of the anthropos, thus revealing the human as the eschatologically deferred being. We began by examining the significance of this dogmatic truth of Mary in relation to the other truths explored earlier in this project. By observing how the assumption includes the total reality of Mary—"body and soul"—we were able to note how it essentially affirms her being *the* theoanthropocosmic synthesis as *mere* creature. And by considering the proleptic reality of this eschatological "event," we also noted how, in fulfilling the entire reality of the human being as such—origin, identity, vocation—this telos seen in Mary reveals the human being to be the apophatically concealed being.

We then were able to explore how pneumatic time—the temporal/eternal dynamic—constitutes the mystery of the assumption as an eschatological "event" that occurs at the end of *this* time, happening at a specific day and hour only known to God, thus a twofold dynamism at work. This furnished a further insight: the assumption is the "omega" to the corresponding "alpha" of our Lady's immaculate conception, and so for the originating (immaculate) and culminating (glorified) events of anthropos as such.

Given what was examined, we then explored in greater detail how the assumption *illumines* anthropological end in a totalizing way, specifically paying close attention to how the body could in fact "continue" beyond the temporal terminus of death. Saint Maximus's theologically informed metaphysics was important for us here as we attempted to think through the query concerning the body/flesh in an eschatological mode, and how that *illumines* the somatic reality of anthropos within the entirety of its frame. This opened space for us to further consider the role of pneumatic time within the relation between the telos and the origin, identity, and vocation of the human being as such, which, in turn,

67. Ratzinger/Benedict XVI, *Dogma and Preaching*, 259; emphasis in original.

revealed how the enacting in time one's maternal identity and virginal vocation—an enactment described in chapters 2–3 of this project—is the dynamic unfolding of theosis, of sanctification. Theosis/sanctification is, then, the proleptic arrival of the *yet unknown*.

This then positioned us to consider the glorious end of our Lady in relation to her Son through the use of Bulgakov's insights, helping us to discover the following: the dormition—assumption—is the hermeneutical lens through which we behold the archetypal pair as the *full* and *complete* expression of anthropos, the theoanthropocosmic synthesis as *mere* creature vis-à-vis Spirit, intrinsically united to the theoanthropocosmic synthesis as God the Logos, according to the providential will of the Father.

Finally, we proceeded to specifically examine how Mary *illustrates* what in fact is given *illuminatively*. By returning to the question of her creatureliness, we explored how human finitude might suggest something more, something beyond what is merely given. Considering what was hitherto discovered in our previous chapters, and with recourse to Falque, Ratzinger, and Przywara, we were able to identify the few ways a philosophical examination of the assumption via the contingency of creatureliness *illustrates* the ineffable culmination of the human being. In the end, theo-philosophically observed, Mary reveals that this unutterable *end*, this glorious culmination apophatically concealed, which also happens to be the essential *beginning* and sustaining *middle*, can in fact be uttered in a single word: Love.

# Conclusion

## OPENING

To bring together our findings within our study of constructive Marian theo-philosophical anthropology, we will conclude this project by summarizing the key insights in relation to the research aims. This chapter will also discuss the value and contribution of this research. Finally, we will note the limitations of the study and propose various opportunities for future research.

## OVERALL FINDINGS IN RELATION TO THE RESEARCH AIMS

This study investigated how Mary, given her unique position in the divine economy, enacts and recapitulates what it means to be human theo-philosophically. Several research objectives were identified in our introduction as ingredient for the constructive approach needed to study the various ways in which our Lady is decisive for anthropology. One objective was to identify a metaphysical basis for situating anthropological reflections under Mariology. The results indicate that, because of our Lady's *intrinsic* relation to the Trinitarian hypostasis (for she is the Theotokos, *Mother* of God), she is the expressed concretization of Erich Przywara's description of the *analogia entis* as *mere* creature. Thus, a Trinitarian ontology, construed along the *analogia entis*, is unveiled in and through Mary's unique person and work, which in turn grants us a pleromatic vision of the metaphysics that establishes her as definitive for anthropology. She is the existential icon of a creaturely metaphysics, ever only as mere creature. Therefore, this initial step in our project was essential because in discerning how Mary is a perfect manifestation of a creaturely metaphysics as a human hypostasis, it then follows that in her person and work she recapitulates and reveals what it means to *be* a creature, and, conjointly with her Son, an authentic human being. Given the above results, we were then able to observe how our Lady inimitably reveals in a personified manner the dynamic, undivided relationship between *nature* and *grace*—and so, coextensively, *faith* and *reason*, *theology* and *philosophy*, and *God* and *creation*. This allowed us to address another research objective we had: to identify how both a theological and philosophical consideration of Mary in view of anthropology is justified given the metaphysical basis aforementioned. Since our Lady is the peaceful interval and rhythmic beat of the Trinitarian unity in difference as *mere* creature, she reveals, in unity with her Son *in* and *by* his humanity received from her, what grace can do with nature, and what nature is called to in grace. In her as in her Child, we see how grace is in and beyond nature, how theology is in and beyond philosophy, and how faith is in and beyond reason, for their undivided relational dynamic is also construed along an analogical interval such that theology does not destroy philosophy, faith does not undo reason, nor does grace negate nature. Thus, we observed that philosophy, reason, and nature—the creaturely correlates to Mary as mere creature—are elevated in a theophanic pitch that not only maintains their creaturely integrity but perfects it, as we see in the Theotokos. Therefore, Mary, as the concrete expression of the analogical ontology as a nonfoundational, decentering, suspended middle, like her Son though in a distinct register, *illumines* anthropology as *Theotokos*, the theological (Mariology) illuminating the philosophical (creaturely being), while also *illustrating* anthropological truths as a mere human person, the philosophical explicating the theological. So, given the metaphysics discernible in Mary—a Trinitarian ontology via *analogia entis* by way of her unique placement in the divine economy—we discovered there are good grounds to offer a sustained theological *and* philosophical meditation on our Lady in view of anthropological considerations.

The third objective for our study was to examine how the church's four Marian dogmatic statements effectively address the perennial questions concerning the human being: anthropological origin, identity, vocation, and destiny. Presupposing the inner unity and coherence of the dogmatic truths, we identified how each dogmatic teaching about Mary offer a response—given the unity of our Lady's being and person—to those questions implicit in human existence: Mary's divine maternity unfolds the maternal identity of anthropos; her perpetual virginity identifies anthropological vocation; her immaculate conception reveals the decisive origin of the human being; and her assumption details the end, the destiny of the anthropos as such. By reflecting on the inner coherence of these dogmatic truths in view of the temporal mechanics discernible therein, we discovered that the crucial mystery of anthropos can only really be apprehended within a temporal/eternal dynamic—called here *pneumatic time*—since, in the light of our Lady, human identity and vocation can only ever be understood by way of the proleptic appearance of the eschatological end, as well as the eternal/temporal beginning of the human being. This is so also since, through Mary, we observe that *God* is indeed the utter origin and end of anthropos, and anthropological identity and vocation are decisively informed by the *eternal* presencing of God (without the undoing of time as such). By way of an anthropological construction predicated upon Mary vis-à-vis the dogmatic truths, we concluded the following: (1) human identity (as maternal) is the *locus of union* between the infinite and finite, the finite paradoxically containing the infinite; (2) human vocation (as virginal) is an *eschatologically oriented exocentricity*; (3) human origin (as immaculate) is the temporal (baptism) realization in grace, revealing an eternal (election) "beginning" (4) human destiny is a twofold end, enacted with the "completion" of this temporal age, and so the "beginning" of the eternal, thus revealing, because of the proleptic realization of the eschatological *within* human identity and vocation, the human being to be the *apophatically concealed, eschatologically deferred being*. In addition, by considering the ways in which our Lady not only enacts and recapitulates the anthropos but also shows us the way forward, we examined how human identity, vocation, beginning, and ending can in fact be realized for those who seek to follow her, the true human being, conjointly with Christ her Son. Through our own fiat, gestation, birth giving, and subsequent parenting of the Word, our maternal identity is enacted, which coincides with our vocation, which is to live a chaste life in pursuit of God, for God, in God, by God's grace. This, as we argued, can be achieved only by baptism/election, and such a life lived will result in the completion of this age and its full, ineffable realization in the eschaton via death. These are the results of our theo-philosophical—theological *and* philosophical—meditations on our Lady.

Finally, our fourth objective, which was to identify the ways in which Mary is the theoanthropocosmic synthesis as a *mere* human being, was addressed throughout our research in the following ways: (1) by virtue of the metaphysics discoverable and articulated in and through her unique position in the divine economy, she *is* such a synthesis; and (2) by way of her unique identity, vocation, origin, and, especially, her ineffably glorious end, she is this synthesis, as *mere* creature (while her Son is this synthesis as God). Thus, by extension, each human being is called to "live out" this synthesis in imitation of our Lady and our Lord.

## CONTRIBUTIONS TO THE FIELD

This research has sought to offer a constructive approach to a Mariologically informed theo-philosophical anthropology. Although theologically and philosophically informed anthropologies abound (see the introduction), and anthropological considerations in view of Mary have been offered, little if any research (to my knowledge) has been done on providing a robust *metaphysically* informed *theo-philosophical* anthropology that draws out the enduring significance of our Lady for anthropological reflection. In addition, I am not aware of any research that simultaneously considers all the dogmatic truths of Mary in view of anthropology, while coordinating those truths explicitly to those questions concerning anthropological origin, end, identity, and vocation. As noted in our introduction, some Mariologically informed anthropologies have examined in a general manner ways in which Mary offers an archetypal and paradigmatic response (typically via a pastoral mode) to contemporary issues, while other research has tended to elaborate on how various dogmatic truths of our Lady (i.e., divine maternity, immaculate conception, etc.) provide certain insights into the human condition. However, these studies have tended to focus either only on certain aspects of Mary in relation to anthropology or on a general appraisal of anthropological insights observable given her place in the divine economy. Thus, this project contributes toward addressing these gaps in the current fields of theological and philosophical anthropology, as well as Mariology in general, in the following way: developing (1) a robust *metaphysically* informed theo-philosophical anthropology that draws out the enduring significance Mary has *for* anthropology; (2) a full-bodied Mariological anthropology that considers *simultaneously all* the dogmatic truths of our Lady, especially in the light of perennial questions concerning human origin, identity, vocation, and destiny; (3) a Mariologically informed anthropology that recognizes the significant role both theology *and* philosophy have in exploring the ways in which Mary mutually *illumines* (grace/faith/theology) and *illustrates* (nature/reason/philosophy) anthropology.

In addition, by identifying a Trinitarian ontology as the shape of the analogy of being uniquely revealed in Mary (ch. 1), metaphysical justification for research in both theological and philosophical anthropology vis-à-vis Mariology is provided. By coordinating the dogmatic claims of our Lady to those perennial anthropological queries, this research also shows the inner coherence of those questions implicit to the human being as such, a unity that reveals an *intrinsic* and thus necessary relation among the origin, identity, vocation, and telos of the human being. This intrinsic relatedness among the various facets and qualities of anthropos also shows how a proper reckoning of time and eternity is ingredient to apprehending the deep mystery of the human being since the origin and end, the identity and vocation of such a being is inscribed by a temporal/eternal dynamic: pneumatic time. Thus, any attempt at understanding the human being without recourse to the simultaneity of time and eternity—pneumatic time—will effectively be futile, given what we observe in our Marian theo-philosophical anthropology. These discoveries, I believe, are significant contributions to the field of theological and philosophical anthropology.

Other ways in which this research contributes to anthropology, especially theologically, can be noted as follows: (1) We discovered that Mariology safeguards an anthropology that is informed by a *mere* human being and person, thus the creaturely reception and response to the person of Christ, external to Christ's human nature, yet inclusive of it. (2) We also observed how Mariology reveals the preeminent expression of a human hypostasis in the economy of grace; thus (3) Mariology unveils decisive "modes" in which the human being and person relates to God in complementarity to Christ the God-anthropos, thus the synergistic partnering that comes from one who is not a divine hypostasis, which allows for the expression of faith and other virtues from the side of human hypostasis as manifestations of divine grace. (4) We also discerned how Mariology "fleshes out" the unity ingredient to the one Lord Jesus the Christ, thus sustaining the inherent logic of the hypostatic union of the dual natures of Christ and so safeguards the hominization of God and the deification of anthropos, while also grounding the complementarity of the new Adam and the new Eve. Absent these discoveries, an impoverished anthropology will ensue, thus leading theological and philosophical anthropology astray—and all theology subsequently. Thus, as we have observed implicitly throughout this study, a Christomonistic approach to anthropology fails to discern the significant role Mary has in revealing the human being, as a mere creature, in the economy of grace as decisively shaped by a synergistic partnering with the God-anthropos. "Christ alone" cannot account for a full complementarity that is given only along with Mary, and, by extension, the human being as such.

This research also contributes to pastoral considerations concerning human growth and development by way of discipleship. Since Mary enacts and sums up what it means to be human, by turning to her one orients oneself toward the truth of human origination and ending, and discovers authentic human identity and vocation. By closely examining the ways our Lady enacts the robust truth of anthropos, a model and pathway is given such that one could practically enact those very truths in one's life to fully actualize the truth of one's very being and personhood.

## LIMITATIONS

There are several limits to this study. First, as stated in the introduction, the scope of this research was confined to a theological and philosophical investigation of Mary with respect to anthropology in general. Therefore, this was not a study on Mariology *as such*. In addition, our investigation assumed the inner unity and coherence of the Catholic Church's dogmatic teachings about our Lady—while also clearly presupposing the truth-value of such statements from the dogmatic tradition of the Catholic Church—and that it is indeed possible to coordinate these teachings with various anthropological questions in view of elucidating a deeper insight into the mystery of human being. Additionally, explicit questions about the role of gender and other socio-politico-cultural items were not discussed in this project. While these are no doubt important areas of investigation, this project was limited to the metaphysical and architectonic structure of Mary (in concert with her Son) to offer a constructive account of anthropos both theological and philosophical.

This investigation was also limited methodologically to a qualitative and constructive approach. And while an anthropological investigation was pursued in the light of each of the four dogmatic truths theo-philosophically, this investigative approach was not exhaustive. Rather, the researcher sought merely to establish the architectonic structure inherent to the anthropos within a theo-philosophical mode, a structure revealed uniquely in our Lady. Therefore, the constructive approach offered in this study is rooted in a modest appraisal of the datum given from both revelation (faith-reason) and nature (reason-faith) discernible in Mary vis-à-vis the dogmatic tradition of the Catholic Church in view of anthropology. Finally, the researcher's own limited experience in research as extensive as this study required no doubt posed an overall restriction to this investigation.

## RECOMMENDATIONS FOR FUTURE RESEARCH

Since this project focused on offering a generally modest appraisal of the anthropological insights engendered by a close look at our Lady, future research could concentrate on human origin, identity, vocation, and/or ending in the light of what has been offered here, building forward. There is a good deal of space to elaborate on the findings in this research, including the possibility of investigating other potential metaphysical models discernible in Mary *for* anthropological investigation. Further research could explore the temporal/eternal dynamic that constitutes the anthropos, perhaps in reference to Henri Bergson's *la durée*, for example. Several philosophers have been referenced in this project (i.e., M. Merleau-Ponty, M. Henry, M. Blondel, etc.), but much more could be said as to how their respective work indeed gestures toward what is in fact revealed decisively in Mary, and how their philosophical insights could help to continue to explicate what is revealed. Indeed, further investigation into the fathers and doctors of the church, as well as the magisterial teachings and Scripture, could yield even deeper insights only initially articulated in this work, providing more fodder for greater philosophical explication that would further illuminate and illustrate the mysteries ingredient to anthropology.

I envision this research possessing a generative dynamic that could far exceed the life of this project. Given the scope of this work, it could potentially impact the fields of psychology, sociology, anthropology "proper," and other similar domains, while also having a reverberating effect within the intersecting fields of theology and philosophy. Given, for example, a phenomenological approach rooted in a metaphysical context that is experientially opened and thus amiable to testing (via human experience), the research findings could potentially be examined through a series of introspective and meditative methodologies while also providing a particular "model" of the human being that could be tested and explored considering various empirical methodologies. Given this, the evidence of a clear pathway to potential scientific engagement seems intrinsic to the very nature of this research and overall project.

## CLOSING SUMMARY

Guided by a qualitative and constructive methodology, this research offered an exploratory account of Mary, Mother of God, in view of cultivating a theo-philosophical anthropology. By way of the church's four dogmatic statements about our Lady, this project investigated human origination, ending, identity, and vocation theologically and philosophically. Given her unique position in the divine economy, we conclude that Mary enacts and recapitulates what it means to be human—the anthropos—theo-philosophically.

# Bibliography

Allen, Prudence. "Mary and the Vocation of Philosophers." *NBf* 90 (2009) 50–72.

Augustine. *The Confessions of Saint Augustine*. Edited by Hal McElwaine Helms. Brewster, MA: Paraclete, 2010.

Balthasar, Hans Urs von. *Dramatis Personae: Man in God*. Translated by Graham Harrison. Vol. 2 of *Theo-Drama: Theological Dramatic Theory*. San Francisco: Ignatius, 1992.

———. *A Theology of History*. Communio. San Francisco: Ignatius, 1994.

Balthasar, Hans Urs von, and Joseph Cardinal Ratzinger. *Mary: The Church at the Source*. San Francisco: Ignatius, 2005.

Barth, Karl. *The Doctrine of Creation*. Edited by G. W. Bromiley and T. F. Torrance. Vol. III/2 of *Church Dogmatics*. Edinburgh: T&T Clark, 1960.

Barth, Karl, and Eduard Thurneysen. *1921 to 1930*. Vol. 2 of *Briefweschsel*. Gesamtausgabe. Zurich: Theologisch, 1974.

Behr, John. *Becoming Human: Meditations on Christian Anthropology in Word and Image*. Crestwood, NY: St. Vladimir's Seminary Press, 2013.

———. *John the Theologian and His Paschal Gospel: A Prologue to Theology*. 2nd ed. Oxford: Oxford University Press, 2019.

———. *The Mystery of Christ: Life in Death*. Crestwood, NY: St. Vladimir's Seminary Press, 2006.

Benedict XVI. *Anthropology and Culture*. Edited by David L. Schindler and Nicholas J. Healy. Vol. 2 of *Joseph Ratzinger in "Communio."* Ressourcement. Grand Rapids: Eerdmans, 2013.

———. *See also* Ratzinger, Joseph; Ratzinger, Joseph/Benedict XVI.

Blondel, Maurice. *Action (1893): Essay on a Critique of Life and a Science of Practice*. Translated by Oliva Blanchette. Notre Dame, IN: University of Notre Dame Press, 1984.

———. *"The Letter on Apologetics" & "History and Dogma."* Edited and translated by Alexander Dru and Illtyd Trethowan. Ressourcement. Grand Rapids: Eerdmans, 1994.

———. *Philosophical Exigencies of Christian Religion*. Translated by Oliva Blanchette. Thresholds in Philosophy and Theology. Notre Dame, IN: University of Notre Dame Press, 2021.

Bonhoeffer, Dietrich. *Act and Being: Transcendental Philosophy and Ontology in Systematic Theology*. Edited by Wayne W. Floyd. Translated by Hans-Richard Reuter and H. Martin Rumscheidt. Minneapolis: Fortress, 2009.

———. *Creation and Fall. Temptation: Two Biblical Studies. Creation and Fall* translated by John C. Fletcher, revised by editorial staff of SCM Press; *Temptation* edited by Eberhard Bethge, translated by Kathleen Downham. New York: Simon & Schuster, 1997.

Bouyer, Louis. *The Meaning of the Monastic Life.* Translated by Kathleen Pond. New York: Kennedy and Sons, 1955.

———. *The Seat of Wisdom: An Essay on the Place of the Virgin Mary in Christian Theology.* Translated by A. V. Littledale. New York: Pantheon, 1960.

———. *Woman and Man with God: An Essay on the Place of the Virgin Mary in Christian Theology and Its Significance for Humanity.* Translated by A. V. Littledale. London: Darton, Longman and Todd, 1960.

Bulgakov, Sergius. *The Burning Bush: On the Orthodox Veneration of the Mother of God.* Translated by Thomas Allan Smith. Grand Rapids: Eerdmans, 2009.

Cabasilas, Nicholas. "Homily on the Annunciation." *Communio: International Catholic Review* 46 (2019) 386–98.

———. *The Life in Christ.* Translated by Carmino J. DeCatanzaro. Crestwood, NY: St. Vladimir's Seminary Press, 1974.

Calloway, Donald H. Foreword to *Mother Thrice Admirable: An Introduction to the Mariology of Fr. Joseph Kentenich,* by Danielle M. Peters and John Larson, 5–7. Stockbridge, MA: Marian, 2019.

———, ed. "The Virgin Mary and Theological Anthropology." Special issue, *Mater Misericordiae: An Annual Journal of Mariology* 3 (2018).

———. *The Virgin Mary and Theology of the Body.* Stockbridge, MA: Marian, 2005.

Catholic Church. *Catechism of the Catholic Church: Revised in Accordance with the Official Latin Text Promulgated by Pope John Paul II.* Washington, DC: United States Catholic Conference, 2000.

Chardon, Louis. *The Cross of Jesus.* Translated by Richard Murphy. 2 vols. Petersham, MA: Stella Maris, 2018.

Chrétien, Jean-Louis. *The Ark of Speech.* Translated by Andrew Brown. London: Routledge, 2004.

———. *The Call and the Response.* Translated by Anne A. Davenport. Perspectives in Continental Philosophy. New York: Fordham University Press, 2004.

Clifford, Anne M. "When Being Human Becomes Truly Earthy: An Ecofeminist Proposal for Solidarity." In *In the Embrace of God: Feminist Approaches to Theological Anthropology,* edited by Ann O'Hara Graff, 173–89. Maryknoll, NY: Orbis, 1995.

Congregation for Catholic Education. "Magisterial Documents: The Virgin Mary in Intellectual and Spiritual Formation." Seminary of Christ the King, Mar. 25, 1988. https://sck.ca/wp-content/uploads/2020/02/The-Virgin-Mary-in-Intellectual-and-Spiritual-Formation.pdf.

Cunningham, Conor. "*Natura Pura,* the Invention of the Anti-Christ: A Week with No Sabbath." *Communio* 37 (2010) 243–54.

Cunningham, Mary B. *Gateway of Life: Orthodox Thinking on the Mother of God.* Foundations 7. Yonkers, NY: St. Vladimir's Seminary Press, 2015.

———, trans. *Wider Than Heaven: Eighth-Century Homilies on the Mother of God.* Popular Patristics. Crestwood, NY: St. Vladimir's Seminary Press, 2008.

Dante Alighieri. *The Divine Comedy.* Translated by Allen Mandelbaum. Everyman's Library Classics Series. New York: Knopf Doubleday, 1995.

———. *Paradiso*. Translated by Allen Mandelbaum. Vol. 3 of *The Divine Comedy*. Bantam Classics. New York: Bantam, 1984.

Denzinger, Heinrich Joseph. *The Sources of Catholic Dogma*. Translated by Roy J. Deferrari. 30th ed. Self-published, CreateSpace, 2013.

Dillon, Martin C. *Merleau-Ponty's Ontology*. 2nd ed. Evanston, IL: Northwestern University Press, 1997.

Doherty, Cathal. *Maurice Blondel on the Supernatural in Human Action: Sacrament and Superstition*. Brill's Studies in Catholic Theology 4. Leiden: Brill, 2017.

Duffy, Stephen J. "Anthropology." In *Augustine Through the Ages: An Encyclopedia*, edited by Allan Fitzgerald and John C. Cavadini, 24–31. Grand Rapids: Eerdmans, 1999.

Dunn, Rose Ellen. *Finding Grace with God: A Phenomenological Reading of the Annunciation*. Eugene, OR: Pickwick Publications, 2014.

Dupré, Louis. *Passage to Modernity: An Essay on the Hermeneutics of Nature and Culture*. New Haven: Yale University Press, 1993.

Edgar, Orion. *Things Seen and Unseen: The Logic of Incarnation in Merleau-Ponty's Metaphysics of Flesh*. Veritas. Eugene, OR: Cascade Books, 2016.

Falque, Emmanuel. *Crossing the Rubicon: The Borderlands of Philosophy and Theology*. Translated by Reuben Shank. Perspectives in Continental Philosophy. New York: Fordham University Press, 2016.

———. *God, the Flesh, and the Other: From Irenaeus to Duns Scotus*. Translated by William Christian Hackett. Evanston, IL: Northwestern University Press, 2015.

———. *The Metamorphosis of Finitude: An Essay on Birth and Resurrection*. Translated by George Hughes. Perspectives in Continental Philosophy. New York: Fordham University Press, 2012.

Fehlner, Peter Damian. *Theologian of Auschwitz: St. Maximilian M. Kolbe on the Immaculate Conception in the Life of the Church*. Hobe Sound, FL: Lectio, 2019.

Florensky, Pavel. *The Pillar and Ground of the Truth: An Essay in Orthodox Theodicy in Twelve Letters*. Translated by Boris Jakim. Princeton: Princeton University Press, 1997.

Fourth Lateran Council. "Constitution 2." In *Decrees of the Ecumenical Councils*, edited by Norman P. Tanner, 1:231–32. Washington, DC: Georgetown University Press, 1990.

Foster, David Ruel, and Joseph W. Koterski, eds. *The Two Wings of Catholic Thought: Essays on "Fides et Ratio."* Washington, DC: Catholic University of America Press, 2003.

Galot, Jean. *Maria: La donna nell'opera della salvezza*. 3rd ed. Rome: Ed. Pontificia Universita Gregoriana, 2005.

Gambero, Luigi. *Mary and the Fathers of the Church: The Blessed Virgin Mary in Patristic Thought*. Translated by Thomas Buffer. San Francisco: Ignatius, 1999.

———. *Mary in the Middle Ages: The Blessed Virgin Mary in the Thought of Medieval Latin Theologians*. Translated by Thomas Buffer. San Francisco: Ignatius, 2005.

Gilson, Étienne. *On the Art of Misunderstanding Thomism*. McAuley Lectures 1966. West Hartford, CT: St. Joseph College, 1966.

Gonzales, Philip. "Thinking Towards an Analogical Mariology." In *Commitments to Medieval Mysticism Within Contemporary Contexts*, edited by Patrick Cooper and Satoshi Kikuchi, 111–28. BETL 290. Leuven: Peeters, 2017.

Gregory of Nyssa. *The Life of Moses*. Edited and translated by Abraham J. Malherbe and Everett Ferguson. Classics of Western Spirituality. New York: Paulist, 1978.

Gutiérrez, Gustavo. *A Theology of Liberation: History, Politics, and Salvation*. Maryknoll, NY: Orbis, 1988.

Haffner, Paul. "The End of Our Blessed Lady's Earthly Life, Her Glorious Assumption and Their Implications for Today." In *De Maria Numquam Satis: The Significance of the Catholic Doctrines on the Blessed Virgin Mary for All People*, edited by Judith Marie Gentle and Robert L. Fastiggi, 69–91. Lanham, MD: University Press of America, 2009.

Hart, David Bentley. *The Hidden and the Manifest: Essays in Theology and Metaphysics*. Grand Rapids: Eerdmans, 2017.

Hauke, Manfred. *Introduction to Mariology*. Translated by Richard Chonak. Washington, DC: Catholic University of America Press, 2020.

Healey, Kilian J. "The Assumption Among Mary's Privileges." *Thomist* 14 (1951) 72–92.

Heidegger, Martin. "The Problem of a Possible Determination of Finitude in Human Beings." In *Kant and the Problem of Metaphysics*, translated by Richard Taft, 153–62. 5th ed. Studies in Continental Thought. Bloomington: Indiana University Press, 1997.

Heintz, Michael. "Mariology as Theological Anthropology: Louis Boyer on Mary, Seat of Wisdom." In *Mary on the Eve of the Second Vatican Council*, edited by John C. Cavadini and Danielle M. Peters, 204–25. Notre Dame, IN: University of Notre Dame Press, 2017.

Hemmerle, Klaus. *Theses Towards a Trinitarian Ontology*. Translated by Stephen Churchyard. Brooklyn: Angelico, 2020.

Henry, Michel. *Incarnation: A Philosophy of Flesh*. Translated by Karl Hefty. Studies in Phenomenology and Existential Philosophy. Evanston, IL: Northwestern University Press, 2015.

———. *Words of Christ*. Translated by Christina M. Gschwandtner. Interventions. Grand Rapids: Eerdmans, 2012.

Hugon, Édouard. *Mary, Full of Grace: Plena Sibi, Superplena Nobis*. Edited and translated by John G. Brungardt. Providence, RI: Cluny, 2019.

International Theological Commission. "Communion and Stewardship: Human Persons Created in the Image of God." Vatican, July 23, 2004. https://www.vatican.va/roman_curia/congregations/cfaith/cti_documents/rc_con_cfaith_doc_20040723_communion-stewardship_en.html.

———. "The Dignity and Rights of the Human Person." Vatican, 1983. https://www.vatican.va/roman_curia/congregations/cfaith/cti_documents/rc_cti_1983_dignita-diritti_en.html.

———. "Theology, Christology, Anthropology." Vatican, 1982. https://www.vatican.va/roman_curia/congregations/cfaith/cti_documents/rc_cti_1982_teologia-cristologia-antropologia_en.html.

———. "Unity of the Faith and Theological Pluralism." Vatican, Oct. 10–11, 1972. https://www.vatican.va/roman_curia/congregations/cfaith/cti_documents/rc_cti_1972_fede-pluralismo_en.html.

Jacobi, Friedrich Heinrich. "Open Letter to Fichte." In *The Main Philosophical Writings and the Novel "Allwill,"* translated by George di Giovanni. McGill-Queen's Studies in the History of Ideas 18. Montreal: McGill-Queen's University Press, 1994.

Janicaud, Dominique, et al. *Phenomenology and the "Theological Turn": The French Debate*. Perspectives in Continental Philosophy. New York: Fordham University, 2000.

John of Damascus. *The Mother of the Lord: Memory, Presence, Hope*. Translated by Thomas A. Thompson. Staten Island, NY: St. Paul, 2007.

———. "An Oration on the Nativity of the Holy Theotokos: No. 5." In *Wider Than Heaven: Eighth-Century Homilies on the Mother of God*, 53–70. Translated by Mary B. Cunningham. Popular Patristics Series 35. Crestwood, NY: St. Vladimir's Seminary Press, 2008.

John of the Cross, St. *The Collected Works of St. John of the Cross*. Translated by Kieran Kavanaugh and Otilio Rodriguez. 2nd ed. Washington, DC: ICS, 1991.

John Paul II. "*Fides et Ratio*: On the Relationship Between Faith and Reason." Vatican, Sept. 14, 1998. https://www.vatican.va/content/john-paul-ii/en/encyclicals/documents/hf_jp-ii_enc_14091998_fides-et-ratio.html.

———. *Man and Woman He Created Them: A Theology of the Body*. Translated by Michael Waldstein. Boston: Pauline, 2006.

———. "*Mulieris Dignitatem*: On the Dignity and Vocation of Women on the Occasion of the Marian Year." Vatican, Aug. 15, 1988. https://www.vatican.va/content/john-paul-ii/en/apost_letters/1988/documents/hf_jp-ii_apl_19880815_mulieris-dignitatem.html.

———. "*Redemptor Hominis*." Vatican, Mar. 4, 1979. https://www.vatican.va/content/john-paul-ii/en/encyclicals/documents/hf_jp-ii_enc_04031979_redemptor-hominis.html.

Kapic, Kelly M. "Anthropology." In *Mapping Modern Theology: A Thematic and Historical Introduction*, edited by Kelly M. Kapic and Bruce L. McCormack, 121–48. Grand Rapids: Baker Academic, 2012.

Kempis, Thomas à. *The Imitation of Mary*. Edited by Albin de Cigala. Translated by a Dominican sister from the French ed. Brooklyn: Angelico, 2020.

Kentenich, Joseph. *Das Katholische Menschenbild*. Edited by Herta Schlosser. Vallendar: Schönstatt, 1997.

Kierkegaard, Søren. *Philosophical Fragments; Johannes Climacus*. Edited and translated by Howard V. Hong and Edna H. Hong. Kierkegaard's Writings 7. Princeton: Prince-ton University Press, 1985.

Koerpel, Robert C. *Maurice Blondel: Transforming Catholic Tradition*. Thresholds in Philosophy and Theology. Notre Dame, IN: University of Notre Dame Press, 2019.

Lacoste, Jean-Yves. "Perception, Transcendence and the Experience of God." In *Transcendence and Phenomenology*, edited by Peter M. Candler Jr. and Conor Cunningham, 1–20. Veritas. London: SCM, 2007.

Lamb, Matthew L. *Eternity, Time, and the Life of Wisdom*. Faith & Reason: Studies in Catholic Theology & Philosophy. Naples, FL: Sapientia, 2007.

Laurentin, René. *A Short Treatise on the Virgin Mary*. Translated by Charles Neumann. Washington, NJ: AMI, 1991.

Lavigne, Jean-François. "The Paradox and Limits of Michel Henry's Concept of Transcendence." *International Journal of Philosophical Studies* 17 (2009) 377–88. https://doi.org/10.1080/09672550902948985.

Lehrberger, James. "The Anthropology of Aquinas's '*De Ente et Essentia*.'" *Review of Metaphysics* 51 (1998) 829–47. https://www.jstor.org/stable/20130298.

Lemna, Keith. *The Apocalypse of Wisdom: Louis Bouyer's Theological Recovery of the Cosmos*. Brooklyn, NY: Angelico, 2019.

Loudovikos, Nikolaos. *A Eucharistic Ontology: Maximus the Confessor's Eschatological Ontology of Being as Dialogical Reciprocity*. Translated by Elizabeth Theokritoff. Brookline, MA: Holy Cross Orthodox, 2010.

Lubac, Henri de. *The Mystery of the Supernatural*. Translated by Rosemary Sheed. Milestones in Catholic Theology. New York: Crossroad, 2018.

Maguire, Matthew W. *Carnal Spirit: The Revolutions of Charles Péguy*. Philadelphia: University of Pennsylvania Press, 2019.

Manelli, Stefano Maria. "Mary Coredemptrix in Sacred Scripture." In *Mary: Coredemptrix, Mediatrix, Advocate*, edited by Mark I. Miravalle, 59–104. Vol. 2 of *Theological Foundations: Papal, Pneumatological, Ecumenical*. Santa Barbara, CA: Queenship, 1995.

Marion, Jean-Luc. *God Without Being*. Translated by Thomas A. Carlson. 2nd ed. Religion and Postmodernism. Chicago: University of Chicago Press, 2012.

Maximos the Confessor. *On Difficulties in the Church Fathers: The "Ambigua."* Edited and translated by Nicholas Constas. 2 vols. Dumbarton Oaks Medieval Library. Cambridge: Harvard University Press, 2014.

———. *See also* Maximus the Confessor.

Maximus the Confessor. *The Life of the Virgin*. Edited and translated by Stephen J. Shoemaker. New Haven: Yale University Press, 2012.

———. *See also* Maximos the Confessor.

Meconi, David Vincent. "Philosophari in Maria." In *The Two Wings of Catholic Thought: Essays on "Fides et Ratio,"* edited by David Ruel Foster and Joseph W. Koterski, 69–90. Washington, DC: Catholic University of America Press, 2003.

Merleau-Ponty, Maurice. *Phenomenology of Perception*. Translated by Donald A. Landes. New York: Routledge, 2012.

———. *"The Primacy of Perception": And Other Essays on Phenomenological Psychology, the Philosophy of Art, History and Politics*. Edited by James M. Edie. Studies in Phenomenology and Existential Philosophy. Evanston, IL: Northwestern University Press, 1964.

———. *The Visible and the Invisible*. Translated by Alphonso Lingis. Studies in Phenomenology and Existential Philosophy. Evanston, IL: Northwestern University Press, 1968.

Milbank, John. Foreword to *Notes on Bergson and Descartes: Philosophy, Christianity, and Modernity in Contestation*, by Charles Péguy, ix–xxxiv. Veritas. Eugene, OR: Cascade Books, 2019.

MMMO Database. "Gaude Maria Virgo cunctas haereses sola." MMMO Database, n.d. https://musmed.eu/chant/232709.

Naumann, M. Isabell. "A 'New Creation in Christ' (2 Cor 5:17)—Mary, the Immaculata, as Anthropological Model." In *Theological Anthropology at the Beginning of the Third Millennium*, edited by Kevin Wagner et al., 171–84. Theology at the Beginning of the Third Millennium. Eugene, OR: Pickwick Publications, 2022.

Newman, John Henry. *Mary: The Virgin Mary in the Life and Writings of John Henry Newman*. Edited by Philip Boyce. Grand Rapids: Eerdmans, 2001.

———. *Meditations and Devotions of the Late Cardinal Newman*. Edited by Wm. P. Neville. 2nd ed. London: Longman, Green, 1893.

———. *Meditations on Mary, Our Mother*. Edited by TAN Books. Gastonia, NC: TAN, 2019.

———. *The Mystical Rose: Thoughts on the Blessed Virgin from the Writings of John Henry Cardinal Newman*. Edited by Joseph Regina. Princeton: Scepter, 1996.

Nichols, Aidan. *There Is No Rose: The Mariology of the Catholic Church*. Minneapolis: Fortress, 2015.

Origen. *Commentary on the Gospel According to John, Books 1–10*. Translated by Ronald E. Heine. FC 80. Washington, DC: Catholic University of America Press, 1993.

Orr, James. *God's Image in Man and Its Defacement in the Light of Modern Denials*. London: Hodder & Stoughton, 1905.

Ott, Ludwig. *Fundamentals of Catholic Dogma*. Translated by Patrick Lynch. London: Baronius, 2018.

Pannenberg, Wolfhart. *Anthropology in Theological Perspective*. Translated by Matthew J. O'Connell. Philadelphia: Westminster, 1985.

Pascal, Blaise. *Pensées*. Translated by A. J. Krailsheimer. Penguin Classics. London: Penguin, 1966.

Paul VI, promulgator. "*Gaudium et Spes*: Pastoral Constitution on the Church in the Modern World." Vatican, Dec. 7, 1965. https://www.vatican.va/archive/hist_councils/ii_vatican_council/documents/vat-ii_const_19651207_gaudium-et-spes_en.html.

———. "*Marialis Cultus*: For the Right Ordering and Development of Devotion to the Blessed Virgin Mary." Vatican, Feb. 2, 1974. https://www.vatican.va/content/paul-vi/en/apost_exhortations/documents/hf_p-vi_exh_19740202_marialis-cultus.html.

Perrin, Xavier. *The Radiance of Her Face: A Triptych in Honor of Mary Immaculate*. Kettering, OH: Angelico, 2017.

Pius IX. "*Ineffabilis Deus*: The Immaculate Conception." Papal Encyclicals, Dec. 8, 1854. https://www.papalencyclicals.net/pius09/p9ineff.htm.

Pius XII. "*Munificentissimus Deus*: Defining the Dogma of the Assumption." Vatican, Nov. 1, 1950. https://www.vatican.va/content/pius-xii/en/apost_constitutions/documents/hf_p-xii_apc_19501101_munificentissimus-deus.html.

Pontifical International Marian Academy. *The Mother of the Lord: Memory, Presence, Hope*. Translated by Thomas A. Thompson. Staten Island: St. Paul, 2007.

Prokes, Mary Timothy. *Toward a Theology of the Body*. Grand Rapids: Eerdmans, 1996.

Prosperi, Paolo. "'Fixed End of the Eternal Plan': Rereading Cabasilas's 'Homily on the Annunciation.'" *Communio: International Catholic Review* 46 (2019) 207–36.

Przywara, Erich. *Analogia Entis: Metaphysics: Original Structure and Universal Rhythm*. Translated by John R. Betz and David Bentley Hart. Ressourcement. Grand Rapids: Eerdmans, 2014.

Ratzinger, Joseph. *Daughter Zion: Meditations on the Church's Marian Belief*. Translated by John M. McDermott. San Francisco: Ignatius, 1983.

———. *Eschatology: Death and Eternal Life*. Edited by Aidan Nichols. Translated by Michael Waldstein. 2nd ed. Washington, DC: Catholic University of America Press, 1988.

———. *Principles of Catholic Theology: Building Stones for a Fundamental Theology*. Translated by Mary Frances McCarthy. San Francisco: Ignatius, 1987.

———. *See also* Benedict XVI; Ratzinger, Joseph/Benedict XVI.

Ratzinger, Joseph/Benedict XVI. *Dogma and Preaching: Applying Christian Doctrine to Daily Life*. Edited by Michael J. Miller. Translated by Michael J. Miller and Matthew J. O'Connell. San Francisco: Ignatius, 2011.

———. *See also* Benedict XVI; Ratzinger, Joseph.

Rowland, Tracey. "Theological Anthropology at the Beginning of the Third Millennium." In *Theological Anthropology at the Beginning of the Third Millennium*, edited by Kevin Wagner et al., 1–22. Theology at the Beginning of the Third Millennium. Eugene, OR: Pickwick Publications, 2022.

Scheeben, Matthias Joseph. *Mariology*. 2 vols. Translated by T. Geukers. N.p.: Ex Fontibus, 2015.

Schelling, F. W. J. *System of Transcendental Idealism (1800)*. Translated by Peter Heath. Charlottesville: University Press of Virginia, 1978.

Schmemann, Alexander. *The Virgin Mary*. Vol. 3 of *Celebration of Faith*. New York: St. Vladimir's Seminary Press, 1995.

Slesinski, Robert F. *The Theology of Sergius Bulgakov*. Scholarly Monographs 2. Yonkers, NY: St. Vladimir's Seminary Press, 2017.

Speyr, Adrienne von. *Handmaid of the Lord*. Translated by E. A. Nelson. 2nd ed. San Francisco: Ignatius, 1985.

Steenberg, Matthew C. *Of God and Man: Theology as Anthropology from Irenaeus to Athanasius*. London: T&T Clark, 2009.

Tagore, Rabindranath. *Stray Birds*. New York: Macmillan, 1916.

Tanner, Norman, ed. *Vatican II: The Essential Texts*. New York: Image, 2012.

Teevan, Donna. "Challenges to the Role of Theological Anthropology in Feminist Theologies." *Theological Studies* 64 (2003) 582–97.

Teilhard de Chardin, Pierre. *The Future of Man*. New York: Harper & Row, 1964.

———. *The Human Phenomenon*. Translated by Sarah Appleton-Weber. Brighton, UK: Sussex Academic, 2003.

Thandeka. *The Embodied Self: Friedrich Schleiermacher's Solution to Kant's Problem of the Empirical Self*. SUNY Series in Philosophy. Albany: State University of New York Press, 1995.

Thunberg, Lars. *Man and the Cosmos: The Vision of St. Maximus the Confessor*. New York: St. Vladimir's Seminary Press, 1985.

Torrance, T. F. *Calvin's Doctrine of Man*. 1957. Reprinted, The Torrance Collection: θεολογος. Eugene, OR: Wipf & Stock 1997.

Troeltsch, Ernst. *The Christian Faith*. Edited by Gertrud von le Fort. Translated by Garrett E. Paul. Fortress Texts in Modern Theology. Minneapolis: Fortress, 1991.

Vallin, Philippe. "Un filo rosso antropologico, sacramentario ed etico attraverso i documenti della Commissione Teologica Internazionale (1969–2019)." Address before the International Theological Commission, Pontifical Lateran University, Rome, Nov. 20, 2019.

Vatican. "Litany of Loreto." Vatican, n.d. https://www.vatican.va/special/rosary/documents/litanie-lauretane_en.html.

Williams, Rowan. *Christ: The Heart of Creation*. London: Bloomsbury Continuum, 2018.

Wingren, Gustaf. *Man and the Incarnation: A Study of the Biblical Theology of Irenaeus*. Translated by Ross Mackenzie. London: Oliver & Boyd, 1959.

Wood, Ralph C. "Flannery O'Connor, Benedict XVI, and the Divine Eros." *Christianity and Literature* 60 (2010) 33–62.

Woznicki, Christopher G. *T. F. Torrance's Christological Anthropology: Discerning Humanity in Christ*. Routledge New Critical Thinking in Religion, Theology and Biblical Studies. London: Routledge, 2022.

www.ingramcontent.com/pod-product-compliance
Lightning Source LLC
LaVergne TN
LVHW100527110826
845146LV00002B/808